NOBLE ROT

W. W. NORTON & COMPANY

NEW YORK LONDON

NOBLE ROT

A

BORDEAUX

WINE

REVOLUTION

William Echikson

For information about permission to reproduce selections from this book, write to
Permissions, W. W. Norton & Company, Inc., 500 Fifth Avenue, New York, NY 10110

Manufacturing by Courier Westford
Book design by Barbara M. Bachman
Production manager: Julia Druskin

Library of Congress Cataloging-in-Publication Data

Echikson, William.
Noble rot : a Bordeaux wine revolution / William Echikson.—1st ed.
p. cm.
Includes index.
ISBN 0-393-05162-5 (hardcover)
1. Wine industry—France. 2. Wine and wine making—France. I. Title.
HD9382.7.B6 E24 2004
338.4'76632'009447144—dc22

2003027565

ISBN 0-393-32694-2 pbk.

W. W. Norton & Company, Inc., 500 Fifth Avenue, New York, N.Y. 10110
www.wwnorton.com

W. W. Norton & Company Ltd., Castle House, 75/76 Wells Street, London W1T 3QT

1 2 3 4 5 6 7 8 9 0

For my mother, Barbara Gross Echikson (1936–2003),

who sent me to France in the first place

and encouraged me ever after

CONTENTS

—

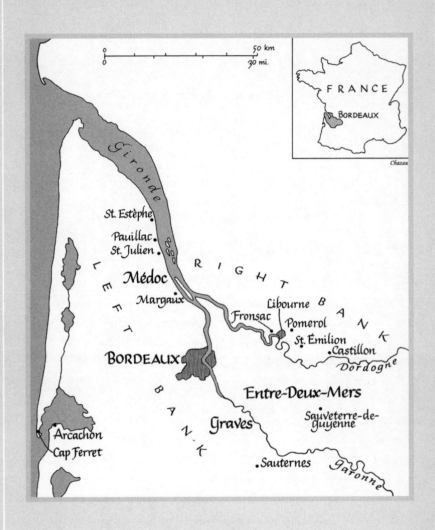

WHEN I FIRST TRAVELED TO FRANCE, I WAS ONLY FIFTEEN years old. It was 1975. My parents enrolled me in a summer study program. A French family hosted me for a full month in the seaside resort of Arcachon, just west of Bordeaux and a summer retreat for the region's winemakers and merchants.

Before crossing the Atlantic, I spent a grueling week with other ninth-grade high school students preparing in Massachusetts. We wrestled with the French subjunctive. We followed Napoléon Bonaparte from Austerlitz to snowy Moscow. We attempted to decipher, line by line, short stories by Flaubert and Camus. It was like boot camp, and we were the draftees training for the imminent invasion of a foreign land. Our teachers warned us about "cultural" differences. One cautioned us to pack a large bottle of deodorant. Hot water was expensive in France and cleanliness not up to American standards.

"The French take a shower only once a week," the professor warned.

For the first few days in Arcachon, I dared only to wash my face. I began to smell ripe. My host family, the Vellys, soon wondered about American "cultural" differences. Their seventeen-year-old daughter, Anne, finally asked why I wasn't washing. When I told her about my teacher's warning, she laughed. "I take a shower every day," she assured me.

Obviously, this wasn't a "primitive" country and I had a lot to learn. The Vellys had their own special recipe for *joie de vivre*. The ingredients started, naturally enough, with food and drink. Madame Velly was a terrific cook. She could take simple tomatoes and transform them into a thing of beauty by adding some onions and drizzling delicious vinaigrette over them. Monsieur Velly loved wine. At lunchtime, he would head down to his cellar and return with a bottle from the Bordeaux region of Graves—*"mon petit Graves,"* he called it.

The only wine I had tasted before was sweet Manischewitz at Jewish holidays. Monsieur Velly would always propose a sip. His rich, ruby red Graves tasted wonderful, and so did the long, unhurried lunches. The wine fueled animated conversation. We discussed serious subjects such as Franco's regime in Spain, which ended with his death a few months later, and how Basque separatists were exploding bombs near the French-Spanish border. And we laughed about simple adventures such as skinny-dipping in the ocean. My French advanced in gallops.

Monsieur Velly's birthday fell on July 4. I teased him that he was celebrating America's independence. We assembled at Tante Yvonne's apartment for a festive lunch. I don't remember the menu except for the dessert, a sumptuous, thin pastry wafer filled with *crème pâtissière* called, appropriately enough, *le succès*. I had never tasted such a delectable concoction. Four hours passed by the time the plates were cleared, tablecloths brushed, and coffee served. A lazy early evening swim lay ahead, followed by a drink in a local café. What an Independence Day celebration!

During the month in Arcachon, the school group took three field trips. The first was to a local paper factory. Dull. The next took us to nearby Bordeaux, where we visited the elegant eighteenth-century Grand Théâtre. More interesting. The final excursion was to the sweet-white-wine-growing district Sauternes and a winery called Château d'Yquem.

Although I had never heard of Sauternes or Yquem and I don't recall much about the château itself, I do remember descending into the luxurious cellar and being offered a sip of the golden elixir made there. In my memory, it was extraordinary, sweet and perfumed with flavors I never imagined to exist. The guide explained how the grapes were harvested only after they shriveled and developed a certain mold. In one glass, all the magic of the Old World came alive.

TWO AND A HALF DECADES LATER, I had been living and working in Europe most of my adult life. Bordeaux remained synonymous with fine wine. The region's top winemakers were enjoying an unprecedented period of millennium-fueled prosperity. Their wines fetched hundreds of dollars a bottle and served as the reference point, setting standards for quality and luxury.

Below them, however, French preeminence was being challenged. Where once France had dominated Europe, it now was one of fifteen members of an increasingly united European Union, trailing Germany in population and Great Britain in military prowess. When the French mocked America, I sensed jealousy and insecurity in reaction to a super-power's overwhelming influence.

During the 1990s, the United States exploded with innovation and prosperity. In the same period, the French economy, for the most part, stagnated. The result: unemployment stayed high and crime soared. Tensions between native French people and young Arab immigrants mounted. Even after the terrorist attacks of September 11, 2001, America exuded optimism hard to find among the more pessimistic French, whose contribution to toppling the Taliban or fighting terrorism was limited. When the world-champion French national soccer team played against Algeria in the Stade de France just outside of Paris in the fall of 2001, the crowd jeered the French national anthem. "Americans salute their flag and sing the national anthem, standing tall, hand in hand, while in France we boo anyone who sings the 'Marseillaise,'" wrote Alain Genestar, editor in chief of the country's most popular magazine, *Paris-Match*. "In America, you are proud to be American. In France, you don't know what to be proud of anymore."

This malaise was visible in the French wine industry: from the hills of

Beaujolais to the valley of the Loire, the prospect was gloomy. For centuries the French had reigned supreme. Now huge conglomerates from Australia, California, and elsewhere were outflanking France's fragmented, family-run vineyards. Giant New World companies such as Gallo and Mondavi were spending millions to create consistent brands recognized around the world, while many French growers were turning out low-quality table wine with complicated, hard-to-understand labels.

It looked like another painful lesson in globalization, the latest chapter in France's ongoing and mostly losing struggle to balance its artisan traditions with the unyielding demands of the marketplace. Brewers and liquor companies, with their deep pockets and marketing reach, were buying up winemakers and introducing the concept of branding. Australia's beer baron, Foster's, gobbled up America's Napa Valley–based Beringer Blass, while Australia's Southcorp, owner of the prestigious Penfolds and the more budget-minded Lindemans brands, took over family-owned premium winemaker Rosemount. As giant supermarkets all over the world sold more and more wine, these multinational conglomerates were able to supply them with large quantities of reliable, if homogeneous, mid-priced wine.

During this big bang, France stood sulking on the sidelines. Of the world's ten largest wine companies, only one, a cooperative called Val D'Orbieu, producing what the British call plonk—simple, often undrinkable table wine—was French. While three Australian companies dominated 80 percent of their home market, in France Bordeaux alone boasted almost ten thousand different producers. With the exception of isolated joint ventures such as those by one branch of the Rothschild family (Opus One with the Robert Mondavi Winery in California and Almaviva with Concha y Toro in Chile), French wine companies remained provincial. Bordeaux growers found it difficult to cooperate even with Burgundy or Côtes du Rhône producers. "We stick to our own home regions when we must begin to compete in a universe of consumers dressing in Nikes, Reeboks, or Adidas, eating Big Macs and drinking Coca-Cola," lamented an official French government critique of its wine industry published in 2001.

Gallic tempers rose as the bleak scenario unfolded. In 1999 a cheese maker named José Bove from the Mediterranean region of Languedoc won widespread popular support by destroying a McDonald's outlet in protest against U.S. trade sanctions on Roquefort cheese. A year and a half later, he and other farmers in that same region—which produces a third of all the wine made in France—derailed an attempt by the California-based Robert Mondavi Winery to create a sprawling corporate vineyard and produce premium wines. Around the same time, growers demanding higher prices for their grapes publicized their demands by ransacking highway tollbooths and supermarkets that sold foreign wines. "Each bottle of American and Australian wine that lands in Europe is a bomb targeted at the heart of our rich European culture," said one Languedoc winemaker.

Tensions flared even in the top end of the market, where Bordeaux continued to dominate. In some blind tastings, California Cabernets surpassed the best of Médoc. When I revisited Château d'Yquem after a quarter century, Sauternes seemed plunged into a deep slumber. Consumers had lost their taste for the world's most famous sweet wine. What seemed like a fairy tale setting to a fifteen-year-old had become a cobwebbed castle. The family owners had been fighting among themselves for years, and their battle to re-create the golden world of the past seemed lost.

Luckily, in the rubble of Bordeaux's decaying old order I also discovered a revolution. Starting two decades ago, some high-end winemakers, enologists, and merchants modernized how they tend the land, crush and ferment the grapes, and sell the wine. They are challenging foolish regulations imposed by a heavy-handed bureaucracy in Paris. Their wines are in hot demand and sell for hundreds of dollars a bottle, keeping France dominant among global connoisseurs. Who is buying? Americans enriched by a decade of prosperity and encouraged by an American wine critic whose verdict can make and break the market. Instead of losing sleep over New World hegemony, these entrepreneurs are confronting the competition.

Some of these new wave French winemakers grew up in Bordeaux and have climbed the social ladder by producing wines superior to those made by many of the traditional estates owned by long lines of aristocrats. Others are nouveau riche newcomers, attracted by the glamour of making wine. Together, they show that it is possible to resist the industrialization of winemaking and respect *terroir,* a French word that literally means soil but contains philosophical, existential connotations for those who make and market wine.

"Selling wine shouldn't be just like selling pork bellies," explained one American wine merchant based in Bordeaux. This expatriate has dedicated his career to preserving and promoting variety in winemaking from the onslaught of homogeneous New World products—generic Chardonnays and Cabernet Sauvignons. A Chardonnay produced in Chablis in northern Burgundy tastes drier and more mineral than a rich, buttery one produced less than a hundred miles south in Burgundy's Côte d'Or. "We shouldn't lose these differences," he insists, echoing the angst of Europeans who bemoan the incursion of everything from standardized, greenhouse-grown tomatoes to Hollywood blockbusters.

Just as France must come to terms with American political, economic, and military power, French winemakers must regain pride in both their history and their present achievements. Despite the crisis currently facing their industry, signs of a renewal are visible. The Bordeaux Wine Board has doubled its advertising budget and launched a new campaign. One ad features a sexy model dressed in red silk lingerie hovering over a muscular man. "Let the Mood Take You to Bordeaux," reads the caption.

New World competition is forcing French winemakers to improve, and even some in the wine establishment welcome such a change. "When I see Gallo trying to sell wine in Paris, I celebrate because it's the only way to wake us up from our slumber," says one Bordeaux merchant.

AS I WRITE, the United States and France are going through their worst spat in memory. President Jacques Chirac and his flamboyant foreign minister, Dominique de Villepin, led the global opposition to President Bush's war in Iraq. The French goal seems to be to create a Europe that operates as a new global power to serve as a check on U.S. interests and influence—with Paris in the driver's seat. This vision is contested, and not just in Washington. Britain, Spain, and many eastern European nations with fresh memories of freedom from tyranny want a Europe that is strong, but one that also works with the United States to promote shared values and interests.

The argument is being played out on both sides of the Atlantic, and wine, not surprisingly, has its role. Anti-French American consumers have begun shunning many expensive French bottles. One New Jersey restaurateur publicly poured a bottle of costly Champagne down the toilet. French leaders similarly have aggravated tensions. When asked who he wanted to win in Iraq, foreign minister de Villepin stumbled for an answer. More than one-third of French people polled with the same question answered, "Saddam Hussein."

With time, though, I'm confident friendship can be rebuilt. France and the United States have been allies for more than two centuries. France helped us win independence, and our founding fathers led by Thomas Jefferson developed a taste for fine French wine. We still admire the French for their style and success in enjoying life. In our minds, France remains the arbiter of *bon gout* and *joie de vivre*. Similarly, even if frightened by American power, most of the Bordelais who befriended me admired American energy and entrepreneurship.

Ever since my month as a teenager in Arcachon, I knew that France and its favorite drink would play a role in my life. The Vellys had opened up their house—and a window onto an attractive way of life. When I returned to Bordeaux as an adult to write this book, they and many others again opened their homes and their best bottles. With everyone I visited, every tasting I attended, all eyes would turn to me as I raised my glass. Is it good? Can I make it better? How? The passion was palpable and the winemakers' efforts produced unforgettable wines, bursting with rich, distinct flavors.

Just before leaving Bordeaux, I lunched with the Vellys. The meal began with thick slabs of foie gras. A *confit de canard* followed. Then came salad and cheese. For dessert, Anne remembered my initial love—*le succès*. The old pastry shop had closed, but the owner had passed on the recipe to another local baker. After lunch we visited Tante Yvonne, going strong at age eighty-six. She hadn't forgotten me and remembered our July 4 festivities two and half decades before.

We sipped some red Bordeaux. It wasn't a great bottle, but it served the purpose of fueling happy memories. I put aside my concerns about the future of France and its emblematic wine industry. I stopped worrying about whether wine is important in a world hit by an economic downturn and fears of deadly terrorism. I simply looked forward to telling the story of those who have resisted the Bordeaux wine revolution and those who are leading it.

November 2003
Brussels, Belgium

NOBLE ROT

CHAPTER 1

—

Millennium Madness

THE SCENE LOOKED, AT FIRST GLANCE, LIKE AN ELEGANT COCKTAIL party, but serious business was at stake. Wine merchants, importers, and writers from around the globe crowded into Château Angélus's vaulted reception hall. Outside, vineyards stretched up to the hilltop village of Saint-Emilion, its medieval bell towers and weathered limestone glistening under a rich blue spring sky. Inside, gentle lights bathed the hall's creamy white walls and terra-cotta floor. Glass doors within gave onto a huge temperature-controlled cellar filled with rows of oak barrels of fermenting wine. Each guest was given a notebook, pencil, and wineglass. Silence soon enveloped the large room. Anyone who chuckled or even whispered was scolded with a searing "Shhhh."

It was the morning of March 27, 2001, the opening of the annual spring tasting event hosted by the Union des Grands Crus de Bordeaux. The Union is a promotional group for some 140 of the top Bordeaux châteaux that stand at the pinnacle of the five thousand estates that bottle Bordeaux wine. The wine world was judging whether they were worth buying, and if so, at what price. Decisions about quality would make or break fortunes, and this was no ordinary year. The wine had been made from grapes harvested the previous September and would be bottled as the 2000 vintage. Winemakers were counting on the millen-

Black-tie parties are an important part of Bordeaux's
annual tasting week.

nium effect to spur sales. Florence Cathiard, co-owner of Château Smith-Haut-Lafitte and one of the most dynamic, richest newcomers to the region, called it "the magical three zeros."

Almost all wine in the world is sold only after it's bottled. The top couple hundred or so Bordeaux estates represent a notable exception. They offer their products starting the spring after the harvest, while the fermented juice remains in barrels. These "futures" are delivered bottled to buyers only two years later, giving the elite winemakers early access to cash and allowing wine connoisseurs early access to rare wines.

Selling futures is a complicated process. Unlike producers in other regions, Bordeaux châteaux almost never sell direct to consumers. Journalists, enologists, growers, brokers, merchants, and importers joust for power and profits. The marketplace is known locally as the *place de Bordeaux*. The *place* isn't a physical square with a fountain or monument. It refers to the process by which the world's most famous wine gets from cellars to consumers.

Once the tasters return home after their week in Bordeaux, they publish notes on the quality of the vintage and on individual estates. The "campaign" then opens. Brokers act as go-betweens among the château owners and the merchants. They fan out across the region and sound out winemakers about how much they want for each bottle—as much as possible—and the amount the merchants are willing to pay—as little as possible. Brokers attempt, with more or less success, to nudge each side toward a compromise. Estates then announce a price and determine how much wine will be allocated to each trader. These merchants turn around and resell the wine to importers, who pass it on in the United States to distributors, who then send it to retailers, who in turn sell to consumers.

The system resembles a grown-up version of the French schoolyard game *barbichette*, "in which children hold one another by the chin to see who laughs first," notes journalist William Langewiesche. "The child who loses gets a slap in the face." Each château negotiates its own prices, a function of what the market will pay and of what the owner anticipates his or her neighbor will receive. Prices are important not just for the revenues they bring in but also because the higher the sticker prices, the higher an estate's prestige.

The Bordeaux marketplace is not efficient. The broker takes 2 percent. The merchant adds another 10 to 15 percent. Importers and retailers worldwide then add their own margin. By the time the wine makes it from the grower to the consumer, the price has doubled or even tripled. Expensive though the system is, it does create a marketing mystique. Since some merchants specialize in the U.S. market and others in the Asian or Latin American, producers too small to ensure their own distribution around the globe are confident that their wines will be stocked in cellars from Miami to Moscow.

Like speculating in flower bulbs or cocoa beans, buying Bordeaux wine futures is a chancy business. The region's cool, rainy climate injects one degree of uncertainty. Despite improvements in viticulture, vintages vary in both quality and quantity. Areas around the Mediterranean, not to mention sunny California or Australia, benefit from hotter and drier growing seasons. During at least three years each decade, Bordeaux suffers from too much cold or rain for grapes to ripen properly.

Excitement soared in the run-up to the 2000 tastings. Most of Bordeaux's greatest vintages have been the product of exceptionally hot, dry summers, with below average rainfall and above average temperatures. If it is too cold in June or July, the vines don't flower evenly and suffer from *millerandage,* a condition that causes bunches of grapes to mature unevenly. The summer of 2000 was appropriately hot and dry. Although July started cold and unstable, temperatures rose and stayed high through the end of the month and August. A tiny amount of rain arrived in early September. Then a month of bright hot weather ripened the red wine grapes to perfection. A good vintage was in the making. Just how good would be determined at these March tastings.

MOST OF THE WORLD'S famed wine regions are crammed into small, compact valleys such as the Moselle and the Napa, or circle even smaller villages such as Chablis and Châteauneuf-du-Pape. Bordeaux is different. It's huge. France's largest high-quality wine region stretches from the Atlantic Ocean to the Dordogne Valley, producing almost a billion bottles a year. That's a lot of wine to sell, particularly since it ranges in quality from the simple to the sublime.

Northwest of the city of Bordeaux lies the Médoc peninsula, which extends west toward the sea. Often called the Left Bank, the Médoc is the heart of traditional Bordeaux, home to the most famous red wines, from Latour to Lafite, Margaux to Mouton.

To the northeast, rolling hills create sweeping vistas around the villages of Saint-Emilion and Pomerol. This is the Right Bank. In politics, right means conservative. In the world of Bordeaux winemaking, the Right Bank is dominated by radical new wave winemakers bent on overturning many of the region's traditions.

South of Bordeaux, vineyards stretch for almost twenty miles, starting with the Graves, a region of gravel-filled soils that produces smoky, tobacco-scented red wines and classic, crisp dry whites. The Graves gives way to Sauternes, home to some of the world's most exquisite sweet wines.

Below the top estates, all of these areas produce a sea of undistinguished wine—under a vast array of different labels. Simple Bordeaux and Bordeaux *supérieur* both refer to lesser wines made throughout the entire region. The next steps up the ladder in prestige are regional labels such as Haut-Médoc and Entre-Deux-Mers. Another step up and bottles are marked with the names of villages such as Margaux and Saint-Emilion. These are made from grapes grown only in those villages.

In France, a village or region is defined as an *appellation,* literally a denomination or namesake. The theory is that wine from Margaux doesn't taste like wine made in Saint-Julien. In 1934 the government legislated an official system of Appellation d'Origine Contrôlée. This control system defines the hundreds of different wine districts and awards the right to use the term *appellation* only to those vineyards located within specific boundaries. The variety of grape that can be grown in an area also is specified, as are the maximum percentage of alcohol allowed for each wine and the maximum yield for each acre. To codify and enforce these laws, Paris established a division of the Ministry of Agriculture called the Institut National des Appellations d'Origine.

On top of these *appellations,* Bordeaux has developed its own separate rating system over the past three and a half centuries. The pinnacle of the traditional system is reserved for "classified growths." Several hundred estates benefit from the label *grand cru,* or great growth. At the very, very top stand a few select *premiers crus,* or first great growths. It's these select classified growths and a few other wines that aficionados have flown here from all over the world to taste.

About 250 Bordeaux properties produce these mouthwatering, stupendous wines that are sold as futures after the spring tastings. The thousands of other growers struggle to keep up. Many have banded together into large cooperatives designed to provide economies of scale and regular incomes. The problem is, Australian, American, and Chilean winemakers work in steady, hot climates, which produce regular harvests and consistent wines. They can plant whatever types of grapes they want, wherever they want. Bordeaux winemakers must cope with heavy-handed regulators who control the amount and types of vines they can plant. "I needed eight different types of government approvals before replanting some vines," complains Dominique Bécot, co-owner of a leading Saint-Emilion estate, Beau-Séjour Bécot, situated on a limestone plateau above Angélus.

Other hurdles prevent French growers from innovating. Many New World wineries have begun throwing oak chips into the wine as it ferments in steel tanks, adding an appealing oak taste without going to the expense of aging the wine in oak barrels. In France, though, this technique is illegal—leaving many winemakers feeling handicapped. "It's like playing rugby when the Australians can pass the ball forward and we can only pass it backwards," complains Jean-Marie Chadronnier, CEO of one of France's largest wine merchants, Compagnie des Vins de Bordeaux et de la Gironde.

The Australians and Americans are demystifying wine in other ways, too. Compared with the intimidating tongue twisters on French labels, some of the best-selling Aussie brands—Wolf Blass, Penfolds, and Rosemount—are easy to pronounce and remember. What's more, Australian labels tell what grapes the wine is made from—Merlot, Cabernet Sauvignon, or Chardonnay. In contrast, the Bordeaux system of blending different grape varieties and labeling according to geographic origin results in widespread confusion. In Bordeaux, fifty-seven different *appellations* compete for recognition. It almost requires an enology degree to make sense of the differences—plus an encyclopedic knowledge of the hundreds of growers in each village, many bottling their own wines of vastly different quality. Many estates even bottle their best wine under the château label and also release a second or third wine of lesser quality under different names. Even connoisseurs can spend years trying to understand all the different labels.

Consumer demand for Bordeaux's high-end wines has risen and fallen alongside the larger economy. Historically, prices have swung between euphoria and depression, rocketing up and down like a roller coaster by as much as 30 to 40 percent each year. Quality in 1971, for example, was decent and prices reasonable. Demand rose, driving up prices and production. The 1972 vintage was terrible. "The wines tasted of green peas and asparagus: they were, quite simply, made from unripe fruit," recalls Stephen Brook, a British wine writer and critic. Instead of lowering prices, however, the producers demanded even higher sums, as much as four times the 1971 levels. Merchants felt obliged to buy. Otherwise, they feared losing their allocations from the best châteaux.

By the time 1973 arrived, many merchants were struggling to stay afloat. Richard Nixon's presidency was unraveling under the pressure of Watergate, and Bordeaux was soon wrestling with its own scandal, dubbed Winegate. A Bordeaux merchant named Pierre Bert masterminded a scheme to "improve" the *appellation* designation of inferior wines, altering the paperwork between inferior red wine from southern France and real Bordeaux. The police Fraud Squad, the feared Répression des Fraudes, was called in. Prominent merchants including members of the Cruse family were found to be aware of the scam. After a much publicized trial, family patriarch Yvan Cruse jumped to his death off Bordeaux's Pont d'Aquitaine suspension bridge. Pierre Bert went to prison.

That same year, the Yom Kippur War unleashed an oil crisis followed by a global recession and a dramatic drop in luxury wine consumption. Many merchants who had stocked up on credit suddenly found themselves with large inventories of unsold goods and banks were calling in their loans. A typical traditional merchant, the Bartons, owned several prestigious estates and a wholesale business through which they bought and resold wines from all over Bordeaux. They were forced to unload their namesake Barton & Guestier merchant house to Seagram's in order to hold on to Château Léoville Barton and Château Langoa Barton, both of which they had owned for almost two centuries. "My uncle Ronald had a choice: sell the merchant business or sell the châteaux," said seventy-one-year-old Anthony Barton, Ronald's eldest living relative.

Recovery came only in the 1980s. Large numbers of wealthy Asian buyers began buying expensive wines for the first time. Big corporations decided to take advantage of this trend. The French insurance company AXA bought up five Bordeaux estates and poured millions of francs into upgrading their vineyards and facilities. Then, in the 1990s, rich outsiders who had made huge amounts of money on start-up companies arrived. When they sold their businesses, they settled in Bordeaux and soon began producing some of the region's best wine. Overall quality, particularly in top-end wines, rose, though the mass of small growers in cooperatives continued to struggle to find needed resources to improve their wines.

Many futures bought by wealthy connoisseurs during this period generated an investment bonanza. A case of 1990 Latour went for $370 while still in the barrel—and before bottling. A decade later, it was worth $3,800—a refreshing increase in value. The rarer the wine, the higher the potential gain. Only about 6,000 bottles a year are produced of a new wave Pomerol called Le Pin. When it began to surpass all other Pomerols in blind tastings, prices soared. By 2000 a case from 1982 fetched $18,000 at auction—a 1,775 percent return on the futures price.

The 1990s were a golden era for top-notch Bordeaux, just as they were for the global economy. The 1995 vintage was superb. Producers sold at a reasonable price and the merchants made a killing. The 1996 vintage also was good and prices went up—Saint-Emilion's Angélus jumped by 80 percent. In 1997 the wine was good but not great and yet prices still rose, on average by 29 percent. "We saw all the money the merchants made the year before and thought we should get part of the cake, too," recalled Florence Cathiard.

When she set her price, merchants resisted. "They would tell me, 'Oh, we just don't have the money this year,'" said Cathiard. "I knew I was being blackballed." Cathiard, a onetime advertising executive and the wife of the former owner of a supermarket chain, picked up her phone and began peddling her Château Smith-Haut-Lafitte to other merchants. Within twenty-four hours she was sold out. Merchants felt powerless to fight back. "We had to buy or risk losing our future allocations," recalled merchant Jeffrey Davies, who bought 1997 Smith-Haut-Lafitte.

He and other merchants soon regretted their decision. Consumers saw that the 1997 wines were much more expensive than the superior 1995 and stayed away. Stocks grew in importers' cellars. Merchants unloaded to supermarkets, which began offering deep discounts.

And yet the disaster was fast forgotten. The 1998 vintage, particularly from the Right Bank, came out demonstrating decent quality and consumer demand returned. Even though the 1999 vintage proved mediocre—better than 1997, but less worthy of aging than 1998—the high-tech boom kept prices moving up. By the spring of 2001, even though dot-com frenzy had already subsided and stock markets were falling, particularly in the United States, a lot of leftover money was still waiting to be spent.

If the spring tasting showed that the millennium vintage was good, Bordeaux's merchants and growers were confident that investors and wine lovers would open their wallets to celebrate. Until recently, the weeklong event was little known. But the spread of Bordeaux's popularity set off an explosion of interest among importers and the press alike. For the particularly promising 2000 vintage, the Union des Grands Crus received requests for 4,000 invitations, a third more than in previous years. For the first time, the group began turning down journalists or traders it didn't consider worthy. The 120 journalists who received invitations were treated to a gala dinner at the beginning of the week and five-course lunches between their tastings. On their free evenings, château owners offered them sumptuous dinners accompanied by fabulous old bottles.

The tasters had a busy schedule. In just four days, they sampled wines from all around Bordeaux. Conscientious critics supplemented the Union's own sessions with personal visits to individual châteaux. The Union split its invitees into groups. All the visitors sampled the wines, but the journalists were offered separate tastings at which they were asked,

"Blind or not blind?" At Château Angélus, blind tasters were brought to one end of the hall and directed to bottles identified only by a simple number. The others were shown to bottles with the labels exposed.

Opinion is split on the question of blind versus nonblind tasting. The blind taster's argument is simple: it is the only way to arrive at an impartial verdict about the wine. Tasting blind focuses the attention on color, bouquet, flavors, and texture. Non-blind tasters protest that the process takes longer and can be misleading. The question today at the opening of the tasting week wasn't whether Angélus—or any of the other wines sampled—would be good. Even in poor vintages, these high-class wines always assure a minimum of quality. The questions to answer were how good and at what price? Tasting with the labels uncovered or marked out doesn't alter the answer, or at least so goes the argument.

Blind or not, the tasters each poured samples, filling only about a quarter of a glass to give the wine room to breathe. Holding the glass by its stem—in order to avoid warming the precious liquid—the taster tilted the glass away from his body and checked first for the wine's appearance. Cloudiness or fuzziness suggests problems. Although red wines become paler and browned with age, Bordeaux's best young wines exhibit a deep purple color, and the glossier the color the better.

Next, the taster swirled, moved the glass to the nose, and sniffed. Agitating helps release the wine's bouquet. Aromas, ranging from floral violets to fruity cherries to vegetal herbs and spicy cloves, begin to appear.

Finally, the glass was brought to the lips. A small sip was poured onto the tongue and air sucked in noisily to agitate the liquid and distribute it throughout the mouth. The top of the tongue senses the wine's sweetness and saltiness, the sides its fruit acidity, the back the bitterness. The cheeks measure the tannins, the astringency given off by the skins and seeds. Does the flavor linger? Without swallowing, the taster leaned forward and spat out the wine into one of the porcelain funnels placed at the center of each table. The funnels drained into buckets encased in wooden barrels. When they were full, lanky young hostesses arrived with new buckets and carried off the other ones through the crowd. The owners of the estates stood around the room, eyeing the "jury" of tasters.

Most tasters keep the wine in the mouth for at least five seconds, and some as long as ten, to discern the wine's full aromatic palette. After spitting out the wine, they hesitated for an instant and concentrated on the residual flavors. Most jotted a few notes or typed a few words into their portable computers. Complicating their lives, the new vintage's wines were still babies, difficult to judge. The newly fermented juice had been put into oak barrels only six months before and had yet to display mature complexity and sophisticated aromas. At such an early stage, the best one could say was whether a particular wine was robust, made from ripe, not rotten, fruit. If the fruit is harvested immature and green, the wine can never be great. If it is harvested too late, the resulting wine will have a pruny, overcooked flavor. Alain Raynaud, Union des Grands Crus president and a château owner himself, once suggested postponing the tasting until June so the wines would offer a more accurate picture of their potential. But his fellow winemakers refused, saying that the late date wouldn't leave them enough time to complete the annual sales campaign before summer vacation.

Although the wines took a year to produce, within an hour judgment was passed on more than a dozen of Saint-Emilion's rarest and finest. Another Union tasting was scheduled in the afternoon south of Bordeaux. Despite spitting out everything, the tasters had absorbed enough alcohol to create a mild buzz. Sniffing, swirling, sipping, sucking, and spitting so many great wines may sound like fun. It's also hard work.

A FEW OF THE TASTERS left Château Angélus and proceeded to another Saint-Emilion winemaker. This time no vaulted reception hall awaited them. Michel Gracia greeted his guests in the cold, damp garage that serves as his wine cellar. Instead of offering a drink from carefully prepared bottles, Gracia picked up a long *pipette,* a clear glass instrument that resembles a turkey baster, placed it deep into a barrel, extracted some young wine, and poured it into a waiting glass. The tasters stamped their feet to ward off the chill, swirled the liquid to warm it up, and tried to imagine what it would smell and taste like in more comfortable surroundings.

In contrast to Château Angélus, which, amid golden vines, looks up toward the hillside village, Gracia's garage is tucked away on a narrow street in the middle of Saint-Emilion, the world-famed wine center

Michel Gracia is challenging Bordeaux's old order.

twenty-five miles northeast of Bordeaux. Leaving the city on the four-lane highway, the visitor soon enters deep countryside sprinkled with occasional signs of the south, fields of sunflowers and cypress trees and villages with the patina of age. Limestone is the main building material here and the villages, including Saint-Emilion, are constructed of the soft beige stone. Even modern cement buildings here are covered with thin stucco of a similar color.

Saint-Emilion's origins date back to the second century, when the Romans established an outpost and began planting vines. In the eighth century, monks settled there. Between the ninth and twelfth centuries, a church, now called the Monolithic Church, was carved into a massive stone outcropping. In subsequent centuries a Gothic bell tower was built literally on top of it. Narrow cobblestoned streets feed off the main square. Despite Saint-Emilion's fame, which attracts more than a million tourists annually and supports dozens of wine stores and boutiques, it counts only a few hundred inhabitants.

Before becoming a wine cellar, Gracia's garage stored building equipment. The 450 square feet of space is divided into two small rooms and looks primitive. The floor is fashioned from simple clay tiles. The walls are whitewashed, to fight off odors. The ceiling is simple red construction brick. In one room, two dozen oak barrels are lined up. In the other stand two squat stainless steel tanks. There is no tasting table. A few Pyrex graduated cylinders, the type used in high school chemistry classes, represent the only visible equipment. Gracia uses these to blend wine from the various barrels.

Despite the simple surroundings, Gracia makes no *vin ordinaire*. He produces a dark, dramatic wine called, simply, Gracia, which he sells for as much as Angélus and other top-ranked *grands crus*.

Quixotic? Certainly. Crazy? Not at all. For the past two decades, some of Gracia's neighbors in Saint-Emilion have been producing special small-production wines. They don't require large vineyards or big crews. A few workers suffice. Hard work on average land takes the place of hundreds of years of history. And while any decent-minded Bordeaux winemaker wants to host glittering receptions in a comfortable manor house, *garagistes* such as Gracia are satisfied with, literally, garages.

In 1996 Gracia's stepmother died at the age of 102, leaving him a small parcel of vines on a modest hill above Saint-Emilion. Like most growers of her generation, she had pushed for quantity over quality, producing three times more juice per acre than the village's best growers. "She made the vines piss wine," was the way Gracia put it. Once harvested, the bloated grapes were sold in bulk to the local cooperative, where they produced a diluted, bitter drink.

Gracia, following in his neighbors' footsteps, turned his stepmother's recipe upside down. Instead of encouraging the vines to grow as many grapes as possible, he worked hard to reduce the crop. He trimmed and tailored his vines, cutting away leaves and bunches of excess fruit, so that the remaining grapes, in Darwinian fashion, became concentrated and strong. Rich and ripe fruit allowed him to make rich and ripe wine.

Harvesting, too, differs from the traditional methods. It takes place weeks later than in the past, when the fruit has reached optimal ripeness. And the precious fruit is brought in by hand and sorted "berry by berry," to remove all underripe grapes and stray branches that might give the wine a green, bitter taste. The juice is then fermented as slowly as possible, to extract maximum color and concentration. He called the wine by his own name—Gracia—not even bothering to add the word "Château."

By the time Gracia decided to make wine, he was fifty-seven years old. The son of an immigrant construction worker from Spain, Gracia himself is an artist. In his youth, he studied sculpture for two years at Bordeaux's Ecole des Beaux-Arts and apprenticed with a professional stonemason. This earned him a prized government-bestowed diploma that allows him to work on historic monuments.

His masonry and construction company, Gracia Enterprises, renovated the bell tower above Saint-Emilion's Monolithic Church, and in 2001 was restoring its arched doorways and stained glass windows. Gracia can even resculpt gargoyles. Over three decades, he has renovated many of the fancy wine estates around Saint-Emilion, including Château Angélus. During the 1990s, as money poured into Bordeaux, his business boomed. By now it had fifty full-time employees and generated $5 million in annual revenues.

Despite his success, Gracia knows his place in France's rigid social hierarchy and doesn't feel at ease in the upper-class wine world. While most Bordeaux mandarins are rarely seen in public without a tie and jacket, Gracia favors jeans and open-collar polo shirts. He was a star soccer player in his youth, but his love of good food has betrayed him and produced a hefty stomach. He is balding, but lets his remaining gray hair grow out curly, almost hippie-style.

Gracia's favorite expression is *"putain."* Literally, that means "whore." But to the stonemason, the vulgar term is not an insult. It expresses, depending on emphasis, everything from mild interest to wild surprise to deep disapproval. If he's watching a local soccer game and the center forward makes a nice move, he yells, *"Putain."* When he found out that Jeffrey Davies, the merchant who has been helping him bring his wine to market for the past several years, drives a BMW, he was more emphatic.

"PU-TAIN."

Gracia works in the center of the village but lives modestly in a nondescript ranch-style bungalow a few minutes away, near the main road leading from Libourne, the nearest commercial center. His front yard serves as an open-air warehouse for stones and building materials of all sizes and shapes, and his offices are in two mobile homes. Gracia has often said he will fix up something more permanent, but he never seems to get around to it. "Construction workers always build for themselves last," he observed.

Aristocrats running prestigious estates don't appreciate this simple worker's efforts to make an expensive wine. "My clients will be furious if my wine sells for more than theirs," he said, smacking his lips, half in fear and half in anticipated delight. For Gracia, wine was becoming a passion. If you grow up in Florida, you want to become a scratch golfer. If you come from Saint-Emilion, you want to become a *vigneron*. When he started out, Gracia was like a talented amateur golfer who tries to qualify for the U.S. Open. If he succeeded with his garage wine, he would prove himself as good as the counts and countesses who had inherited their vineyards. His two daughters, both in their early twenties, were relying on him. They weren't interested in the construction business. They wanted to make wine.

Gracia believed he could make a first-class product. "If I can restore a twelfth-century stone archway, I believe I can make a great wine," he said. And yet, without any pedigree, how could he sell it? It is much easier for an American amateur to go to the supermarket and buy Beringer or Rosemount than a Bordeaux Château No-name. Even within Bordeaux the word *château* has become debased. It may sound grand, but only a few of the region's winemakers boast the turrets and tall fortified walls, the keeps and gates of storybook tales. Anybody can put a château label on the wine as long as it comes from a specific parcel of vines. Many winemakers do, no matter what the quality of their product.

French vintners have adopted various strategies in order to raise their images above the tangle of competing châteaux. A few count on centuries of tradition and a fancy name. Others pack up their trucks and peddle their wares at food markets and wine fairs. And yet others put up billboards and sell to passing tourists. But these strategies target the lowest common denominator. Few tourists pay top dollar, and the general rule in French wine country is, "The bigger the sign, the worse the wine."

Gracia couldn't sell centuries of tradition and needed something more powerful than a peddler's truck or a big sign. He knew what it was: *"PUUUUTTTTTAAAIIIN!"* he exclaimed. "I need a good Parker score."

Parker is Robert Parker, a bulky, top-heavy, hardworking, and straight-shooting American wine critic. He lives half a world away from Bordeaux, north of Baltimore in the backwoods of Maryland, surrounded by dairy farms. He travels only twice a year to Bordeaux.

But his power is uncontested. Since 1978 Parker has written and published almost single-handed a dry monthly newsletter called the *Wine Advocate*. For each issue, Parker tastes several hundred wines, giving each a blunt commentary of several lines and scoring each like a schoolteacher between 50 and 100. A wine rated in the 70s is poor. One in the 80s is average. Anything over 90 is good—and gives the wine a commercial lift.

For centuries France's wine capital was known for producing complex, light-colored wines; hence the English moniker "claret." Many years when it rained or turned cold too soon, the region's wines were thin, acidic, and astringent. Apologists might mistake the thinness for subtlety. The wine could not be consumed soon after harvest. It needed to be cellared and drunk decades later. By then, if it still proved thin on the palate, at least few of the original buyers would be around to complain.

Parker, by contrast, favors rich-colored, intensely flavored wines that can be downed young. Tradition? Pedigree? Parker doesn't care. "I don't give a shit that your family goes back to pre-Revolution and you've got more wealth than I could imagine," he told one journalist. "If the wine's no good, I'm gonna say so."

During the 1990s, Parker became so powerful that he stopped attending the Union des Grands Crus spring tasting events. Too many people watched him taste and followed his every move. He dismissed the show as a circus. "How can you taste with all that commotion?" he asked. For the past few years he has traveled to Bordeaux before the Union tasting and worked alone, in merchants' offices and at individual estates. He stays at the basic Sofitel on Bordeaux's beltway. "It's a convenient location," he explained. Every evening he returns there early, eats a simple dinner, and goes to sleep. "You can't do this job seriously unless you've had a good night's sleep," he said.

Other critics rush to publish. In 1999 James Suckling of the *Wine Spectator*, the best-selling wine magazine in the world, published his scores— also ranging from 50 to 100—on the Internet even before the Union des Grands Crus tastings began. Few noticed. The market waited for Parker and Parker took his time, releasing his scores only at the end of April. Only after his verdict came out were prices set.

Already in 1999 Parker had called for a 30 percent reduction in prices. It had rained a lot and the wines weren't outstanding by Parker's high standards. He worried aloud about retailers dumping the mediocre 1997s and the marginally better 1998s. That wasn't all. Bordeaux's growers and merchants had gotten greedy, Parker wrote. "If arrogance prevents them from understanding this," he wrote about the estate owners, "they will see the irresponsibility of their ways." The threat was clear.

Before Parker's rise, wines without a pedigree had no chance of joining the small world of futures. Even then, they never commanded top prices. But if Parker gave him a good score, Gracia believed he could sell his wine the spring after it was harvested for almost $50 a bottle. That required putting a sample under the guru's nose and hoping for the best.

For Gracia, today's tasting represented more pleasure than business. He liked receiving visitors and seeing their faces as they sipped his wine. But the merchandising impact was minimal. Parker had tasted his wine the week before, at Jeffrey Davies's office in Bordeaux. Afterward, the American critic had given the American merchant few hints about his thinking. His verdict was secret. Gracia would have to wait to find out his fate.

—

LATER IN THE TASTING WEEK, Yves Vatelot brought some journalists and importers to visit Château Lascombes. Lascombes is on the Médoc peninsula, just down the road from Château Margaux. The previous owners had decorated the dining room in a mix of black marble fixtures and gold-framed mirrors. "It looks like a bordello," Vatelot complained.

Entrepreneur Yves Vatelot shows investors around Château Lascombes.

Out back, Lascombes's cellar looked in even worse shape, like a concrete barn rather than a historic estate. Its walls were dark and gray, pocked with unrepaired holes. "We'll fix it up," Vatelot promised. He described plans to gut the cellar's interior and install a sparkling three-story winery in its place. Galvanized aluminum staircases would rise. Modern elevators would be put in place to lift freshly harvested grapes in small baskets to the top floor to be sorted and placed in new stainless steel tanks to begin the winemaking process. "We won't bruise the fruit by pumping it up," Vatelot said, expressing disdain for the standard method of most Bordeaux winemakers. "Everything will fall gently by gravity."

Vatelot, who already owned a château near Saint-Emilion, was putting up some of his own money and serving as the chief consultant to American investors who were about to buy the estate. They were scheduled to sign final papers on April 5. Although he had not been present for the 2000 harvest, the aggressive new owner had already changed the way Lascombes blended its wine. In an attempt to obtain a decent Parker score, he picked and chose from the best barrels. The vast majority of the production was relegated to a less expensive second wine called Chevalier de Lascombes. Only the best lots were reserved for the "château" wine. Vatelot was showing off his and the investors' soon-to-be acquisition by offering a few busy tasters a tour.

Like the upstart *garagistes,* newcomers with money to burn are storming the bastions of traditional Bordeaux. Vatelot doesn't need to live off the proceeds of his winery. Where giant insurers such as AXA dominated the 1980s, he and other rich entrepreneurs supplanted them during the 1990s. Purchasing a château makes sense for the ultrarich, particularly those who have sold their businesses. If they don't reinvest their money, they become liable for capital gains. If they buy another business—and a Bordeaux winery qualifies—they pay no tax while running it. Highly educated people who in another generation would have earned their living in white-collar professions have now focused their sights on producing a better bottle of wine. Financial freedom has allowed them to open their checkbooks. They can buy vineyards and live like princes.

Vatelot, the son of a journalist at the conservative daily newspaper *Le Figaro,* started out in Paris as a real estate developer. His career took off in the early 1980s when he had a girlfriend who was a model. Watching this woman laboriously wax her legs every time she prepared for photo shoots gave him the idea of inventing a razor with circular rotating blades that painlessly removed the hair from female legs. He called it Silk-Epil. By 1990 Vatelot's company employed three hundred and produced 3.5 million electric shavers a year. But, tiring of the business and facing a court case over his patent, the restless entrepreneur sold Silk-Epil to Gillette.

Several hundred million francs richer, Vatelot decided to live the life of a Bordeaux château owner. Ever since childhood, he has loved wine. Although his father didn't drink, his mother kept a large cellar of fine bottles, and whenever she received guests, the teenage son was allowed to taste. In high school, Vatelot participated in a wine club. As soon as he started earning money, he began collecting. By the time he was thirty years old, he owned six thousand bottles, many from the fine vintage of 1961, and many from the most renowned estates. "They weren't expensive then," he recalled.

His passion led him to Bordeaux, where about halfway between the city and Saint-Emilion, he settled on an elegant seventeenth-century château called Reignac. "I saw this magnificent place and knew at once that I wanted to live there," he said. When Vatelot moved into Château de Reignac in 1990, giant machine harvesters were used to bring in grapes and dump them into huge tanks. The result was barely drinkable table wine that sold mostly in bulk to the local cooperative. The wine is classified as a humble Bordeaux *supérieur*. Even the best Bordeaux *supérieur* never sold to consumers for more than $10 a bottle at the time.

But a local geologist told him he had perfect gravelly soil for growing grapes. In 1995 the ambitious Vatelot hired world-famous enologist Michel Rolland, based in nearby Pomerol, who advised him to follow the Gracia's *garagiste* recipe: slash yields, push back harvest dates by several weeks, and discard the machine harvesters. A shiny new winery was built in two short months, in time for the harvest. Thousands of new oak barrels were purchased from top barrel makers Seguin-Moreau, Demptos, and Sylvain. Whatever it cost, Vatelot was determined to make the best possible wine.

The next year, Parker gave Reignac's *cuvée speciale* scores in the high 80s and soon he was winning scores in the low 90s. "Reignac is the reference point for what can be achieved in Bordeaux's less prestigious *appellations*," he wrote of the 1996. This allowed Vatelot to sell Reignac as a future for $10 a bottle to Bordeaux merchants who passed it up the chain for $20 to consumers, almost unheard of for a Bordeaux *supérieur*. American consumers, less concerned than Europeans about historic labels, bought three-quarters of the production.

Only a little more than a decade after arriving in Bordeaux to live full-time, the ambitious Vatelot now aimed to join the wine major leagues. This meant investing in another château, this time in the Médoc. Here are situated the red wine world's holy of holies, châteaux such as Latour, Lafite Rothschild, Mouton Rothschild, and Margaux. The Médoc is vast and these are all large estates, covering as much as 250 acres and producing hundreds of thousands of bottles of wine each year. Their brand names are immediately recognizable, and the people who produce these legends are more than proud of their calling. As Paul Pontallier, the general manager who runs Château Margaux, put it, "We are bottling history."

Not surprisingly, Left Bank mandarins look down upon Vatelot and his fellow nouveaux riches who live around Saint-Emilion on the Right Bank of the Gironde River. In part, it is a question of size. Even the largest and most exalted Right Bank estates, such as Cheval Blanc and Pomerol's Pétrus, are much smaller than these vast domaines. In part, it's a matter of history. High-end Left Bank estates have enjoyed global reputations for several centuries. Right Bank stars won their laurels only within the last few decades, and in many cases, only within the last few years.

It's a social battle as well. Like Vatelot, most of the Left Bank owners made fortunes in banking or commerce. Ever since the nineteenth century, when Napoléon III's nouveaux riches, led by the Rothschilds, snapped up Médoc estates, Left Bank château owners have lived in Paris or Bordeaux. Rich businessmen wouldn't dream of getting their hands dirty in the vineyards, even though they profit from the wine produced on their lands. They employ peasants to do the hard work. To the vineyard owners, a château is less an investment than what the French call *danseuses,* pretty feminine jewels to show off. François Pinault, Château Latour's master, provides a good illustration. Once, on a trip to New York, he noticed that none of the Big Apple's elite cared that he was the owner of the Printemps retail chain and one of France's richest men. "But when I was in a restaurant and I said that I owned Château Latour, I suddenly was treated with respect," he said.

By contrast, Vatelot and his Right Bank friends live full-time on their estates and direct the winemaking themselves. Most wear jeans. Vatelot doesn't care about appearances. He refuses to chop off his thinning blond hair and dresses in smart, casual clothes even when meeting his bankers.

The Right Bank–Left Bank war is about winemaking, too. Left Bank wines taste more austere than Right Bank ones, a result of differences in land, cultivation, and grape varieties. While most modern wines, particularly in the New World, are made from single grape varieties, Bordeaux wines are blends. Back in the nineteenth century, as many as thirty different types of grapes grew in the region. Since then, for red wines, the varieties have been reduced to a mere half dozen. Two grapes dominate: Merlot, concentrated around Saint-Emilion, and Cabernet Sauvignon in the Médoc. Merlot thrives on clay soil, ripens early, and produces high-alcohol, richly colored wines that can be drunk while young. Cabernet Sauvignon is a much more brooding fruit. It ripens late and, when harvested ripe, requires time before revealing its perfumes of black currant and black cherry.

The Médoc mandarins consider the Right Bank's deep, dramatic concoctions made largely from the velvety Merlot to be "common wines." Their fickle Cabernet Sauvignon grapes produce wines that are hard and firm in their youth, requiring at least a decade before they are ready to be drunk. Of course, the Médoc produces some Merlot and uses Cabernet Franc and Petit Verdot for spicing. And despite its dominant Merlot, Saint-Emilion has some Cabernet Sauvignon and even more of its offshoot, the Cabernet Franc. But the proportions are small and the Médoc's princes believe that the Saint-Emilion recipe of fresh, fruit-driven Merlots is inappropriate for them. "Our wines have more finesse and gain complexity over time," boasts Château Margaux's Pontallier.

Upstart Vatelot scoffed at this discourse. He dismissed the aristocrats and *haute bourgeoisie* from the Médoc as lazy and arrogant, saying they kept yields too high and harvested before the fruit was mature. Cabernet Sauvignon may be a difficult grape, he admitted, but he was sure he could soften its hard edges and make it fruitier in youth.

"You harvest bitter grapes and you get bitter wine," insisted Vatelot.

How about complexity and aging?

"If it's shit the first year, it will be shit a decade later," he responded.

Vatelot didn't just aim to show the Left Bank princes the error of their ways. He wanted to make a fast buck. Throughout the Médoc, he saw underperforming estates. What if their wines were upgraded? The price of their bottles would increase. That wasn't all. The price of their vineyards would rise. Over the previous decade, the price of top Bordeaux vineyards had soared. At the turn of the millennium an acre of a generic Bordeaux vineyard still went for only about $33,000. Top estates were going for as much as $666,000 an acre. "More than anything else, Bordeaux is becoming a real estate play," Vatelot said.

That is why Vatelot zeroed in on Château Lascombes, founded in the seventeenth century by a knight named Antoine de Lascombes. When classifications were determined, it received a second-growth title, not bad. In recent years, however, Parker and other critics had derided Lascombes as weak and weedy. The 1995 had received a lowly 79. "This wine is now a candidate for drying out, given its hollow middle and hard, austere, angular finish," Parker wrote. The effects had been devastating. By the time Vatelot came on the scene, a bottle of Lascombes sold at a mere tenth of the price of one from Château Margaux located across the street.

Once he determined to invest in a Left Bank château, Vatelot knew he needed financial backing. His search for potential investors began in the summer of 2000 and led him to Sébastien Bazin, who worked for a group of American real estate investors called Colony Capital. The two soon joined forces. Colony was a Los Angeles–based company created to buy up distressed real estate from struggling savings and loans. Its major investors were pension funds such as CalPERS, the California public employees' pension fund. Colony bought low, revamped the asset, and then sold it off. During the 1990s, the company invested more than $7 billion.

In Europe, Colony concentrated on hotel and office properties in big cities, particularly Paris. A building boom in the 1980s followed by a recession in the early 1990s had left the French capital with far too much unused space. Colony picked up properties at half of their cost in 1998 and 1999, just before the French economy revived. Its investors cashed in, making 50 percent returns in less than two years.

Luckily for Vatelot, Colony was eyeing new opportunities. The Paris real estate market was fully valued and vineyards suddenly appeared a more promising investment. In the Napa Valley, Colony had already acquired numerous vineyards and made a killing as demand boomed for California wines. In France, the key was finding a property that was undervalued, improving its wine fast, and then cashing in. Before targeting Lascombes, Vatelot looked first at another Margaux estate, Château Prieuré-Lichine. It was owned by the descendents of the Russian-turned-American wine merchant Alexis Lichine, the man who did so much in the 1950s and 1960s to popularize top Bordeaux in the United States, both with the wines he sold and with the books he wrote. But they thought Prieuré's price was high and the inventory of past vintages in the cellar of doubtful quality.

Vatelot and Colony's sights next moved to Lascombes. British brewery and hotel group Bass Charrington hadn't paid much attention to the property, which it had purchased in the 1960s. It used the château to entertain high-ranking managers and their customers. "It was a trophy asset," recalled Bazin. Bass had recently sold the rest of its liquor division and decided to concentrate on running hotels. It wanted to sell.

Bazin's Colony and Vatelot agreed to pay $67 million. Colony took a 53 percent stake. Goldman Sachs and its partners, including discount airline Ryanair's founder Tony Ryan, took the rest, leaving Vatelot with only a symbolic financial stake but a strong position as their on-site representative in Bordeaux. In the year ahead, Vatelot planned to spend another $5 million of his investors' money cleaning up the vineyard and building the new, modern cellar. In future years, the business plan called for $5 million more in investment for transforming the château building itself into a luxury estate. The 2001 Lascombes would receive a sparkling Parker score, he promised. This would allow him, as his business plan demanded, to raise the price of Lascombes's wine by half next year and to triple it within five years. "Then we will sell off the property for a big profit," he vowed.

In the glow of the millennium year, no ambition seemed too grand.

—

FOR COUNT ALEXANDRE DE LUR-SALUCES, spring tasting week represented only a minor event. He refused to participate in the Union's scheduled tastings, considering himself above such crass commercialism. Although he held a cocktail party for select visitors during the week, he opened only older bottles. No outsider was allowed near the maturing wine still in barrels. His wine was always released four years after the vintage, and

Count Alexandre de Lur-Saluces (left) speaks with supporter Jean-Paul Kauffmann in front of Château d'Yquem for a French television program.

only then could critics get a taste. And unlike those in charge of other famous Bordeaux wines, the count had refused so far to sell his as a future.

This balding, bespectacled, and rumpled sixty-six-year-old man didn't look aristocratic. Yet he was the face of the world-renowned sweet white wine produced at Château d'Yquem, perched on a hill just outside the village of Sauternes, twenty-five miles southeast of Bordeaux. Here, since 1593, the Lur-Saluces family had put its name on the nectar. Through the centuries, Yquem has attracted an impressive array of admirers—

Thomas Jefferson among them. When Bordeaux's wines were classified, Yquem warranted a unique category on top of all others—first great growth, or *premier cru supérieur*. Other great wines, such as Château Margaux, were designated *premier cru*. Yquem alone got the extra *supérieur*.

Yquem is a glorious, mostly fourteenth-century edifice topped by limestone towers and parapets, one of the few Bordeaux châteaux worthy of the name. It stands atop a hill commanding a fairy-tale view of vines stretching down the slope, fading into a shimmering landscape of amber, green, and gold foliage and a gentle river meandering through the vineyards. Early evening sunlight reflects off the castle's polished limestone and the medieval sundials that grace two of the towers. In the spring of 2001, on another tower, this one added in the sixteenth century, the clock stood still.

Sauternes is the most traditional of Bordeaux regions, a place where the French Revolution never seemed to have an impact. Elsewhere in Bordeaux, most aristocrats have departed in recent years, replaced by rich entrepreneurs or peasants. Here, gilded châteaux still grace the hills, inhabited by many of their original noble families.

Even at the dawn of the twenty-first century, life at Yquem seemed a throwback to prerevolutionary times. A dozen houses for workers were spread about the property, and the houses and jobs were handed down from generation to generation. Until recently, individual employees didn't receive their own paychecks. Families did. "The count is so generous with us," said one woman who refused to give her name as she fed chickens in her yard. "He gives us everything." In 1999 the newspaper *Le Monde* mocked Lur-Saluces for feeding harvesters soup made from one of the least expensive, most pedestrian of vegetables, cauliflower. Lur-Saluces defended himself against the charge of practicing feudal paternalism. "Rural society permits social relations that would escape the understanding of Parisian journalists," he insisted.

The count always seemed to be on guard, wary of ordinary outsiders peering into his well-protected world. Signs to Sauternes's other châteaux line the narrow two-lane roads that cut through the vines. At one time, arrows pointed the way to Yquem, but the local mayor said visitors kept tearing them down as souvenirs. Now only the discreet and weathered Latin letters chiseled into stone centuries ago mark Yquem's main gate. "Tourists come all the time asking how to get there," reported an official at the Sauternes Tourist Office. Visitors sign up weeks in advance for a short guided tour, and even so, no hotel can lodge them in Sauternes. The isolation pleases Lur-Saluces. "We don't want to become like Mondavi in the Napa Valley," he said. "One must merit a visit to Yquem."

Producing Yquem requires similar patience. Sauternes and its splendid isolation are blessed with a special microclimate. From Yquem's sacred hill, one can see the Garonne River, which merges with its colder tributary, the Ciron. In autumn, mists form overnight and creep up the vineyards in the mornings. By the end of the morning, the sun has blazed through and burned them off. God forbid that Lur-Saluces should add sugar to his wine. He lets the fruit go rotten, and a fungus called *Botrytis cinerea* attacks it, shriveling the grape skins into brown pulp. Water escapes, concentrating the remaining sugars and flavors in the juice, producing the singular bouquet of sweetness for which Yquem is noted.

This is the work of nature the French call *pourriture noble*—noble rot.

Since the natural sugar adds to the wine's aging potential, certain vintages of Yquem may last more than a hundred years and still taste fresh. Noble rot develops at different times on the same vine, so pickers pass as many as six times through the vineyards during a single harvest, choosing the best moment to snip each berry.

Getting the right amount of rot is never a sure thing, much chancier than a good harvest for red wines. About once a decade the crop freezes. Other times, it doesn't get cold enough and most picking is delayed from traditional mid-October into cooler November. A little precipitation is required. But if it rains too much, the vines will be swamped and the fruit diluted. Three times over the past three decades, in 1972, 1974, and 1992, Lur-Saluces made the tough but wise choice not to bottle a single drop of Yquem. In those years, heavy rain persisted through the end of the month and into November. The water seeped into the vines' roots and bloated the berries. They rotted. But this rot was not noble. It was *pourriture gris*—an ignoble condition called gray rot.

Each year's production of the prized elixir is something of a divine miracle. Bordeaux châteaux that produce red wine on average generate one bottle per vine; at Yquem, an entire vine produces a single glass. Only the wealthiest estates indulge in this expensive technique to cultivate the ultimate dried-out, overripe noble condition. "Such a legacy is not easy to uphold," Lur-Saluces has often said. In his view, Yquem epitomizes the power of French traditions rooted in the nation's rich soil. The raw force of the global marketplace should not contaminate it.

Great Sauternes, given the difficulty of making it, is extremely expensive to produce. In recent decades, many growers struggled to avoid bankruptcy. Poor-quality sweet wines from other French regions proliferated, undercutting Sauternes's general image and eroding its market share. While red wine won a healthy image among consumers, sweet whites suffered from the perception of being calorie-filled and unhealthy, even if they were no more so than dry wines. In response, some Sauternes winemakers began mixing noble and less noble grapes, in hopes that lower costs and larger supply somehow would mean larger profits. Another difficulty is that Robert Parker favors red wines, expending little energy on whites, and rarely tastes Sauternes, nor does he include them in his all-important spring tasting scores. The American finds it difficult to match sweet wine with food. "Sauternes are wonderful wines, but too heavy before a meal and too heavy afterwards," he complains.

Other owners in Sauternes resent Lur-Saluces's arrogance. While few new wave winemakers settle in the tradition-bound region, some home-grown innovators are producing lighter, fruitier wines than Yquem—among them the Dubourdieu family at Château Doisy-Daëne. When Denis Dubourdieu tastes Yquem, he finds it heavy. "It gives me a stomach ache," he said. Yquem's failure to participate in the spring show angers Dubourdieu and he complains that it deprives the region of attention at a crucial period of the year. Many in the press don't even bother to make the trip south to Sauternes.

The millennium year tested the count and all Sauternes winemakers. September and the first half of October stayed warm and clement. Red winemakers smiled and harvested. Sauternes growers were optimistic. A smoky vapor began rising from the grapes. Noble rot appeared and the first few batches were brought into the cellars in perfect, moldy condition.

Then, on the morning of October 15, 2000, storm clouds gathered. Heavy rain continued through the end of the month and into November. Although winemakers tried to harvest, gray rot set in. About three-quarters of Yquem's harvest was ruined. Just a few weeks before, the growers of Bordeaux red wines had fêted a successful harvest. The red wine celebration now turned into a sweet white wine wake. Some other prestigious Sauternes châteaux, such as La Tour Blanche, refused to release a 2000 vintage, citing quality that wasn't "up to snuff." Doisy-Daëne released only a small amount and almost none of its luxury wine called Extravagant.

Since the 1970s, Lur-Saluces had skipped entire vintages three times, and he now left everyone to wonder if he would he do it again. The millennium spring tasting came and went. But the count remained mum. Bordeaux's power brokers waited for his decision.

THE TASTERS' VERDICTS arrived at the end of April and they were near unanimous: the 2000 vintage of top red Bordeaux was terrific. Parker called it "a phenomenal year that might turn out to be one of the greatest vintages that Bordeaux has ever produced." He went on CBS's *60 Minutes* and PBS's *Charlie Rose* and repeated his praise. He even published a list of twenty-four wines that he reckoned would be "legends of the future."

The unanswered question: How much would the legends cost? Once the campaign began, the first estate to release its futures was a new wave Parker favorite named Château Quinault L'Enclos, owned by Union president Alain Raynaud. Parker gave it a 94–96 rating, "outstanding." Raynaud decided to set an example. He raised his prices for merchants only 20 percent over 1999, from $25 to $30 a bottle, which, when passed through importers and retailers, translated to almost $60 by the time it reached consumers. "If Bordeaux doesn't want to create a bad taste in the consumer's mouth, it must stay reasonable," Raynaud said. Many merchants and retailers were still complaining that they had lost money on the 1997 vintage and had too much Bordeaux in stock. Quinault's 2000 production of 57,000 bottles sold out in a single day.

But no one else listened. On June 5, 2001, top names Château Margaux, Château Latour, Château Mouton Rothschild, Château Lafite Rothschild, and Château Haut-Brion set a record for young Bordeaux. Each tested the market by releasing a small amount of wine at $100 a bottle to merchants, a 71 percent increase from their 1999 price. Other estates followed with similar increases over 1999. Yet despite complaints by some merchants, the wines sold.

The following week, Château Margaux offered a second batch for $125 a bottle. Veteran traders called the price "crazy." But it was snapped up within minutes. Other top estates followed at the same price. A third and fourth release of Margaux soon appeared on the market. By the middle of June, Château Cheval Blanc, one of the two top-rated estates from Saint-Emilion, had increased its price to $200 a bottle. Château Latour went further, pushing its price up to $215 per bottle.

Amid the euphoria, a few voices of caution emerged. Cooler heads worried about the long-term impact of dramatic price increases. A rise of 10 percent would have been enough, insisted Anthony Barton of Château Léoville Barton. "We need to look to the future, and not make it so that only the ultrarich can drink good Bordeaux," he explained. He priced his own 2000 vintage at a moderate $30 a bottle.

Within hours of his announcement, however, the price of Léoville Barton in London retailers had quadrupled, reaching $120 a bottle. Barton was one of Bordeaux's few remaining traditionalists, who remembered the tough times as well as the present good ones. Other producers weren't going to let a merchant make a 200 percent profit overnight.

Michel Gracia worried about offering his Gracia too cheap. In 1997 Parker devoted several paragraphs to his debut vintage, judging the wine "powerfully extracted, rich, full-bodied, and concentrated, with abundant quantities of smoky oak intertwined with liqueur-like, intense black cherry and berry fruit." He rated it 89. Gracia had only 3,500 bottles to sell. He charged $25 a bottle and sold out within an hour to four merchants. The second year, 1998, Parker scored Gracia an outstanding 92, lauding the wine as "a spectacular effort" that "exhibits an opaque purple color as well as a gorgeous bouquet of overripe black cherries intermixed with blackberries, blueberries, licorice and smoky oak." Garcia charged $35 and sold out again. By 1999 he had added another acre of vines and had 6,000 bottles to sell. Parker again graded his wine a 92, and since Bordeaux prices rose across the board, he sold it at $40 a bottle.

The Gracia 2000 was "even better than the 1998 and 1999," Parker wrote. It is "a thick, unctuously textured Saint-Emilion with a dense purple color and gorgeous aromas of black cherry jam intermixed with graphite, earth, Asian spices and vanillin. Full-bodied and sweet because of fruit ripeness, it finishes with an explosive, voluptuous texture." The score? A splendid 92–94, as good as that for any of the wines with top pedigrees. Gracia sold out again in an hour, at $45 a bottle. "Just give me a little more time and I'll sell for as much as a first growth," Gracia predicted.

Yves Vatelot's golden touch seemed to be paying off as well. Parker called his 2000 Reignac "an awesome generic Bordeaux," adding, "It boasts a dense purple color as well as a sweet nose of *crème de cassis*, intermixed with mineral, toast and spice box aromas." The score was a sterling 90–91 and his final verdict stunning. "This 2000—believe it or not—is of classified-growth quality. If you don't believe me, insert it in a blind tasting against some of the best classified growths and see for yourself." Parker also approved of the changes at Château Lascombes, saying Vatelot had improved its wine by severe selection. Whereas the 1999 had received a failing 77–79 score, the 2000 Lascombes got a 90–92 and a nice write-up as a "charming, sexy wine."

By late June, frenzy had swept the market. Merchants felt they had to jump in right away or risk paying $100 more a bottle the following week. "I'd get a call in the morning with a price and the broker would say, 'Take it or leave it,'" said merchant Jeffrey Davies. Since it was still the middle of the night in the United States, he didn't know how most of his customers would react. "I began calling them at 3 A.M. to find out," Davies said. Often, though, he just had to gamble that they would buy, no matter how costly.

One of Davies's favorite wines was a Saint-Emilion *premier grand cru,* Château Pavie, made by a nouveau riche supermarket magnate named Gérard Perse. It cost $45 a bottle for merchants in 1998. On June 20 Perse's broker called Davies offering the 2000 vintage at $110 a bottle. Many of Davies's major customers were unreachable that day, en route to Bordeaux for the semiannual Vinexpo, one of the largest wine fairs in the world.

"I had two hours to make a decision or lose my allocation," said Davies. Pavie had received a 96–99 rating from Parker, who wrote that "except for some provincial knuckleheads (who resent outsiders), this is widely acclaimed as one of the region's most singular and greatest wines." Davies bought 3,684 bottles. For a small business, the $405,000 outlay represented a giant gamble.

The euphoria even swept up Alexandre de Lur-Saluces. He finally decided to go ahead and release a 2000 vintage as a future. It was the first time he had ever sold Yquem before bottling it. Quantities were limited, only 20,000 "future" bottles versus the 100,000 usually released four years after the vintage. It didn't benefit from any score, Parker or otherwise, good or bad, since critics had not tasted. Skeptics snickered that the count was succumbing to commercial thirst. Lur-Saluces insisted that the grapes harvested before the October rainfalls were excellent. His wholesale price was a staggering $400 a bottle.

Bordeaux's merchants swallowed hard. It was a lot to pay for a bottle of wine, even a mythic one. They hesitated. In the end, most bought a small quantity and resold it as quickly as possible at cost.

As the campaign petered out in the summer of 2001, the global economy was turning down. The next vintage would be crucial. With dot-com fever faded and New World wineries producing better and better wines, a poor harvest could cool the zeal of the remaining high-end buyers. The eyebrow-twitching prices suggested that many were buying top Bordeaux as financial investments to be sold later at auction rather than to be sipped. Even Bordeaux's cooler heads couldn't resist temptation. "We are running the risk of speculation," admitted Pierre Lurton, Château Cheval Blanc's director. By this time, he was selling his Cheval Blanc 2000 for $200 a bottle to merchants.

From his Maryland perch, the same Parker who had praised the millennium vintage watched with horror at how it was being sold. "I don't write for rich businessmen," he declared. "The consumer is getting screwed by all this market manipulation." With the all-powerful Parker demanding a correction, Bordeaux needed to be careful. Otherwise, its millennium-year bonanza could end up producing a nasty hangover.

CHAPTER 2

—

Broker Business

ACH MORNING AT ABOUT NINE, MANY OF SAINT-EMILION'S
winemakers, brokers, and merchants congregate at a village café. It is a
nondescript place—linoleum flooring, a couple of cheap tables, and a
zinc bar where drinks are taken standing up. Over cups of thick, dark
espresso, the locals discuss everything from soccer results to who is sleep-
ing with whom—and, of course, who is making good wine.

One morning at the café in the spring of 1996, a thirty-two-year-old
broker named Thierry Castells first learned about Michel Gracia's winemaking plans. "When I heard Michel was getting his hands on some vineyards, I thought he would do something exceptional because he is so
meticulous and respected in his restoration work," Castells said.

If Castells becomes excited about a wine, it is a good omen because
he has a knack for discovering some of the best. Brokers play a pivotal, if
controversial, role in Bordeaux. When they first appeared in the fourteenth century, brokers acted as consumer advocates, tasting the wine
before it was exported and certifying to the authorities that it was "loyal
and without any defaults," as the saying went. Over the centuries, they
became middlemen for merchants who didn't have the time to visit all

their suppliers. When a grower wanted to offer his wine to the market, he consulted with a broker, who suggested what price he could expect to receive. The broker then approached merchants with a proposal. He received a flat 2 percent commission on sales.

In 1739 Abraham Lawton emigrated from Ireland to France. His family brokerage remains in business, run by a direct descendant, Daniel-Georges Lawton. While growers and merchants came and went, the brokers remained. Their deep knowledge, passed down in ledgers recording prices, weather, quality, and sales, gave them great influence. When the decision was made to compile an official classification of Bordeaux wines in 1855, the brokers were assigned the task. Only they had the detailed historical track record of sales over a century of vintages on which the ratings were based.

In recent years, brokers have largely become an entrenched class. Newcomers find it hard to enter the business because the most famous châteaux, such as Yquem, have sold the same amount of wine to the same merchants for decades. In these cases, all the broker has to do is draw up the paperwork for the transaction. That takes a maximum of ten minutes per deal. Not surprisingly, many brokers earned such derisive nicknames as *porteur d'échantillons*—sample carriers—or even worse.

But some brokers such as Castells still play a key role today, particularly in discovering promising new wines. While the traditional practitioner dealing with well-known estates spends most of his time in comfortable offices, this new-style operator does the difficult groundwork. Pearls among Bordeaux's ten thousand growers are rare. The successful modern broker must find them, cultivate them, and convince a merchant to buy them. This calls for detective skills worthy of a police investigator and diplomacy befitting a local politician. Different merchants favor different types of wine. One might be looking for a fresh Sauvignon Blanc. Another might favor soft, round Merlots. And a third might desire aromatic blends of Cabernet Sauvignon and Merlot. The broker has to know how to identify the talents of his suppliers in order to quench the specific thirst of his buyers. "We are the eyes and ears of the merchants," said Castells.

Until recently, the division of labor between brokers and merchants was clear. Merchants were the traders who managed contacts with importers in foreign markets. Brokers were the scouts with the contacts among growers. These once clear lines now have blurred. Powerful critics such as Parker, renowned enologists such as Michel Rolland, and even some dynamic merchants such as Jeffrey Davies have started performing some of the scouting role themselves.

Clever brokers only survive by lending these other Bordeaux power players a helping hand, and that is the case with Castells. The wiry broker with a terrierlike face had originally trained to be a navy pilot. When he wasn't chosen to fly the latest jets, though, he struggled to find a place as a civilian pilot and didn't have his heart in it. "Flying a Mirage is like driving a Ferrari," he said. "Flying an Airbus is like driving a bus."

Castells returned home to Bordeaux, studied enology at the state-run Château La Tour Blanche's school in Sauternes, and took over managing his family's ten-acre vineyard in a village near Saint-Emilion. But he soon realized he could never pay the heavy inheritance tax that would come due on his parents' death. A friend of his was a broker and needed an assistant. He convinced his parents to sell their vineyard to a British businessman and began brokering. He soon carved out a specialty, discovering small promising producers. Since he drank coffee almost every morning with Michel Gracia at the Saint-Emilion café, Castells was well placed to become his friend's go-between. Gracia told him to go find a merchant for his wine. "I needed someone who was sensitive to this type of project and who had access to wine critics, particularly Parker," Castells said.

His first call was to Jeffrey Davies, one of the leaders of a new generation of merchants in Bordeaux. Davies concentrates his business on *garagistes* such as Gracia and nouveau riche winemakers such as Yves Vatelot. Davies sees himself, correctly, as a revolutionary, democratizing Bordeaux. "It takes no genius to procure and propose the *grand cru* wines," said Davies. "What does take time and perseverance is uncovering those producers in the less revered *appellations* who are determined to make the most exceptional wines possible."

This philosophy appeals to the world's most important nose: Robert Parker. Davies is on a first-name basis with Parker. Every winter, on one of his two annual visits to Bordeaux, Parker spends four or five hours tasting in Davies's office in the city. "Jeffrey knows how to ferret out over-achievers," says an admiring Parker.

American Jeffrey Davies follows a long tradition of foreigners playing a key role in the Bordeaux wine trade.

Born and raised in California, Davies still looks and dresses like a Californian. With his light hair and casual Levi's, he always stands out among the dark-haired, formally dressed French merchants.

Davies first arrived in Bordeaux in 1972 as a nineteen-year-old exchange student from the University of California. For a youngster brought up in sunny California, Bordeaux's Atlantic climate was a problem. "It rained and was dreary and I became depressed," he recalled.

Within a few months his spirits improved. He met his future wife, Françoise, at a college coffee party. She was eighteen, with a fine, angular face and sharp figure. How worldly and sophisticated she seemed to the young Californian. Jeff could often be carefree, spending his last centime, not to mention spending more time in the vineyards than in college classrooms. Françoise was serious, and she brought order and discipline.

He bought a motorized bicycle the French call a *mobylette* in order to visit châteaux. One night he crashed into the side of a car on the rue Saint-Catherine, one of the city's busy commercial thoroughfares. He ended up in the hospital. His chin had been cracked open and, worse, a key artery severed. The first surgeons did a lamentable job fixing him up and Davies nearly died on the operating table. Françoise was off in England working as an *au pair* to improve her English, but he kept thinking about her. She returned to nurse him back to health. The lasting memory of his brush with death was a scar under his chin—and a commitment to the Frenchwoman who had helped him. In 1974, he finished his undergraduate studies at the University of California, and the next year he returned to Bordeaux, to Françoise, and to the local university's Institute of Enology. He proceeded to graduate from the enology institute, one of the first two Americans to do so.

In 1976 he and Françoise moved to the States and married. He first worked as a wine salesman at 67 Wine & Spirits in New York, then as an importer in Kansas City, where he became the midwestern director of one of the first wine appreciation clubs, Les Amis du Vin. He also wrote for the club's newsletter.

But Françoise soon tired of the Midwest and in 1982 they returned to France, where they ran a country hotel north of Bordeaux. Davies supplemented his income by freelancing for a number of magazines. One of his articles was a year-by-year description of Bordeaux vintages. When he later met Parker, the critic said his work had helped inspire him.

But Davies couldn't make enough of a living to support Françoise and their two young boys. In 1987 he moved to the city and began selling wines on a commission basis. His formula was to search out good but unknown producers and take a percentage for selling their wines to American importers. The producers invoiced the importers. This allowed Davies to avoid the risk of financing large amounts of inventory. But it also meant importers received dozens of different bills. They told Davies that they wanted to pay only a single invoice.

In response, the American set up Signature Selections and became a full-fledged merchant. Unlike the traditional French houses, Davies didn't work in a fancy office above extensive cellars of wine. He operated out of a home office, with one secretary and a single tasting room where he received brokers bringing him samples to taste. More often than not, he was in the vineyards and cellars.

Davies's business soon prospered. By the millennium year, he and his family lived in more than comfortable fashion. He had just spent a tidy sum renovating his home and office, as well as buying a black Mercedes sedan and a BMW sport-utility vehicle.

Despite these outward trappings of success, Davies remains a rebel. He bemoans the *place de Bordeaux,* considering it outdated and ossified. The *place*'s clubbiness frustrates him. He neither cares that he was never invited to join their exclusive tennis and golf clubs nor wants to spend the summer with them on the beach in Arcachon or Cap Ferret. He prefers to take his family back to the States. "When I take a vacation, I don't want to see the same people that I work with," he said.

Davies has little respect for brokers and merchants who survive just because of their pedigree. "It seems like you have to be around for a century before the first growths will even consider selling to you," he observed. Since these exclusive properties bottle their own wines, the old-style merchants don't need to keep any stock or participate in the winemaking process. They need only to contact their buyers in the United States or Britain or Germany. "They're *faxistes,*" he mocked, in his idiomatic French that sounds native, without even a trace of an American accent.

Davies does business differently. He concentrates on discovering small unknown winemakers and working with them to make top-quality wines. When he began traveling to the hinterlands of Bordeaux, he found out the traditional merchants never went there. The *place de Bordeaux* still worked well for those who already had money and a brand name. Unknown winemakers needed a new-style merchant like Davies, who would sell their wines—and even help produce them. If new oak barrels are needed to age the wine, Davies finances the barrels. If a consulting enologist needs to be called in, Davies makes the contact. Once the grapes are harvested and fermented, he designs an attractive label for the front of the bottle and writes a poetic description for the back. Only then does he pitch the wine to specialty wine distributors, primarily in the United States. In the 1990s, Davies began working with winemakers elsewhere in France, even producing small amounts of his own garage wine, Clos des Truffiers, in the Mediterranean region called Languedoc.

Earlier in his career, Davies attempted to work without brokers, buying direct from growers. The brokers naturally resisted, but so did growers, who refused to sell to him. "Jeffrey was like Don Quixote," recalls Olivier Sèze of Château Charmail. "He's learned now that you can't fight the system. You need to work within it." Reluctantly, Davies agreed to pay the brokers' 2 percent fee and share consignments with other merchants.

When Davies began representing Yves Vatelot's Château de Reignac, the deal was that he would do so exclusively, at least in the United States. In 1996 Davies sold 2,500 cases at $8.50 a bottle. Vatelot was pleased. The next year, the price increased by 30 percent and Davies still bought his full allotment of 2,500 cases. In 1999, when Robert Parker heaped praise on Vatelot's wines—"a terrific effort," the critic called them—it was Davies who sold the most Reignac as a future.

The success, however, led to a clash. Vatelot decided he wanted a wider distribution. That meant selling his wine to other merchants on the *place*. He worried that Davies sold only to distributors on the U.S. East and West Coasts and believed his wine needed to be available throughout Europe and the Far East. Vatelot also thought his wine should be sold in Britain. Davies said no major U.S. markets existed outside the coasts, with the exception of Chicago, and he could arrange to distribute Reignac for sale in Britain. In 1999 Vatelot went ahead anyway and offered his wine to other merchants on the *place de Bordeaux*.

Both men ended up disappointed. Vatelot discovered that few other merchants were interested in his wine because, as good as it is, Reignac remains only a Bordeaux *supérieur*. Davies felt burned because he hadn't received enough supply from Vatelot, and he soon found that other merchants were offering it to his customers in the United States. "Yves didn't expand the market," he complained. "He just split it up among several merchants." Vatelot hoped to get $13 a bottle, which meant that the wine would be sold for $26 in stores. That proved too high. The price came down and Vatelot's business relationship with Davies deteriorated into a series of mutual recriminations. Vatelot criticized Davies for insufficient distribution outside the U.S. coasts. Davies accused Vatelot of betraying him and his distributors by ending their exclusive arrangement. "I made Yves's wine a success in the U.S. and then he turned around and allowed other merchants to benefit from my hard work," Davies complained.

Michel Gracia knew the bitter history between Davies and Vatelot and warned Castells, from the beginning, that he wouldn't repeat the experience. Gracia equated exclusivity with serfdom. He remembered how, until the 1950s, merchants owned or leased many properties. The exclusivity system proved bad for both the producer and the merchant. If the winemaker sold to a number of merchants, he couldn't skimp on quality without fear of being noticed. If he had a captive customer, though, there was a risk of going to sleep.

For merchants, too, an obligation to buy an entire harvest could be dangerous. The Ginestet family was a case in point. When they owned Château Margaux, they sold the wine only through their own merchant house. In 1973 and 1974, the merchant branch was forced to buy huge amounts of Margaux's poor vintages. It plunged into bankruptcy and survived only by selling off its crown jewel. Although Davies wasn't proposing the same ingrown system of producing and selling his own wine—he could stop selling Gracia anytime and Gracia could, like Vatelot, begin selling elsewhere—the *garagiste* was adamant. Gracia refused to be "owned" by any one merchant.

Castells didn't like exclusivity, either. In Castells's opinion, that showed the American was a lone cowboy, unable to cooperate with others. Just as France fears it will be overwhelmed by American power, Castells's skepticism was rooted in a deep-seated fear of losing leverage. "Like many Americans, Jeffrey goes overboard and wants to control," Castells criticized.

But the French broker swallowed his dislike. He knew Davies was the best bet to market an unknown such as Gracia. The American had a record of spotting good wines, and his customers in the United States were much more willing to open their wallets than French connoisseurs. "Jeffrey doesn't care about your background, just how the wine tastes," Castells said.

Early one hot July morning, only a few months after Castells first learned of the stonemason's winemaking plans at the café, the three men convened in Saint-Emilion at Michel Gracia's garage. Gracia handed out tasting glasses, plunged his *pipette* into the barrel, and poured each man a glass. Silence. Each man tasted and spit out onto the floor.

"How do you plan to harvest?" Davies asked.

"By hand, just as with some of your other producers," Gracia answered. More tasting and questions followed about barrel makers and winemaking techniques. Within a few minutes Davies had made up his mind: he wanted in. Gracia would set the price the following spring, only after Davies had presented his new find to Parker. Castells stood silent on the sidelines during this entire discussion. But now he had an important point to make.

"No exclusivity, Jeffrey," he said. "We want at least three merchants involved."

Davies's smile faded.

"You brokers are just pimps," he said, only half in jest.

The demand angered the American. Davies understood that winemakers feared a merchant with exclusivity would never pay as high a price as if the wine were on the open market and that fewer retailers might sell his wine. But he wanted at least to be the sole distributor for the United States. Few Bordeaux wine merchants are willing to take the risk of launching a new, unknown winery such as Gracia. If he helped the stonemason gain a global reputation, he knew other merchants would arrive in droves telling the growers what a great job they were going to do in such and such a market. "Courageous conduct, isn't it?" he says he thought to himself.

But Davies liked Gracia and believed in him. He knew Castells might find someone else to replace him. The American took a final sip, smiled, and shook hands with both Gracia and his "broker," issuing a rallying cry: "Let's sculpt some great wine."

—

AS AN AMERICAN ABROAD, Davies is following in a long tradition. Foreigners like him have dominated the wine trade for much of Bordeaux's history. When the city was founded in the first century, it was linked with the Roman colonies of the Mediterranean, not Paris. In 1154 the local princess Eleanor of Aquitaine married King Henry II and England took control. For the next three hundred years, Bordeaux blossomed under English rule. During the fourteenth century, nearly a third of England's imports consisted of wine, almost all from Bordeaux. Even after French kings regained control in the next century, the trade with Britain continued.

By modern standards, the wine exported to England was weak, resembling modern rosé. The French called it *clairet,* meaning clear and light in color. The English deformed this word and came to call Bordeaux wines "claret." Most claret came from the area on the city's outskirts, especially the Graves district. Other vineyards existed on the steep banks of the Gironde and around Saint-Emilion. At this time, most of the Médoc peninsula was a vast marshland where few grapes were grown.

In addition to the English, the Dutch played an important role in transforming the region into a global wine capital. Dutch traders had already introduced tea and coffee from the Far East into Europe and spread the practice of using hops to improve the quality of beer. In the sixteenth century, they moved on to wine. The Dutch drained the Médoc, opening up large areas for cultivation of vines.

Dutch technology also allowed wine to be stored and aged for the first time. Until the mid-sixteenth century, Bordeaux's best wines were drunk young, within a year of harvest, before they could spoil and turn to vinegar. The Dutch perfected ways of keeping the drink healthy for longer periods. For Bordeaux, they developed a more effective trick to stabilize wines—sulfur. A wick was dipped in the chemical and burned in the barrel before it was filled. This prevented spoilage by inhibiting the growth of bacteria. Through such techniques, the Dutch supplied their customers—not only in northern Europe but also across the globe in their far-flung colonies—with wines that could survive a long sea voyage.

But the thrifty Dutch concentrated on cheap wines and Britain remained the prime market for Bordeaux's expensive bottles. In 1660, when the hedonistic Charles II was restored to the British throne once the Puritan teetotaler Oliver Cromwell had died, the stage was set in London for a wine renaissance. On April 10, 1662, the thirty-year-old Samuel Pepys spent an evening drinking at the Royal Oak Tavern on Lombard Street in the City of London. The next day, Pepys set down the first Parker-style review for a Bordeaux wine. "Drank," he wrote, "a sort of French wine called Ho Bryan that hath a good and most particular taste that I ever met with." He had tasted Haut-Brion, the first Bordeaux wine ever to be sold under the name of the estate that produced it. It was the beginning of "château" wines.

In Pepys's time, the Pontac family owned Haut-Brion. The Pontacs were landowners and lawyers, upper-class professionals who only later would gain aristocratic titles through marriage. They followed a family tradition of public service. At the same time Arnaud de Pontac began exporting Haut-Brion to London, he also served as mayor of Bordeaux.

In Burgundy, monks introduced the vine and produced the best wines. Only they had the necessary time, energy, and funds to make wine. In Bordeaux, rich politicians and professionals such as the Pontacs played the key role. Their winemaking recipe sounded strikingly similar to that of the modern-day *garagistes:* limit yields and reject moldy grapes. These Bordeaux winemasters stored their wine in bottles with proper corks, not in large hard-to-transport barrels. Their new aged and bottled wine commanded high prices.

The Pontacs opened a tavern in the British capital to sell upscale wine. Pontack's Head, as the bar was called, was located behind the Old Bailey, where wealthy barristers practiced. A good wine in a restaurant normally went for two shillings. Haut-Brion was sold at Pontack's Head for seven shillings. Both the tavern and the wine were an immediate success.

Already some of the world's smartest minds questioned the logic of paying giant sums for a bottle of fermented grape juice. English philosopher John Locke visited Haut-Brion in 1677. "A tun of wine of the best quality at Bordeaux, which is that of Médoc or Pontac, is worth 80 to 100 crowns. For this the English may thank their own folly," he wrote. "Very good wines may be had here for 35, 40 and 50 crowns." The celebrated free-market economist Adam Smith questioned the pricing of wine. He acknowledged that "the vine is more affected by the difference of soils than any other fruit tree" and "this flavour, real or imaginary, is sometimes peculiar of the produce of a few vineyards." High prices could be expected for wines where demand exceeded supply. On the other hand, the expensive wines don't cost much more to make than cheap ones. "The high price of the wine seems to be not so much the effect as the cause of careful cultivation," Smith concluded. His argument cuts to the heart of the modern debate about *garagistes* such as Gracia: are wines from certain parcels intrinsically better than others cultivated with greater care from less promising land?

Although the Frenchman Pontac exported his own wine to England, English-speaking merchants soon set up shop in Bordeaux to encourage the trade. Most of the early British merchants actually came from Ireland, starting with Tom Barton. "French Tom" set up in Bordeaux in the 1720s and soon became the biggest buyer of the most expensive wines, which he exported to Britain. Later came the Schröders and Schÿlers from Germany, the de Luzes and Mestrezats from Switzerland, and the Cruses from Denmark. The merchants called themselves *négociants éléveurs*—buyer-growers. They aged and stored wines themselves.

The merchants faced a dilemma: how to distinguish good from bad wines? Tasting is subjective. Prices paid by real customers provide a more objective guide. Brokers have long kept careful note of their sales, recording them year by year, and often month by month. Sales ledgers from the eighteenth century already showed Haut-Brion as the most expensive, followed by Latour, Lafite, Margaux, and Mouton.

In the years leading up to the French Revolution, the merchants succeeded in interesting customers outside Britain in these exotic and expensive wines. The most famous was Thomas Jefferson, who was dispatched as ambassador to France in 1784. He hated the reactionary French royal regime, filling his diary with complaints about how the nobles mistreated the peasantry, leaving it on the verge of starvation. But the American democrat loved the country's exclusive wines. In May 1787, Jefferson traveled to Bordeaux. He approved of the city's reds, particularly Haut-Brion, calling it "Haubrion."

The future American president's preference was for white wines, however, and in particular the Sauternes of "M. Diquem." Yquem, benefiting from its position on the top of a hill, started out as an English fortress in the twelfth century. When the English were defeated, the property reverted to the French crown. In 1593 the king donated it to a knight, Jacques Sauvage d'Yquem. In 1785 the estate's sole inheritor, Françoise-Joséphine Sauvage d'Yquem, married the young Count Louis-Amédée de Lur-Saluces. Both the d'Yquems and the Lur-Saluces were *noblesse de l'épée*, who owed their status to military exploits and had far smaller ambitions and fortunes than the Bordeaux merchants and politicians. Louis-Amédée was a colonel. In 1788, just before the Revolution, he fell off his horse on maneuvers and died. The widowed Françoise-Joséphine took over and nurtured the estate to true fame.

How Yquem came to create the recipe for its elixir is not well understood. Some historians say the technique of noble rot arrived from eastern Europe. Beginning in the eleventh century, growers in Hungary's Tokay produced late-harvest wines for the imperial Austrian court. The technique spread to Germany's Rhineland and could have come from there to Sauternes. As evidence, scholars point to the arrival in the 1830s in Sauternes of a Mr. Focke from the Rhineland. He bought Château La Tour Blanche.

But strong evidence exists that Yquem's masters were already aiming to produce a nobly rotten wine. In the seventeenth century, all white wine makers strove to produce sweet wines. A dry white was considered thin. In a document dated October 4, 1666, Yquem's then owner, François Sauvage, specified that "in order not to harm the reputation of the said wine, harvesting shall be done only when the grapes are fully ripe." He specified that this meant about October 15, a month after the harvest elsewhere. By that time, the grapes must have been at least partially rotten.

In the seventeenth century, the harvesters did not make several passes through the vineyards as they do today. Each year was a hit-or-miss affair.

Seventeenth-century grape pickers just picked grapes late, and thanked God for the proper weather to produce suitably shriveled and nobly rotten fruit. In Sauternes, the practice of making several passes through the vineyard "was installed progressively, over time, due to observation," said Alexandre de Lur-Saluces. "Only little by little did consumers become enthusiastic for the type of wine that requires extravagant efforts."

Customers for nobly rotten Sauternes appeared in the second half of the eighteenth century. Jefferson was only the most famous. He was a connoisseur willing to pay a premium for superior quality. He demanded that his wine come from certain barrels and be bottled at the property so as not to be altered by unscrupulous merchants. "I know yours is one of the best growth of Sauternes, and it is from your hand that I would prefer to receive it directly, because I shall be sure of receiving it natural, good and sound," he wrote to Count Louis-Amédée de Lur-Saluces.

Jefferson ordered 250 bottles of Yquem's 1784 vintage. The wine pleased him so much that in November 1788 he wrote from Philadelphia to the American consul in Bordeaux: "The Sauternes sent me by the Marquis de Saluces turns out very fine." The next year Jefferson bought 250 more bottles, some for himself, others because he had "persuaded our President, General Washington, to try a sample."

Back in Bordeaux, payments from satisfied customers, along with a dramatic surge in colonial trade, ignited a building boom. Prosperous businessmen erected splendid country mansions in Sauternes. Within the city, the transformation was even more dramatic. A fortress outpost that had begun the eighteenth century surrounded by medieval walls became one of France's most modern metropolises. Wide boulevards were carved between the old fortress, the Château Trompette, and a new, elegant public garden. In the 1740s, the grand Place Royale was built on the crescent-shaped port. Its classical symmetry and sculptural details rivaled the Place Vendôme in Paris or even stupendous monuments further away. In the summer of 2001, the municipality put up posters depicting the Place Royale with the tag line "St. Petersburg? No, ten minutes from here!"

As Bordeaux prospered in the 1780s, its citizens celebrated by building an opera house, the Grand Théâtre, which architecture critics consider the most impressive theater erected anywhere in Europe in the eighteenth century. A dozen monumental Corinthian columns frame a magnificent façade. The gilded interior boasts fine acoustics. When Paris revolted in 1789, the Grand Théâtre was completed and the streets of Bordeaux remained calm.

EVENTUALLY THE REVOLUTION swept through Bordeaux. Lafite's and Margaux's owners were guillotined and their heirs fled the country. Some of the largest merchant houses went into liquidation. Many foreigners were forced to leave. Hugh Barton, Tom's son, placed his business in the hands of his French assistant, Daniel Guestier, and the merchant firm Barton & Guestier was born. But Barton was able to hang on to his ownership by proving to the authorities that he was a citizen of neutral Ireland, not of enemy England.

Wars with the English continued, intermittently, through 1815. British ships blockaded France and even closed off shipping routes to the newly independent United States. Perhaps even worse, Napoléon Bonaparte was not a drinker of Bordeaux: he preferred Burgundy. Bordeaux's vineyards declined in size by about a third from 1789 to 1808. Prices fell by a half during the period, despite some excellent vintages.

When the dust settled, however, not much had changed. Peasants won control of small parcels in Burgundy during the revolutionary period. In Bordeaux, most large estates stayed intact. The Lur-Saluces even managed to consolidate their control in Sauternes. Although the revolutionary government had imprisoned widow Françoise-Joséphine from December 1793 to the end of January 1794 and expropriated Yquem, the property was returned to her soon after her release. She lived at Yquem in the château until her death in 1851. Through astute marriages, the Lur-Saluces were able to take over many of Sauternes's other key vineyards, including Filhot, Coutet, and Malle.

During the nineteenth century, Hugh Barton and most of the other foreigners returned and helped usher in a new era of prosperity. They concentrated in a suburb just north of the city center on the Quai des

Chartrons, operating as both brokers and merchants, traveling from property to property to buy up wines, then storing and aging them themselves. Their cellars stretched both under and above ground half a mile behind their offices. Since they were bottling and sometimes blending the wine themselves, the merchants often put their own names in larger type than such celebrated names as Château Lafite or d'Yquem.

Foreign merchants soon became so powerful and rich that they began buying châteaux, particularly in the Médoc. Some of these same merchant families continue to own these estates. In 1826 the Bartons purchased the magnificent Château Langoa in Saint-Julien, and a few years later Château Léoville. In 2001 Anthony Barton still held sway. Unlike French clans that usually divide up their estates equally among children, often losing them in the process, the Bartons kept theirs within the family by always giving 100 percent to the eldest child. Anthony Barton was born and educated in London, and even after decades in France, speaks better English than French. "We Anglo-Saxons are more pragmatic, less sentimental than the French about these family matters," says Barton.

By the mid-1800s, the merchants owned almost all of the best lands in the Médoc. Their ostentatious palaces mixed historical styles, giving the region its present-day flavor—rolling expanses of vineyards punctuated by overblown manors and impoverished villages. Red brick Château Cantenac-Brown echoes a Gothic fortress, Château Pichon-Longueville-Comtesse de Lalande copies the lines of a Renaissance manor, and Château Ducru-Beaucaillou takes on the elegant, symmetrical lines of a classical prerevolutionary Bourbon palace.

Bordeaux's second golden age unfolded. Fright caused by revolutionary upheaval in 1848 faded and the French economy was expanding. Napoléon III's Second Empire was embarked on a massive rebuilding of Paris. Georges-Eugène Haussmann would soon lay out the broad boulevards and build the apartments with their wrought-iron railings that give the capital its present splendor.

In order to celebrate its prosperity, France hosted a Universal Exposition in 1855. It was meant to rival Britain's magnificent Great Exposition held four years earlier in the Crystal Palace, in London's Hyde Park. The Great

Exposition had brought together fifteen thousand exhibitors in the 200,000-square-foot building. It was a hymn to the Industrial Revolution, showcasing the unparalleled prosperity and prowess of the Victorian empire.

Napoléon III ordered the building of two grand palaces in Paris to house the Universal Exposition and named his ambitious younger brother, Prince Jérôme Napoléon Bonaparte, to direct the fair. The Burgundy and Champagne chambers of commerce wanted to show off their wines, and Burgundy's organizing committee wrote to their Bordeaux confederates asking whether they wanted to join in. The Bordeaux committee agreed and asked the city's chamber of commerce to organize the display in Paris. The chamber turned to the brokers, setting them a due date of April 5, 1855, to present "an exact and complete list." The brokers, in turn, set up a rating committee to deal with the chamber's demand.

The simple request should not have caused a commotion. For more than a century the price differentials among wines produced from various properties had stayed steady or shifted only gradually. Even before the Revolution, Jefferson wrote in his notes, "There are four vineyards of first quality." They were Margaux, Latour, Lafite, and Haut-Brion. He went on to mention "second quality wines" such as Léoville, followed by what he called "third class" estates such as Marquis de Terme. In 1816 a French writer named André Jullien published a book called *Topographie de Tous les Vignobles Connus—The Topography of All the Known Vineyards*—citing Margaux, Lafite, Latour, and Haut-Brion as "first growths" and recognizing seven second growths. After that, he listed only villages in order of quality. In 1824 a German merchant named Wilhelm Franck listed a total of thirty-three properties in the Médoc, dividing them into four levels. Then, in 1850, an English professor, Charles Cocks, and a Bordeaux bookseller, Michel Féret, published a comprehensive list in French. Cocks was close to brokers and used their prices to rank wines in five categories. By 1855 the idea of a list based on selling prices was taking hold in the public consciousness.

And yet the chamber of commerce's mercantile desire for a new classification sparked an epic and sometimes farcical battle among château owners and merchants. The brokers realized the sensitivity of their assignment. "You know as well as we do, Sirs, that this classification is a delicate task and bound to raise questions," the chairman of the brokers' rating committee wrote to the chamber. Cocks's guide had publicized the addresses and names of the estates, opening the possibility that the producers could export direct. The merchants, mostly members of the chamber, now attempted to reinforce their control over the growers and insisted that the wines be marked only by a uniform chamber of commerce label, not with the estates' own labels.

Château Lafite's manager, a determined man named Monplaisir Goudal, protested. He wanted the name of his estate printed in bold letters. Prince Jérôme Napoléon decided in favor of Goudal. Despite this defeat, the merchants still won the war. In the final classification, wines were rated by price, not the result of a tasting. "They invented nothing. They only made a transcript of the commercial state of affairs on the *place de Bordeaux,*" says Dewey Markham Jr., an American scholar who spent several years studying the classification.

The listing in Sauternes stirred little debate. By this time, Yquem had already carved out a place for itself above the other Sauternes châteaux. In 1854 its 1846 vintage was selling at twice the price of the next most expensive rival. In contrast, the Médoc first growths were fetching a premium of only 10 percent over the second growths. Because of this wide gap between Yquem and the other Sauternes, the brokers created the unique *premier cru supérieur* category.

The ranking of the red wines caused more controversy. The first growths were Margaux, Latour, Lafite, and Haut-Brion. The Rothschilds had just bought Brane-Mouton in 1853 and renamed it Mouton Rothschild. Their wine was already rising in value. But its track record of prices wasn't long enough to merit the top status, so it became a second growth, though the first of the seconds. Palmer, another recently acquired estate being upgraded, received only third-growth status, well below its true grade. Château Cantemerle, originally ignored, was added as a fifth growth after its owner protested that the estate's wine had been ignored because it was sold only in Holland until 1854. The entry for Cantemerle was written in after the brokers had presented their document to the chamber.

Wines of the southern part of the peninsula around Margaux received more attention compared to wines of potentially higher quality further north in, say, Saint-Estèphe. "Before the construction of the railway up the Médoc in the 1860s, transport costs meant that the nearer the estate was to Bordeaux the more highly it was valued," notes Nicholas Faith in his book *The Winemasters of Bordeaux*. But Markham believes that as the largest *appellation* on the peninsula, Margaux simply received a larger representation than other areas.

All Right Bank wines were excluded, because they sold at prices well below those of even nonclassified Médoc wines. The only Graves included was Haut-Brion, too pricey and celebrated to be omitted. A common perception—that a powdery mildew had swept through the Graves vineyards and no other estates could supply wines for the Paris fair—is false, Markham says. The disease hit all of Bordeaux. Other Graves were excluded because their prices were much lower than those of wines from the Médoc.

At the Universal Exposition, Burgundy and Champagne ended up canceling their plans to show wines. The Bordeaux wines were not displayed in the main exhibition hall. They were placed in the annex devoted to canned foods, a newly developed technique that generated much more interest among visitors than the wines. Lafite and Haut-Brion took over a small stand that had become vacant and exhibited by themselves. A century and a half later the first growths declined to join the Union des Grands Crus's spring tastings.

Although the classification didn't make much of an immediate impact when it was first published in 1855, the rankings soon took hold and became set as if in stone. The grades defined prestige and set prices. Year after year, first growths fetched about twice the price of second growths. In 1859 the brother of the Russian czar, Grand Duke Constantine, ordered 1,200 bottles of Yquem for 20,000 gold francs, 6,000 francs higher than the same amount of Lafite would have cost. Following the grand duke's example, Russian nobility bought almost all of Yquem's subsequent harvests. Demand was so strong that merchants clamored to obtain the wine.

In Russia, many wealthy customers demanded their Yquem be delivered in opulent crystal decanters rather than regular bottles.

Subsequent attempts were made to supplement the 1855 classification, with limited success. Lists were compiled of bourgeois growths, artisan growths, and even peasant growths. None gained much legitimacy. Unlike the 1855 classification, which was based on the objective criteria of prices, the later lists were corrupted by subjective criteria, including location and friendship. The *cru bourgeois* from 1932 lists 444 Médoc châteaux of varying quality. The Graves region, first classified in 1953, ordered wines alphabetically, not by quality. Attempts to make revisions have created major brawls, with disappointed owners protesting favoritism among the judges who tasted the wines.

In comparison, the 1855 classification remained a monument to consistency. Over the years it evolved into the equivalent of the Bible of Bordeaux. When Markham worked as a salesman in the 1980s at New York's Sherry-Lehmann wine store, customers came and asked to buy Bordeaux. They were well aware of the 1855 classification, even if they didn't quite know what the ratings represented. "If I suggested a fourth growth, I could see the disappointment on their face," Markham later recalled. "They would say, 'Fourth isn't very good, is it?' and would ask for a first."

The comments so intrigued Markham that he went to the library and tried to find books about the 1855 classification. None existed. Wine books told all sorts of different stories: that the ratings were based on the emperor's own tastes, that the brokers had decided based on their tastes, that the merchants were decisive or the growers dictated terms. Markham decided to move to Bordeaux and investigate. "It was like trying to understand American history and finding out that nobody had written a book about the Civil War," Markham said.

The task turned out to be a much more difficult undertaking than he had imagined. Many châteaux didn't have any archives. Although owners and managers received Markham with courtesy and offered help, some hesitated to open their archives, not understanding how doing so could fit in with his research or perhaps not wanting to revisit the issue. "They would say, 'Oh, I have archives, but nothing dating back to 1855,'" Markham recalled. At Yquem, Alexandre de Lur-Saluces received the American scholar for an hour and "told me in the nicest way *no*," Markham recalls. Another historian, a local named Philippe Roudié, is the principal archivist at Yquem. Outsiders were not accepted into the count's secrets. Markham did end up writing his book, *1855: A History of the Bordeaux Classification*, published in 1997, but included almost nothing about Yquem and the Lur-Saluces. The message was clear: just as one didn't rewrite the Bible, one couldn't revise the 1855 classification.

THE POWER OF THE broker and merchant families continued to expand during the second half of the nineteenth century. Foreigners dominated the remaining independent growers by locking up the best wines in long-term exclusive contracts. The merchants stipulated how the vineyards should be cultivated, how often the vineyards should be fertilized, when vines should be replaced, and the type of oak to be used in making the barrels. The merchants even put their names on much of the generic wine produced in Bordeaux, creating strong brands such as Calvet and Cruse.

Not only did the old guard do business away from the center of the city on the Quai des Chartrons, they lived apart from the locals. Many were Protestants and they married among themselves, producing a group that often emulated English upper-class lifestyles. They formed "an aristocracy of the cork," according to François Mauriac, winner of the Nobel Prize for literature in 1952. Mauriac was Bordelais himself, born in 1885. "Since the Tuileries were burnt down, the nobility of France has lost its role; but the cellars of Bordeaux are everlasting and our truly royal wine carries with it the right to ennoble the families who serve it."

In his 1921 novel *Préséances,* or *Questions of Procedure,* Mauriac captures the essence of Bordeaux at the turn of the twentieth century. The story centers on a charming young blonde named Florence, the daughter of a timber merchant who has one ambition: to marry a Chartronnais. Mauriac, himself a devout Catholic and moralist, also inherited a family fortune from the timber business. Forests, like vines, were another of Bordeaux's rural riches, but they lacked cachet.

In the narrative, Florence attracts Harry Maucoudinet while bathing at Arcachon, site of the Chartronnais's summer villas. Like the English upper class, the merchants were great sportsmen. They rode to the hunt behind their hounds, founded stud farms, competed in steeplechases, and linked their names to the history of French horse racing. They brought lawn tennis to France. The first French Tennis Championships were held in 1909 at the Societé Athlétique de la Villa Primrose in the Bordeaux suburbs, still called Primrose by locals. In 1910, they founded a golf club, and thanks to their initiative, modern Bordeaux boasts half a dozen championship courses.

Sports and clubs were more important than wives. When Florence finally marries Harry, her entire family rejoices because they may now enter the elite London and Westminster Club, where gambling and good eating hold sway. But Florence broods. Her husband, in good Chartronnais tradition, spends four months a year traveling. When back in Bordeaux, he keeps a mistress, whom he visits each evening between 5 and 7 P.M.—and in France today, just saying "five to seven" is shorthand for a regular tryst. Florence's downfall comes when she takes her own lover and is rejected by her husband's friends as a vulgar outsider. For Mauriac, his novel was a cautionary tale about the dangers of an ingrown, self-perpetuating society.

By the time Jeffrey Davies arrived in Bordeaux in the 1980s, the old guard was in retreat. Many of their warehouses along the Quai des Chartrons stood empty. Urban planners had launched a campaign to renew the district—converting the old commercial spaces into a Bordeaux version of SoHo, full of chic lofts and art galleries. The Calvets, who once ran the giant Maison Calvet, had sold their family's interest in 1971, and scion Patrick Calvet had left the firm in 1974. Now in his seventies, he directs a museum devoted to the Quai des Chartrons's golden era. A Seagram's-trained marketer named Jack Drouant runs Calvet's merchant business. He has borrowed techniques from the liquor business and from New World competitors and attempted to build strong Bordeaux brands, without the benefit of a single château or much reference to tradition or history.

And yet, in the twenty-first century, some of the old Chartronnais families remained in the Bordeaux wine trade. Daniel-Georges Lawton, whose ancestor emigrated from Ireland in the eighteenth century and started the business, worked as a broker at 60 Quai des Chartrons. His offices were modern and brokers sat in a large open "trading" pit. One Friday afternoon in the summer of 2001, the genial, tall, silver-haired septuagenarian was filling an order for fifty mid-priced cases from a Médoc château. Once he had completed the transaction, he turned his attention to the large eighteenth- and nineteenth-century ledgers left by his forebears Abraham and William.

"Look at this magnificent affair," he said, pointing to an entry from 1812 made by William Lawton and detailing a purchase of one hundred barrels of Lafite for 900 francs. His hands whipped over the pages, moving to another entry six months later showing the same wine being resold for 1,510 francs. "That's a 40 percent profit," Lawton explained, his hands coming together in a gesture of satisfaction.

Nowadays, Lawton negotiates on the telephone and by e-mail and fax machine, depending on a computer database. In it are the prices of thousands of wines, their original futures prices, their current prices in bottle, and one other relevant piece of information—Robert Parker's score. The 1855 classification still plays a crucial role in Bordeaux. But its power, like that of the traditional merchants, is finally being chipped away.

CHAPTER 3

—

The Rothschild Revolution

IN THE 1920S, LONG BEFORE PARKER ENTERED THE SCENE, A scion of one of Europe's most powerful families launched the first successful assault against the foreign merchants and the 1855 classification. Philippe de Rothschild was the great-grandson of English-born Nathaniel de Rothschild, the man who bought the Médoc vineyard called Brane-Mouton two years before the 1855 classification.

The purchase of Mouton came when the Rothschilds dominated global banking. Meyer Amschel Rothschild, originally a trader in rare coins, launched the dynasty in Frankfurt, Germany, in the eighteenth century. Four of Amschel's five sons established banks in Vienna, Naples, Paris, and London, while the eldest stayed in Frankfurt. The family financed the allies' fight against Napoléon Bonaparte and profited when Wellington defeated the emperor at the Battle of Waterloo. They built bridges and bankrolled railroads. Oxford historian Niall Ferguson estimates that by 1853, when London-based Nathaniel bought Brane-Mouton, the family's combined wealth equaled $19.1 billion in today's currency.

Mouton was established in the eighteenth century. When Nathaniel Rothschild bought it, the estate had suffered through a period of decline.

Located north of the town of Pauillac, it consisted of sixty-five acres of vineyards together with some stables and the main buildings, which were little more than shacks. No building existed suitable to host a Rothschild. Though Nathaniel immediately set about raising the quality of the wine, his motivations for the purchase remain obscure. In his 1981 autobiography, *Life in the Vineyard,* Philippe de Rothschild wrote that Nathaniel wanted to serve fine wine at his table. It's also possible that he just wanted to own a Bordeaux château because it was fashionable at the time. Many bankers were buying up estates. In 1868 Paris-based James Rothschild purchased his own château, the neighboring first-growth Lafite, giving birth to a family rivalry centered on wine that persists to this day. The two Rothschild branches each tout their own Bordeaux estate as the best and attempt to get the higher price for their wine.

Nathaniel Rothschild had spent some time in France and took an interest in his Bordeaux property. But after he died during the 1870 Prussian siege of Paris, his family neglected Mouton for the next half century. Nathaniel's son James committed suicide and James's widow, Thérèse, was a teetotaler. Her son Henry, Philippe's father, also disliked wine. He was a doctor who had founded his own small hospital in Paris and then turned to writing plays and building his own theater to present them. He visited Bordeaux only a few times in his life. At this time the Médoc estate still had little to attract a wealthy Parisian: no electricity, no running water, and only a primitive outhouse. It took more than a day to get there from Paris, and the final few miles had to be traveled by horse and cart.

Young Philippe discovered Mouton when he was only sixteen years old. He spent most of World War I in Paris at the prestigious Condorcet high school. German cannons threatened the French capital and he was evacuated to Bordeaux to finish his baccalaureate at the Michel Montaigne high school. On the train to Bordeaux, a fellow traveler told him the family owned the château. One morning in April 1918, young Philippe traveled to Pauillac to take a look.

It was love at first sight. "The wine smelled like violets," he said. After pestering his father for three full years, Philippe was given control. He soon fired the vineyard manager and declared war on the merchants, who, he believed, were underestimating the value of his cherished Mouton.

Philippe de Rothschild didn't like being second-rate in anything and vowed to become the best. His rallying cry was adapted from a seventeenth-century rhyme about a French family which, after being deposed from the throne, felt superior to mere nobles.

Premier ne puis
Second ne daigne
Mouton suis

First I cannot be
Second I disdain
I am simply Mouton

Instead of selling his wine in casks to merchants, Rothschild decided to bottle every drop on the property. The consequences were revolutionary, a true Declaration of Independence for Bordeaux winemakers. They were no longer mere vassals for the merchants. In December 1926, Rothschild assembled the owners of the first growths, including Yquem, and convinced them to convert together to château bottling. He also asked the first-growth owners to discuss prices before offering their wines for sale. All agreed.

The only opposition to Philippe de Rothschild, ironically, came from his cousins, the other Rothschilds at Lafite. They were tied to long-term contracts to merchants and didn't want to be associated with their youthful cousin's second growth. Later they would oppose Philippe's efforts to get his Mouton upgraded to the supreme status. Rothschild proceeded to invent a new way of marketing and advertising his revolution. He commissioned the Cubist artist Jacques Carlu to design the label for his wine. The artist created a play on Mouton's logo of a ram's head in black and gray, with the five arrows representing the five different Rothschild families in brown and red. The shock was deliberate. "My wine with my label, not a vague anonymous label," Rothschild wrote in *Life in the Vineyard*.

Without quite realizing it, Mouton's young owner injected showbiz flair into the hidebound world of fine wine while gaining a good shot of global publicity for himself and his product.

Philippe de Rothschild and his daughter Philippine were the original Bordeaux revolutionaries.

CHÂTEAU MOUTON ROTHSCHILD

ANOTHER PHILIPPE DE ROTHSCHILD innovation—and the one that most threatened the power of the Bordeaux merchants—was to start his own merchant business and the first grower's brand, a sort of ready-to-wear for his *haute couture* château. In 1931 Philippe called his second wine Cadet de Mouton, since it was a junior member of the family of Rothschild wines. That was soon changed to the simpler Mouton Cadet and expanded to include wines bought from other growers across Bordeaux. In the last two decades of the twentieth century, Mouton Cadet became the largest French brand sold in the world, selling about a million cases of wine a year.

Since the establishment of Haut-Brion back in the seventeenth century, two distinct markets existed in Bordeaux: classified wines commanding premium prices, which accounted for perhaps 5 percent of production, and bulk table wines, which made up the other 95 percent. Until Rothschild came along, the merchants held a monopoly on the mass-market business. They bought wines made by peasant growers, transported them to their cellars in Bordeaux, and sold them under their own names. The peasants enjoyed little leverage.

The worldwide depression of the 1930s hit Bordeaux hard and prices tumbled, for both fine and bulk wines. Merchants did not even buy many first-rated growths from excellent vintages. Winemakers ripped up their vines. Something needed to be done. The solution was to group together into cooperatives.

Bordeaux's first co-op was founded in 1932 in Saint-Emilion. By the end of the next year, nine co-ops dotted the region—and there were fifty-two by 1939. Joint ownership of production facilities allowed winemakers to survive and even prosper. Costs were reduced. Harvests were saved. "We were the children of misery," goes a common saying among co-op members.

The co-ops spelled bad news for traditional merchants, who could no longer split the producers, pushing down prices. But Rothschild liked the co-ops. They allowed new entrants like himself to build up a foothold in the market, because, unlike small farmers with a few acres of vines, they could supply large quantities.

The arrival of the Nazis interrupted Rothschild's rise. Families with strong British connections such as the Bartons fled. Nazi tanks rolled into the courtyard at Mouton Rothschild, looking for Philippe. The château was confiscated and Wehrmacht regiments lodged there. Rothschild himself had already left for London, where he joined de Gaulle's Free French forces.

Back in Bordeaux, few heroes emerged. Most Bordelais were more concerned about commerce than courage and put money before loyalty and ideology. Admittedly, unlike in the Alps, the winemaking region contained no mountains where rebels could hide. At best, some cellar masters constructed fake walls to conceal their best bottles from thirsty troops. At worst, collaborators such as the future budget minister Maurice Papon did the Germans' dirty work, rounding up Jews and sending them off to Auschwitz.

Many merchants, such as the Cruses and Eschenauers, were of German origin and were only too happy to sell to the Germans. There were no other customers, and they had to survive. Many profited doubly by buying up wine from departing families obliged to sell off their stocks at low prices. Once France was freed, two of the region's most prominent merchants—Roger Descas and Louis Eschenauer—were imprisoned for treason.

The end of the war didn't bring prosperity. Copper sulfate necessary to protect the vines from mildew was still in short supply. Through the 1950s, many prestigious châteaux continued to lose money. When Jean-Michel Cazes was growing up, his family made its living as insurance brokers in Pauillac, not from their Château Lynch-Bages revenue. Young Cazes went off to Paris to study engineering at the equivalent of an American Ivy League college, the prestigious Ecole Polytechnique. He never thought he would return to the Médoc. "Our wine wasn't worth anything," he remembered.

When Philippe de Rothschild returned to his beloved Mouton, his most emotional and exhausting effort lay ahead: a three-decade-long battle to upgrade his wine from a second growth to a first. This campaign put him in direct conflict with the powers that be in Bordeaux, in particular against Marquis Bertrand de Lur-Saluces, the owner of Yquem. If Rothschild was the modernist pushing Bordeaux into the twentieth century, the marquis represented tradition. Politically, Lur-Saluces was a monarchist, even though the Bourbons had been deposed a century and a half before. His father had been the royalist delegate to Parliament for the southwest region and active in the monarchist and conservative Action Française movement. "My family always has had a very strong attachment to the monarchist cause," Alexandre de Lur-Saluces admitted in 2001. "My uncle inherited the same beliefs."

Marquis Bertrand, with his glasses and habitual bow tie, was an intellectual powerhouse. He was a mathematician who didn't quite make it into the elite Ecole Polytechnique. Also a linguist, he dabbled in half a dozen languages. When Alexandre de Lur-Saluces took over the estate in 1968, he decided to brush up on his English and enrolled in courses at the local Berlitz school.

"We had another Lur-Saluces as a customer," the director told him.

Alexandre asked what languages his uncle had studied. The director thumbed through the archives and responded, "Practically all."

The marquis was particularly interested and proficient in Russian. He remembered how the Russian aristocracy had been responsible for Yquem's original rise to glory. Russian literature also fascinated him: Pushkin, Dostoyevsky, and others. He wrote a book in Russian, published in several countries and titled *The Fabulous Moudjik,* about an eighteenth-century Russian philosopher named Mikhail Lomonossov. When Nikita Khrushchev visited Bordeaux in the late 1950s, the marquis put aside his monarchist politics and served as the Communist leader's official translator. "The marquis knows Russian literature better than I do," Khrushchev commented.

In good Lur-Saluces tradition, the marquis had been a military man. During World War I, he served in the cavalry and was injured. At the beginning of World War II, he joined the artillery. Eventually the Germans captured him and imprisoned him for two years. The marquis was a major figure in mid-century Bordeaux. He was among the founders of both the Académie du Vin, which organizes lectures and conferences about Bordeaux's wine and publishes vintage reports, and the Conseil Interprofessionel du Vin de Bordeaux, which gathers data and promotes the region's wines. He also served as president of the Union des Syndicats de Sauternes, representing Yquem's home region, and the Syndicat des Grands Crus, representing the classified growths. He did not live in Yquem's castle, but rather in an elegant town house on the rue Saint-Laurent, right near the city's splendid public gardens. He drove, or, more accurately, was chauffeured in, a Rolls-Royce.

At Yquem, Marquis Bertrand's word was law. He owned a majority of the shares, making it difficult for a troublesome shareholder to question him. When he was imprisoned in 1941, he ordered that the château sell no wine. After the marquis returned to Bordeaux, Yquem's director, who ran the estate on a day-to-day basis, was required to travel to the rue Saint-Laurent each Saturday morning to report on the estate. "I would always go in tie and jacket and didn't dare arrive a second late," recalled Pierre Meslier, who served in the post from the 1960s to the end of the 1980s. "He was a man of a different generation, much stricter and more severe than would be acceptable today."

Philippe de Rothschild, by contrast, never wore a tie and jacket, preferring elegant but informal baggy designer clothes. He sometimes received guests while lounging in his bedroom in a bathrobe. He had the look and bearing of a Romantic poet with his bald pate and muttonchop sideburns. "But his manner throughout the dinner was simple and without pretense," recalled the California winemaker Robert Mondavi about a visit with the baron at his home in the 1970s. "Everything surrounding him that night—the magnificent Château Mouton, his art collection, the library lined with leather-bound volumes of the great poets—all this reminded me of the man's wealth and heritage. He was a Rothschild. But inside all of this, the Baron was very down-to-earth. He speaks little at the table and what he said was always mirthful and right to the point. I also noticed that he hated wine-speak as much as I did. He didn't want to rhapsodize about his hundred-year-old Château Mouton; he wanted to drink it—and do so with delightful gusto!"

Although the strict marquis and the flamboyant Rothschild had little in common, they initially managed to work together. When Rothschild began bottling at his château in the 1920s at the beginning of his career and formed his new trade association for the first growths, the Association des Premiers Crus, Lur-Saluces joined and began bottling Yquem at the estate. Lur-Saluces also overlooked the inconvenient fact that Mouton was not itself a first growth. But three decades later, when Rothschild asked him to sponsor Mouton's elevation, Lur-Saluces refused. Napoléon III had named the Rothschilds as barons only a century before. The Lur-Saluces had owned their title for almost five hundred years. "If you can't inherit a title you can always buy one," Lur-Saluces reportedly told Rothschild when refusing his request for help.

It was a declaration of war. When guests came to dine at Mouton, Rothschild would often serve Yquem frozen as a sorbet. He told a British journalist that the marquis "was isolated in his studies, his passion for his exquisite Yquem." The marquis replied that Mouton was just good enough to serve as a sauce for his beef stew. Alexandre de Lur-Saluces likes to recall how if his uncle Bertrand came down with a cold, his preferred medicine was hot wine with cinnamon. "I will let you determine from what *cru* came the wine," he said.

Rothschild didn't give up on his quest to elevate Mouton. His first steps were innocent enough, improving the château's wine and marketing it so that it sold for prices equal or superior to the first growths. Relentless lobbying—badgering, really—followed. "He would corner anybody of any note and keep on talking about it, and in the end, he made such a pain out of himself that the authorities finally couldn't stop him," historian Markham said.

In 1961 the French government prepared to revise the 1855 Médoc classification. When a proposal was leaked showing that seventeen châteaux would be struck from the honors list, the outcry from the losers was so strong that the project was shelved. Rothschild kept pushing. In 1973 he finally succeeded in convincing the Ministry of Agriculture, which regulates almost everything to do with French wine, to back his demand. Mouton was elevated to first-growth status. No other change was made. Rothschild celebrated by updating his motto:

Premier je suis
Second je fus
Mouton ne change

First I am
Second I was
Mouton does not change

This triumphalism was too much for Lur-Saluces. He sued the Ministry of Agriculture. Mouton's elevation should be nullified, he argued, because only the chamber of commerce, the classification's initial authors, could initiate such a change. The court case failed and the 1855 classification was modified for the first and only time.

But the upstart Rothschild left much of the old order standing. The traditional Bordeaux châteaux reigned supreme in the world of fine wines around the world. While Rothschild himself had done much to modernize their marketing, he had done little to change the way they were produced. Yields still were high. Although some exceptional vintages were produced, the wines were thin and almost bitter in unfortunate years of too much cold or rain.

In 1976 the United States celebrated its bicentennial and an event took place that changed Bordeaux's destiny. A British wine merchant and journalist named Steven Spurrier decided to mark the occasion by organizing a blind tasting between Californian and French wines at Paris's Hotel Inter-Continental. The jury was a Who's Who of eminent French winemakers and gastronomes, including Burgundy's Aubert de Villaine; La Tour d'Argent's sommelier, Christian Vanneque; Michelin three-star chef Raymond Oliver; and Jean-Claude Vrinat, owner of the Michelin three-star restaurant Taillevent. Château Giscours's Pierre Tari represented Bordeaux.

"Since California was near Mexico, they all thought California wines were *hot*," Spurrier later recalled. At the time, it was almost impossible to export American wine to France, and the California samples were brought to Paris by twenty-four different people trusted by Spurrier, each carrying only one bottle so as to remain under the limit imposed by French customs.

Four white Burgundies, all made from 100 percent Chardonnay grapes, were tasted against six California Chardonnays. Three Bordeaux red first growths—Mouton Rothschild, Haut-Brion, Latour, and a second-growth Saint-Estèphe, Montrose—were pitted against six California Cabernet Sauvignons. No one expected much of a battle. Spurrier invited journalists from all over Paris. Only one came—George Tabor from *Time*.

The French experts began to taste. They twirled their glasses. They swished and spat. Grimaces crossed their faces. Then smiles. Some judges were sure of their nose.

"Ah, back to France!" exclaimed Oliver.

He was sipping a 1973 Chardonnay from the Napa Valley.

"That is definitely Californian, it has no nose," said another judge.

He was sampling a Burgundy Bâtard Montrachet 1973.

By the time the tasting was finished and the ballots were cast, the top-scoring red was Stag's Leap Wine Cellars 1973 from the Napa Valley. It beat a Mouton Rothschild 1970, followed by a Haut-Brion 1970 and the Montrose 1970. The four whites were, in order, Château Montelena 1973 from Napa, a French Meursault-Charmes 1973, and two other Californian Chardonnays, Chalone 1974 from Monterey County and Napa's Spring Mountain 1973.

When *Time* published the surprising results, newspapers and magazines in the United States began picking up the story. The French press relayed the news. The "Paris Tasting" took on almost mythic proportions. "Suddenly people had a new respect for what we were doing: they saw we could make wines as good as the best in France," said Robert Mondavi.

Back in Bordeaux, the response to the American challenge didn't come from the old-line estates. By the time the first *garagistes* appeared in the 1980s, Mouton Rothschild, ironically, had become the establishment and Philippe's daughter, Philippine, who inherited the estate and the company that went with it, resisted change. She saw Michel Gracia and the other upstarts as a threat to her world. If anybody could make wine as good as or better than Mouton, then its mystique could be undermined. In return, new wave merchants such as Jeffrey Davies ignored her. Davies doesn't bother to sell Mouton. He doesn't see what value he could add, nor did he much like the Moutons from the 1970s and most of the 1980s.

Robert Parker is equally skeptical. At the beginning of his career, the American critic believed Mouton grew too many grapes on each vine and didn't make a strict enough selection in its choice of fruit. He gave some vintages of Mouton scores as low as a mere 90, disappointing for any first growth. "I have encountered numerous mediocre bottles," he warned.

The 1976 tasting showed that Bordeaux needed to change not just the way it sold its wine. It needed to change the way it made wine. The region's venerable 1855 classification, even if amended by Philippe de Rothschild, had morphed into an injustice. Mediocre wines sold for too much thanks to their classifications and good wines sold for too little for lack of a ranking.

CHAPTER 4

—

Parker Power

WHEN THE 1976 TASTING TOOK PLACE, ROBERT M. PARKER Jr. was working as a lawyer for the Farm Credit Banks of Baltimore. At the time, English wine writers dominated wine criticism. Most had gone to Oxford or Cambridge, and many had studied for an English-invented degree called a master of wine. It was a tough, academic exam that few passed. In Britain, wine was for the upper class, while the working classes went to the pub and downed pints of bitter. Naturally enough, writers such as Edmund Penning-Rowsell, author of the encyclopedic book *The Wines of Bordeaux,* and Michael Broadbent, head of Christie's wine department, remained in awe of the 1855 classification and preferred traditional Médoc châteaux to any others in the world.

In traditional English wine criticism, bad wines didn't exist. There were just varying degrees of wonderful and more wonderful. When the British critics wrote about wine, they rolled out flowery sentences. A wine tasted of everything from the sylvan slopes of gravelly Graves to a hint of sweet silk. It was compared to a pretty girl in the flower of her youth or to the talent of a mature seductress. Parker, an amateur, wondered what those terms meant—simply put, was the wine good or bad?

"When I started out, the whole group of wine tasters were little more than parrots for the powers that be in Bordeaux, just repeating the accepted wisdom," he recalled.

As a student at the University of Maryland in the late 1960s and early 1970s, Parker created an informal wine club with a few friends. He read some British wine books and came away with a sour taste. Even with his

ROBERT PARKER

American Robert Parker overthrew the old
English-dominated order of wine criticism.

little experience, he knew that quality in Bordeaux or elsewhere was variable. He had drunk many expensive wines that were bitter or bland. "I began to ask myself why this Margaux or that Margaux received good reviews when I knew it was terrible," he recalled.

The young American's suspicion soon centered on conflict of interest. Later, during his regular visits to Bordeaux, he learned that when critics arrived at châteaux, car trunks opened and cases of free wine filled them up. Most British wine writers were not just friendly with winemakers. They often worked with or for them. Some were consultants. Others were importers. According to the biography posted on his own web site, the esteemed writer Hugh Johnson, author of a magnificent one-volume history *The Story of Wine,* served on Château Latour's board, was under contract with the mail-order London Sunday *Times* wine club, consulted for the Royal Tokay Wine Company in Hungary, and sold his own ranges of glassware and wine paraphernalia. Most British wine writers, said Parker, "were just riding on the big food and wine gravy train."

From the beginning of his career, Parker never aimed to sell wine, only to write about it. In 1972 he took a course in conflict of interest at the University of Maryland law school. His professor was Samuel Dash, who soon afterward became the chief counsel to the Senate Watergate Committee. The American consumer movement was taking off. Parker admired Ralph Nader and thought he could bring the same sense of integrity and advocacy to the world of wine that Nader was bringing to auto safety and other consumer issues.

When Parker later launched his monthly newsletter, the *Wine Advocate,* he insisted on buying the bottles of wine he was reviewing. His budget rose to about $150,000 a year. Winemakers say they have tried to send him free cases, only to receive letters back saying that Parker donated the cost of the wine to a charity. In his passion to defend his no-freebie policy, Parker pays his own way on trips and rails against those he perceives as less ethical wine critics.

In the United States, the *Wine Spectator* has almost eight times the circulation of the *Wine Advocate,* but unlike Parker's newsletter, accepts ads. "Whatever you say, advertising colors reviews," Parker said.

A subscription to Parker's newsletter costs $85 a year. Each issue contains an editorial or two and about fifty-six pages of short commentaries on hundreds of wines. Parker is talented and hardworking: he has a track record of acute judgments and spotting good wines before they are well known. His comments contain a liberal sprinkling of adjectives such as "diaphanous," "spectacular," and "celestial." They can also be brutal:

wines have been described as having the taste of toothpaste or the smell of the barnyard.

Initially, the newsletter's biggest innovation was how it rated wines—by points. While Parker first thought about using a 20-point system developed at the University of California at Davis, he realized that most Americans were more familiar with a 100-point scale. An A+ wine was from 96 to 100 or "extraordinary." An A from 90 to 95, "outstanding," a B from 80 to 90, "very good," a C from 70 to 79, "average wine with little distinction," a D from 60 to 69, "a below average wine containing noticeable deficiencies," and F from 50 to 59. "We all grew up in school with that grading, so I thought it was logical," he remembered. In his 100-point system, every wine starts out with 50 points. Good color adds up to 5 points. Aroma and bouquet represent another possible 15 points. Flavor and finish account for up to 20 points. Potential for further evolution and improvement adds a final 10 points.

Parker publishes an initial score, typically a two-number range, the spring after harvest. In January the following year, he returns to Bordeaux and tastes the wine a second time while it remains in the barrel. He then publishes an update. And once the wine is bottled, he tastes it again in Bordeaux and often buys a sample back in the United States to make sure it tastes just as he remembers. Only then does he remove his provisional rating and assign a final single number.

British wine critics, who rarely judge these same wines three times, deride this quest for numerical certainty and confidence. They consider putting numbers on a wine a plebeian affront to the poetry locked inside the bottle. How can you be precise about something so subjective? "It remains intellectually fraudulent, in my view, simply because wine is constantly evolving and any tasting note or score is no more than a snapshot," argues Stephen Brook, author of *Bordeaux: People, Power and Politics*. Brook tells how once, at a wine seminar, a British wine lover flashed a slide showing a sculpture by an artist and invited the audience to score it on the 100-point scale. "The absurdity of the suggestion drove the point home," Brook writes. Another British wine mandarin, Jancis

Robinson, wrote in her 1997 autobiography, *Confessions of a Wine Lover,* "I am all too conscious of my own fallibility, that I make my wine recommendations somewhat hesitantly—much less confidently than Parker, for instance—knowing how human preferences, sensitivities and individual bottles can vary."

For Parker, such criticism represents sentimental gibberish. "While some have suggested that scoring is not well suited to a beverage that has been romantically extolled for centuries, wine is no different from any consumer product," he insists. "There are specific standards of quality that full-time wine professionals recognize, and there are benchmark wines against which others can be judged. I know of no one with three or four different glasses of wine in front of him or her, regardless of how good or bad the wines might be, who cannot say, 'I prefer this one to that one.' Scoring wines is simply taking a professional's opinion and applying some sort of numerical system to it on a consistent basis. Scoring permits rapid communication of information to expert and novice alike."

Parker spits out ten thousand wines a year and still remembers them all. Well-known chef Michel Trama remembers asking Parker to taste a wine blind at the end of a multicourse meal. Parker sipped and identified the type of grape, the vintage, and even the wine. "It wasn't a famous wine, either," the chef said. "It was an obscure Spanish bottle." Enologist Michel Rolland recalls how, at a dinner in Bordeaux, the host tried to trick Parker by serving a carafe of red wine and asking him to identify it. "We wouldn't do that to our best friends," Rolland said. But Parker wasn't fazed. "It's a Calon-Ségur 1945," he responded. He was right.

With such certainty, why bother to complicate one's life and taste blind? Although many of his follow-up tastings back in Maryland are often done with a paper bag covering the label, Parker knows what a sample contains when he visits Bordeaux. The more experienced he has become, the more he feels comfortable making a judgment even when the label is visible. "The label doesn't mean a thing to me," he said. "I focus totally on what's in the glass. If a critic can't effectively judge what is in the bottle irrespective of price, pedigree, history, or rarity, he or she shouldn't be writing wine reviews." The key question is whether the critic has the courage to take on established truths. Parker asked, "Does a blind tasting guarantee that the taster will give Lafite Rothschild 65 points once the bag comes off, or change their score?" He adds, "How many great estates get bad reviews from the blind-tasters?"

While most publications employ a team of tasters, Parker has only two assistants, one who handles Burgundy, the Loire Valley, Alsace, and the French Mediterranean region of Languedoc and another who started tasting for him in Italy in 2003. In Bordeaux, he works with a freelance assistant named Hanna Agostini, who translates his articles and books but does no scoring of wines. Parker tastes all the Bordeaux himself. His ratings enjoy consistency. "In my decades doing this, I think I've built up an unrivaled knowledge," he said.

Throughout his career, one of Parker's main motivations is to correct the failings of the 1855 classification. Tradition, history, and land count less to him than the winemaker. "Owners and winemakers change," he insists, "and whereas some famous Bordeaux estates consistently make the best wine possible given the year's climatic conditions, others, because of negligence, incompetence, or just greed, produce mediocre and poor wine that hardly reflects its official pedigree." By the time Parker arrived on the scene, many of the châteaux had changed hands or expanded, so that their vineyards no longer resembled those on which the classification was based. At Château Lascombes, for example, one owner doubled the size of the original estate. Most of the original vineyards were located on prime gravelly land overlooking the Gironde River and adjacent to Château Margaux's property. Many of the new vineyards were situated well inland, on moist clay soil. The grapes grown there proved lower in quality than those from the original vineyards.

In the 1998 third edition of his 1,440-page book, *Bordeaux: A Comprehensive Guide to the Wines Produced from 1961 to 1997*, Parker proposed his own classification, dividing the region's top 160 wines into a five-tiered hierarchy. He includes wines from all major Bordeaux regions, not just Sauternes and the Médoc. Lascombes, prior to the takeover by the investor group led by Yves Vatelot, was not a second growth but, in his opinion, a fifth. Two "garage" wines became firsts. The old classifications "should be regarded by both the wine connoisseur and the novice as informational items of historical significance only," Parker wrote.

The rigidity and complexity of traditional Bordeaux rankings set the stage for the entry of the independent newcomer Parker. During the 1970s and 1980s, the thirst for fine wines expanded beyond the traditional markets. How could these new drinkers sift through hundreds, if not thousands, of offerings? Brokers, merchants, importers, retailers, and the previously dominant British critics had a vested interest in finding a solution. "Buyers in Hong Kong and in the U.S. needed guidance and reassurance and Parker gave it to them," said Jeffrey Davies.

The American critic tastes and rates wines throughout the world and is influential almost everywhere. For example, Parker loves the wines from Châteauneuf-du-Pape in the Rhône Valley. Before he began writing about them, Châteauneufs were considered rustic. Almost single-handedly, the American turned these wines into global phenomena, quadrupling the price of his favorite estates over the last decade. "Parker has been our savior," says Michel Blanc, director of the Châteauneuf Winemakers' Union. In gratitude, the village anointed the American an honorary citizen.

Parker plays less of a role in regions with strong brands. Consider Champagne. While France's other winemaking regions may turn out wines of frustratingly inconsistent quality with hard-to-understand labels, the bubbly pleases with its consistency. All the major names, Moët & Chandon, Veuve Clicquot, Perrier Jouët, Piper Heidsieck, represent reliable bets—clean, crisp wines that will put sparkle in any celebration. "Parker is peanuts here in Champagne," said Benoît Marguet-Bonnerave of Champagne Marguet-Bonnerave. "We can sell everything for a good price without him."

It's in Bordeaux, home to the world's most expensive wines and also to thousands of different châteaux, where Parker's role is most revolutionary—and most contested. In Châteauneuf-du-Pape, he enriched a village full of struggling winemakers. In Bordeaux, his tastes and techniques threaten fortunes and reputations.

—

LIKE THE *GARAGISTES*, Parker isn't overwhelmed by tradition partly because he came from an ordinary middle-class family. He studied at public schools. He rode bicycles. He played sports. In 1952, when Parker was five, his father sold the family dairy farm in northern Maryland and went to work selling heavy construction equipment. Although an interstate has brought his rural hometown of Monkton within a half-hour drive of Baltimore and an hour of Washington, Parker says it seemed much more distant when he was growing up. During his childhood, Parker visited either city only a few times. His universe was dominated by hunting associations and future farmer groups. Parker tasted wine for the first time when he was eighteen years old. It was a sparkling, sugary red concoction called Cold Duck—and it made him throw up.

Parker was a handsome boy. In the tenth grade, he fell in love with a slender, graceful fellow student named Pat Etzel. In college, Pat majored in French, and in the autumn of 1967 she left for a junior year abroad in Strasbourg, in the northeastern French region of Alsace. Parker feared losing her. They planned to meet up in Paris for the December holidays.

When he got to Paris, Pat was waiting for him. Parker reveled in the beauty of the French capital. He visited the Eiffel Tower. He walked up the steps of Nôtre Dame. The young couple stayed in a cheap hotel in the Latin Quarter. It was dingy and dirty, but Parker didn't care. In bistros, he ordered pâtés and smelly cheeses. He was enthralled. Of course, he also loved the wine. It was cheap and ordinary, served in carafes, not the dense, purplish *garagiste* blockbusters he would later admire so much, but light, bubbly reds. He was no connoisseur. He didn't yet know how to describe what he tasted. But he liked it.

His gastronomic future became apparent only when the young couple visited Strasbourg. Pat's host that year was a doctor who invited the couple to enjoy a few meals at some of Alsace's shrines of *haute cuisine*. Included were Parker's first bottles of fine wine. Parker told William Langewiesche, who profiled him for the *Atlantic Monthly*, the story of sipping an Alsatian white.

"There's a little taste of grapefruit and a twist of lemon," he said.

The doctor was astounded.

"You have just defined the main components of a Riesling," he said.

The young American had found his vocation. Later in the trip, Parker decided to take Pat to a lavish going-away bash at Maxim's in Paris, on the prestigious rue Royale and one of France's temples of gastronomy. When they arrived wearing hand-me-down clothes, the maître d' made a nasty comment about Parker's brown shoes and gray trousers. The young Americans were shunted off to a windowless back room full of other foreigners. The lamp on the table didn't work. The meal was barely edible. The wine was just above drinkable. And the bill, well, the bill was enormous. Parker learned that high reputation and high price don't always translate into high quality.

Back in Maryland, he married Pat in 1968 and attended the University of Maryland law school, graduating in 1973. Pat supported him in his studies with a job teaching French in a public school. The young couple lived in a basement apartment in Baltimore. After receiving his law degree, Parker went to work for the Farm Credit Banks of Baltimore. But he was bored. He was much more passionate about wine than about the law and took as much time off as he could to travel with Pat to France. The couple wasn't rich and sometimes they fought over the money Parker spent on wine. She said wine was a romantic, unprofitable profession. But in 1978 Parker decided to put his hobby to use. He typed up the first issue of the *Wine Advocate,* bought a mailing list from Washington retailer Calvert-Woodley, and sent out a few thousand free copies. The newsletter featured no glossy photos, no purple-prose text, no advertising. Its subtitle was *The Independent Consumer's Bimonthly Guide to Fine Wine.* The first year, paying circulation numbered only 600. From the beginning, Parker promised that he would never take freebies and that he would fight just as much against industrialized, homogenized wines as overpriced, tradition-bound bitter ones.

The 1982 vintage proved a turning point. That year in Bordeaux, voluptuous, ripe fruit was harvested at all the elite châteaux, and the wines, even when young, didn't have any of their typical Bordeaux astringency. In a major error, other critics failed to appreciate the grandeur of the vintage. Traditionalists, particularly British, were hostile. They decried the 1982s as "Californian," too dark, too strong, too full of flavor. They said the 1982s lacked acidity and wouldn't last. "When we tasted, it was too hot, too rich, too ripe," remembered Steven Spurrier.

The only critic who disagreed was Robert Parker. "I was convinced 1982 was a scoop, the best vintage I had ever tasted," he said.

At the time, Parker was still working as a lawyer part-time in Baltimore. A rival named Robert Finigan published the preeminent U.S. wine newsletter, *Robert Finigan's Private Guide to Wine*. When he described the 1982 wines as "oafish" and predicted that they wouldn't age well, Parker was frightened. He suffered one of his few moments of self-doubt. Had he made a mistake? He flew back to Bordeaux and began scouring archives. At Château Haut-Brion he found an old diary in which the winemaker worried that the 1929 vintage was too strong at birth and would not endure. In 1982 the 1929s were still going strong. Parker knew he was right.

When the wines were bottled in 1984, they were as splendid as he had said. (In 2003 most were still magnificent.) Doubting critics, including Robert Finigan, began to change their opinion. But it was too late. Most of the 1982s were already sold out and had doubled in price on the auction market. Parker's name was golden. "The 1982 vintage made Parker's reputation," said Jeffrey Davies. By the time the 1982s were released in 1984, the *Wine Advocate*'s circulation had jumped past 10,000. Finigan's *Private Guide*, on the other hand, lost readers and soon went out of print. "The switch to Parker happened almost overnight," according to Spurrier.

In March 1984, betting that he could finally make a living pursuing his passion, Parker quit his job as a lawyer. Several weeks later he signed his first book contract in New York. He told Langewiesche that going home on the train, he felt like Sylvester Stallone in *Rocky*.

OVER THE FOLLOWING two decades, Parker's power mushroomed. His *Wine Advocate* remained a publication for the serious aficionado, with only about 40,000 subscribers. But his influence far outweighed the number of his readers because his readers were connoisseurs and the merchants who sold them their wines. By the second half of the 1990s, Bordeaux producers waited for "the Nose" to weigh in before deciding what prices they would demand for their wine. Merchants abdicated their traditional role of judging wines themselves. If a wine scored 90 or more Parker points, it sold out in two hours, at almost any price the winemaker wanted to set. If the score was lower, he struggled to unload his wine. Retailers took the Parker ratings, copied them, and pasted them next to wines in their stores. "Below 90, you can't sell it," said Jeffrey Davies. "Above 95, you can't find it."

At least partly under his influence, many ambitious Bordeaux winemakers began changing how they treated their vines and made their wines. Throughout the region's winemaking history, yields were small. Growers were always battling nature, and often losing. Frosts, mildew, and other disasters lowered the amount of fruit that could be harvested. While Americans speak of their vineyards' yields in terms of tons of grapes per acre, the French calculate hectoliters per hectare. A hectoliter is about 25 gallons and a hectare 2.47 acres. Before the 1960s, Bordeaux crops as small as 15 hectoliters per hectare were common.

Then, suddenly, new pesticides and other antifungal treatments developed in the 1960s took away much of Mother Nature's uncertainty and yields soared. By the 1970s, Bordeaux winemakers could produce as much wine as they wanted, and did—70 hectoliters per hectare became common, and 100 hectoliters per hectare was not unheard of. Old Bordeaux loved it because more wine meant more money. New Bordeaux believed the end result was a weak, watery drink that couldn't stand up against New World competition.

Traditionally, all fruit, along with green stems and leaves, went into the fermentation tank. This resulted in Bordeaux's trademark bitterness. In reaction, innovative growers took a series of measures designed to produce crops of higher-quality fruit. Vine branches are normally pruned in wintertime. This prepares them to flower the following spring. As soon as summer arrived, Parker-influenced winemakers began removing whole clusters of grapes, a process they came to call green harvesting.

Later in the summer, serious winemakers strip off a portion of the leaves on the vines so the clusters are aired and receive maximum sunlight. The goal is to expose the grapes to more direct sunlight, raising sugar and tannin levels—and avert gray rot. In order to make rich, concentrated wines, vintners became convinced that it is necessary to be brutal in weeding out mediocre fruit. That way, sunshine reaches fewer berries, resulting in more concentrated juice and ultimately richer, fuller wine.

The selection didn't stop there, either. At harvest time, in order to make fresher, fruitier wines, the most progressive New Bordeaux producers introduced sorting tables and a large labor force to discard any rotten, unripe, unhealthy, or blemished berries, and all vestiges of stems and leaves. As much as half of a harvest is often eliminated. Some of it goes into estates' second wines, lower—but still good—quality and sold at lower prices. Truly inferior production is sold as bulk generic wine to merchants.

Has the Parker-driven reaction against high yields gone too far? Médoc traditionalists believe so. Excessive green harvesting is risky. Accustomed to the annual battle to protect fruit, the traditionalists don't understand why anyone would want to reduce the amount harvested. If not enough rain fell during the rest of the summer, they argued, the remaining berries would dry out and produce unbalanced wine. Beyond a certain point, the marginal returns from green harvesting are the subject of much debate. Some say the resulting wine becomes too jammy, too powerful—too Parkerized.

Economic concerns enter into this argument. Throwing out tons of fruit slashes yields too much and leaves less wine. The end result might be better. But it needs to be sold at a high price. Without taking into account the prestige of the estate—and the possibility of capital gains from rising land values—many believe the sweet spot for balancing quality and profits is about 40 hectoliters per hectare. "If we go down any further, then it wouldn't make economic sense—and we wouldn't make much better wine anyhow," insisted Jean-Guillaume Prats, general manager of the Médoc second growth Cos d'Estournel. He and other Left Bankers figure that their prime land allows them to raise yields without losing quality—and to a certain extent, the new generation of Parker-influenced winemakers agrees. If the land is of exceptional quality, then yields can be higher. But if the land is mediocre, flat, and full of clay, instead of hills capped with gravel or limestone, then even greater effort—more pruning and more green harvesting—is required to obtain satisfactory quality.

Similar arguments take place during harvest in the cellar. Once the grapes are safely in their bright stainless steel tanks, they begin to ferment. In the past, when temperatures soared to above 100 degrees Fahrenheit, the yeasts that convert the sugar into alcohol and carbon dioxide were killed and potentially excellent wine turned to vinegar. The introduction of temperature-controlled fermenters and better hygiene eliminated much of the problem.

New Bordeaux winegrowers go one step further and use another technique to delay the onset of fermentation—cold therapy. When injected into a tank of newly harvested grapes, dry ice, which is really solid carbon dioxide, reduces temperatures close to freezing. The onset of fermentation is delayed by four to eight days. Grapes have more time to be in contact with their skins, resulting in rich, dark-colored, fleshy wines with soft tannins. Another new technique used to sweeten and soften the hard edge of many traditional Bordeaux is to inject microscopic amounts of oxygen through a stainless steel or ceramic tube into the fermentation tanks.

The question of barrels is crucial, too. More and more Bordeaux winegrowers are aging their wine in new oak barrels. Critics complain that the wood overwhelms the fruit in many modern Bordeaux. Although Parker himself admits new oak "should be utilized prudently, as a great chef approaches the use of salt, pepper, or garlic," he believes the advantages outweigh the drawbacks. Old oak is a "fertile home for unwanted bacteria, resulting in off flavors and potential spoilage problems." New oak is clean, and if used in moderation, adds an agreeable complexity and vanilla sweetness to the young wine.

A final Parker influence concerns fining and filtering. Both procedures were traditionally used to clarify the wine and to remove the deposit at the bottom of the bottle. But Parker believes they "eviscerate a wine, destroying texture as well as removing aromatics, fruit, and mid-palate flesh." Undergoing less fining and filtering, modern Bordeaux enjoy "more intense flavors, texture, and aroma" than their predecessors.

Parker believes today's finest Bordeaux are far superior to those of a generation ago. Two or three decades ago, fewer than a quarter of "the most renowned estates made wines proportional to their official pedigree," he insists. "Dirty, unclean aromas were justified and disappointingly emaciated, austere, excessively tannic wines from classified growths were labeled 'classic' by a subservient wine press." His verdict was clear: faced with increasing global competition, Bordeaux could stay on top only by changing.

THE WORLD'S MOST powerful wine taster continues to be serious, almost to a fault. At home in Maryland, he wakes up early and starts tasting red wines right after breakfast. Any wine that initially seems to merit 80 points or more is tasted twice, maybe three times before Parker determines its final score. Each time he spits, he scribbles several descriptive lines in his notebook. "He works eighteen hours a day, every day," marveled Pierre-Antoine Rovani, an associate Parker took on in 1996. Parker keeps a similar schedule while on the road, which is almost half the time. In Bordeaux, he has frequently asked Jeffrey Davies to taste at his office on Sunday. "I guess he knew no one else in Bordeaux would see him on the Sabbath," Davies cracked.

By his own admission, Parker is a glutton. He loves to eat and he loves to drink. Although he maintains a strict separation between work and pleasure, always spitting out wines when scoring them, he has compared the pain of not swallowing to being stroked "on the back of your neck by a beautiful, naked woman and yet avoiding the advance by pushing her away." "Bob lives and works in Monkton, not in midtown Manhattan in a penthouse," said Rovani by way of explanation of his boss's penchant for overindulgence on occasion.

As a youth, Parker was trim and athletic. In middle age, he has put on weight. One winter afternoon back in Maryland, during lunch at a local Chinese restaurant in a suburban shopping mall, he didn't drink any wine, just tea. "I have gout," he lamented, "and it's hard for me to taste today." The condition, combined with the difficulty of finding food to match sweet white wines, helps explain why he tastes so few Sauternes. "They can be wonderful wines and I have a lot of them in my cellar, but I almost never find the moment to drink them," he explains.

Even as he became rich and famous, Parker didn't seem all that interested in wealth itself. The *Wine Advocate* isn't a giant moneymaker. With only a little extra work, however, the newsletter has been compiled into half a dozen hefty books that are translated into a series of foreign languages. The royalties run into the millions of dollars each year. And yet Rovani, who started his career as a management consultant and wine retailer, is often frustrated by Parker's inability to leverage his growing brand. His buddy Bob just prefers to go out to a restaurant to drink and talk about wine. "Bob risked a lot of money to give up the safe life as a lawyer and start the *Wine Advocate*," said Rovani. "But he loves to eat and drink and that's more important to him than all the riches in the world."

After more than thirty years, Parker is still married to Pat. They live with their teenage daughter, Maia, a basset hound named Hoover, an English bulldog named George, and 20,000 bottles of wine. It's the house Pat grew up in, and even though it has been expanded to include two wine cellars and Parker's tasting room and office, it bears no resemblance to the mansions inhabited by the investment bankers and movie stars who purchase the wines he recommends. Once you leave the highway, the two-lane road to the Parkers passes through a bucolic landscape of manicured fields and well-maintained farmhouses. Their house is a simple yet comfortable shingled structure in the woods, looking out on a beautiful state park. "I love the peace and quiet here," Parker says. His office is located in one wing. In a separate room work two secretaries, one of whom, Joan Passman, has been with him for several decades.

He likes the anonymity of rural Monkton. One afternoon in 2001, a repairman arrived to fix the office refrigerator. In one corner of the room, Hoover the basset hound lay sprawled on the floor, snoring. In another corner stood a messy desk and a computer, framed by a stereo system stacked with CDs, most 1960s and 1970s classics. His favorite artist is Neil Young. Most of the room was taken up by a large counter-top crowded with dozens of opened bottles of wine, both red and white. There was a rack for wineglasses and a deep sink for spitting. The repair-man walked in, took a brief look, and said, "Guess you like wine." He then proceeded to attend to the refrigerator. Parker made no comment and the repairman seemed to have no idea just who he was visiting.

One frustration, though, of living in Maryland, is that the state gov-ernment exercises tight control over the sale of alcohol; it is a felony to ship wine to an individual from out of state without a permit. Parker derided the liquor authorities as "the pleasure police." The liquor board's director accused him of importing wine illegally. Federal Express and United Parcel Service stopped delivering packages of bottles to him. Parker had to hire a lawyer and travel to Annapolis, the state capital. He finally got his permit to have wine sent to him. Most of the time when he wants to buy wine, he says, he still travels to Washington, D.C., which has more liberal regulations and a better selection.

In Bordeaux the wine trade's more progressive elements view him as a savior of sorts. They have realized that the region has a lot of wine to sell and that Parker helps sell it. The American revolutionary could have championed Californian wines. Instead, his first love is France. He loves French wines, and Bordeaux wines in particular. Without his support, upstarts such as Michel Gracia and newcomers like Yves Vatelot would have had little or no chance. The more forward-looking traditionalists also recognize Parker's positive contribution. "We should name a boule-vard after Bob," said Château Lynch-Bages's owner Jean-Michel Cazes, one of Bordeaux's great modernizers during the 1980s.

On June 22, 1999, in France's equivalent of the White House, the Elysée Palace, President Jacques Chirac pinned his country's highest honor on Parker, inducting him as a *chevalier* in the Legion of Honor. "Robert Parker is the most followed and influential critic of French wines in the world, something I witnessed recently when choosing wine for President Clinton, who automatically referred to Robert Parker as his reference for making a proper wine-buying decision," Chirac said. Napoléon Bonaparte created the Legion of Honor in 1802 to honor the highest level of achievement in France. Parker is one of only a handful of foreigners to have received the award. Parker says the ceremony was one of the highlights of his life. "I saw tears in his eyes," remembered Cazes.

Where there are admirers, there are also detractors. To the critics, Parker is a symbol of American imperialism. Even if his influence has a profound democratizing impact, allowing upstarts such as Gracia with no big castles or capital to thrive and nouveau riche magnates such as Vatelot to make a profit from their immense investments in quality, Gallic critics deride him for McDonaldizing or Coca-Cola-izing the wine world. World-wide, the rise of spicy Asian, Mediterranean, and Latin American cooking is pushing up demand for early drinking, richer, fresher, fruitier—in short, Parker-style—wines. To his detractors, however, a homogeneous Parker style is wreaking havoc on centuries of traditions.

His stylistic consistency leads to suspicions that some winemakers cheat him, lying to him about their yields and use of new oak barrels. Some even suggest that he receives samples different and doctored from the ones they sell to the public, a so-called special Parker batch prepared for the all-important Nose's inspection. Parker acknowledges the danger and says it is one reason that he buys much of his wine from stores. And yet the suspicion that winemakers are creating special Parker batches generated one of Parker's most celebrated defeats. In 1994 a Burgundy winemaker named François Faiveley sued him for libel. Parker wrote in one of his books that some Faiveley wines in the United States tasted "less rich" than the wines he had tasted in Faiveley's cellars. The case was settled out of court. Although Parker didn't pay damages, he did cut the offending comments from ensuing editions of the book and published a statement that he had not intended to suggest that Faiveley made sepa-rate batches for journalists and for the public.

The suit left a bitter taste. "Burgundy doesn't have a lot of wine to sell and never had been criticized before," Parker complained. "When I said they were screwing up badly, that they were taking a magical *terroir* and growing too many grapes, using mobile bottlers and sterilizing their wines, they responded by seeing my influence as sinister." Parker says he remains a fan of Burgundy's main grape variety, the noble Pinot Noir, and together with his brother-in-law he owns a Pinot Noir vineyard in Oregon. After the Faiveley court case, however, he turned over all Burgundy tasting responsibility to his associate Rovani.

In many ways, the argument swirling about Parker stems from different interpretations of one French word—*terroir*. Literally, it means soil, including the subsoil, rocks, and microclimate. It's obvious that all of these factors come into play when wine is made. For the French, though, something more is at stake. *Terroir* doesn't just refer to the physical piece of land. It evokes the metaphysical soil. Just as some people are born princes and princesses, others emerge only as peasants, and the same is true of the land. History, class, tradition—all of these factors go into making noble and less noble *terroir*. In his own mind at least, Parker believes his love of France is rooted in the incomparable variety of its wines, and he says, "I love France because I love the idea of *terroir*." California, he notes, is no longer producing homogenized blockbusters. It is beginning to swallow the French conception that a specific piece of land produces a particular wine. Parker says he appreciates different styles of wines, including light and elegant ones. "I don't just love fruit bombs," he insists.

But Bordeaux's traditionalists have wielded the idea of *terroir* to launch their own anti-Parker crusade. When a Graves château called Bouscaut received a score of only 79–82 in 1999, it ran an advertisement in Bordeaux's daily paper, *Sud Ouest*, with a cartoon mocking a retailer who tells his customer, "A good wine from a real *terroir*? An individualistic wine? No hesitation—find one with a bad Parker score!!!!" At Saint-Emilion's popular L'Envers du Décor wine bar, owner François de Ligneris handed out a poster entitled "Springtime Promotion: Parker Screws." The screw described as "straight and reserved" received a score of only 76. But ones with "elegant notes of ketchup" got a stupendous 95.

A more serious charge concerns cronyism. During the 1990s, Parker became an admirer of Jeffrey Davies. He was also a buddy of Alain Raynaud, a physician as well as winemaker and a similarly bulky and straight-talking man, whom he first encountered as co-owner of Pomerol's

Château La Croix de Gay. In 1982, the year of the terrific vintage that made Parker's name, Raynaud's father harvested at La Croix de Gay by machine and the resulting wine was light and vegetal. Parker scored it a 77, lambasting it as "a good picnic wine." When other Bordeaux vintners received poor Parker scores, they attacked the messenger. But Raynaud went back to the tasting room. He sampled some of the wines Parker had given good scores. And he retasted his father's La Croix de Gay. His conclusion was clear.

"Parker was right," Raynaud said.

The next spring, Raynaud spotted Parker during the annual spring tasting, which Parker still attended then with other wine writers. "I remember seeing Alain coming toward me and I said, 'Oh, no, here we go again. He is going to slam me like everyone else I criticize,'" Parker said. Instead, Raynaud shook his hand and thanked him.

"I was shocked," Parker recalled.

It was the start of a deep friendship. It helped that Raynaud speaks good English. (Parker didn't become fluent in French until much later.) It also helped that Raynaud kept his word. He and his family began to make richer, more concentrated wines. When Raynaud became president of the Union des Grands Crus in 1994, he transformed the spring tasting from an exclusive event for a few journalists into arguably the world's greatest annual wine gathering. Raynaud's friendship with Parker became both his greatest asset and the focus of criticism. Raynaud was responsible for organizing the annual March tastings that do so much to determine the futures' prices. Médoc critics screamed that Raynaud presented Pomerol and other Right Bank wines in an all-too-favorable light, and that he encouraged his friend "Bob" to taste too many garage wines.

In mid-1997, Raynaud borrowed about $3 million from the banks to buy a little-known 25-acre property called Château Quinault. It didn't look like a promising purchase. The estate was near the heart of the town of Libourne, just behind the Intermarché supermarket. But it possessed old vines and its wine was classified as a Saint-Emilion *grand cru*. The former owner, a wine merchant, farmed the vineyard chemically with no tilling of the soil, and got high yields. He speeded fermentation, aged the wine only in steel tanks, not oak barrels, fined and filtered all life out of the wine, and then sold it on the Belgian market. Raynaud built a shiny new winery and cellar, and followed the *garagiste* recipe. Jeffrey Davies signed up to sell a significant portion of the wine, especially in the United States. He also suggested adding the appropriate suffix, "L'Enclos," highlighting the walled-in nature of the vineyards.

For just his second vintage, Parker scored Quinault a 92+. Merchants clamored to buy the wine. Raynaud sold it to them for $15 a bottle in 1998, $25 in 1999, and $30 in 2000. "I could have gotten even double that price, but I didn't want to scare consumers by pricing my wine so high," Raynaud said. Suddenly investors were offering Raynaud $23 million for control of Château Quinault. He turned down the offers.

In March 2001, just before the spring tasting, Raynaud invited Parker to dinner. It was Raynaud's last year as the Union des Grands Crus president and he wanted to offer his friend Bob something special. Raynaud also had something else to celebrate. He was friendly with Yves Vatelot and Vatelot had just hired him to work at promoting and revamping Château Lascombes.

In the middle of foie gras country, about an hour and a half south of Bordeaux, is a two-star Michelin outpost of *haute cuisine,* a restaurant and hotel called L'Aubergade Les Loges. The hilltop village of Puymirol dominates a fertile plain below. It is one of the oldest fortress towns in the Aquitaine region, dating from 1246. In modern days, the agriculture-based region has become one of France's most isolated backwaters, beyond the limits of Bordeaux wine production and not far enough south to be Armagnac country. Other than duck, the main local specialty is corn.

Chef Michel Trama moved there from Paris two decades ago and transformed a thirteenth-century noble home into a member of the luxury chain Relais & Châteaux. Oversized dining chairs, burgundy-colored oak paneling, and dramatic chandeliers create the look of an elegant update of a medieval stage set. In this atmosphere, Trama serves refined dishes such as polenta and foie gras, an "ice cream"–style cone filled with lobster and topped with a *chantilly* of beets and truffles, and a *pot-au-feu* with foie gras and duck breast *confit* instead of the customary boiled beef. "I had eaten at

Trama's a few months before and it was a fantastic meal, so I asked Bob, 'Would you enjoy having dinner there the next time you are in Bordeaux?'" Raynaud said. The gastronomically inclined Parker could not resist.

Raynaud also invited Gérard Perse, the controversial nouveau riche winemaker who took over and improved Saint-Emilion's Château Pavie and was jacking up its prices at a record pace. Into the back of Raynaud's Toyota Land Cruiser the two men loaded all 150 or so samples of the Union's 2000 wines for Parker to taste, then headed to the restaurant.

The plan was to spend two days feasting and let Parker taste the wines during the day in two conference rooms located above the dining room. Parker tasted alone in one room. Raynaud and Perse tasted in another. In between, they shared sumptuous meals. One of the evenings, everyone was celebrating when a woman from the next table rose and approached Raynaud. She identified herself as a journalist from *Sud Ouest* and said she would write about the affair. The three participants all insist nothing untoward happened. "No one was trying to buy Parker because Parker won't let himself be bought," insisted Perse.

But when an article about the dinner was published, the appearance of collusion stung. Parker's critics became Raynaud's critics. "It was typical Bordeaux stupidity, where no one attacks you to your face, but always behind your back, with little barbed comments," said Perse. Soon afterward, Raynaud stepped down early as president of the Union des Grands Crus. "The whole affair was getting blown out of proportion and this was the only way to stop all the bad rumors," Raynaud said.

Parker was infuriated. "I paid for my own meals and room at the hotel," he said. Perhaps the attack shouldn't have come as such a surprise. As his power grew, Parker found himself more and more often on the defensive. He began to become frightened of being set up. "The hysterical reaction from the Médoc aristocracy as well as reactionaries in Pomerol and Saint-Emilion, allied to supportive writers, most notably England's Jancis Robinson, who appears for reasons that escape me to be on a personal crusade against these (garage) wines, has resulted in a shrill and chilling wall of irrational criticism," Parker complained. The criticism led him to ask, "Where is Oliver Stone?"

His fear of a conspiracy may be unfounded, but the opposition can sometimes be daunting. Back in the 1980s, he visited Saint-Emilion's august Château Cheval Blanc. Parker had rated the wine as mediocre. Jacques Hébrard, the château's family manager, called him at his hotel and demanded he retaste. Parker agreed. At the time, the American had no assistant. The next evening, he arrived alone at Cheval Blanc at the appointed time. Hébrard was one of the few Frenchmen as big as the burly American. When the door opened, Parker said, a small, aggressive pit bull came charging at him. Hébrard didn't move to stop his pet. The dog grabbed Parker's leg and hung on. Hébrard still didn't do anything. Parker finally shook off the dog. His pants were torn, his leg bleeding. Hébrard didn't seem to notice. Instead of giving the wounded American a bandage, he pulled out a copy of the *Wine Advocate* and began screaming, "How could you write this about my wine?"

Parker insisted on going ahead with the tasting. The two men went down to the cellar. To his dismay, Parker realized that the wine was indeed better than he had first thought. He revised the rating. Later, Hébrard admitted that the dog did "nip" Parker, but insisted it caused no blood to flow. "It was just like this little dog," he said, pointing to his current pet, which appeared placid enough. "He could do no harm to such a big man as Parker."

But Parker continues to claim that Hébrard's dog bit him and left a scar on his leg for life. He believes that Bordeaux's old aristocracy despises him and he believes he knows why. "The negative, arrogant aristocracy don't like me leveling the field," he said.

The battle lines were set. Alexandre de Lur-Saluces and Yquem would never please the democratic Parker. The American, never a fancier of sweet wines, did not make judgments based only on history and tradition. To Lur-Saluces's horror, foreign, newfangled ideas were sweeping the wine world. Soon he would learn that they didn't come just from Parker, but from within his own family.

CHAPTER 5

Sweet Injustice

Baron Louis Hainguerlot welcomed a visitor one spring afternoon in 2001 into his apartment. It was on the third floor of a seven-story nineteenth-century edifice in the heart of Paris's aristocratic seventh district. The furniture evoked Louis XIV, baroque and opulent. On top of a marble chimney stood an eighteenth-century clock that could have come straight from Versailles or another noble palace. Paintings of Hainguerlot's ancestors stretching back over several centuries hung on the wood-paneled walls.

Hainguerlot is Alexandre de Lur-Saluces's first cousin, the son of his aunt Isabelle de Lur-Saluces. Although the balding sixty-nine-year-old baron looks trimmer and fitter than his jowl-faced, slightly younger relative, the two aristocrats bear a strong resemblance. They had been friends for a long time but now were bitter enemies. To the outside world, Alexandre de Lur-Saluces was the face of Château d'Yquem. Within the Lur-Saluces's clan, though, his stewardship of the family jewel was a matter of dispute and his chief antagonist was Hainguerlot. Their battle would be played out in private over decades before exploding

into a nasty public scandal. It pitted loyalty against fairness, tradition versus modernity, and, of course, revolved around money.

Hainguerlot's father was a naval officer. Louis was born in the
Mediterranean port of Toulon in 1931. His father was second in command of the battleship *Richelieu* and spent the war years away fighting.
Young Louis, his brothers and sisters, and his mother went to the small
seaside resort of Perros-Guirec on the northern coast of Brittany. The
rock-strewn pink granite coast resembles New England both in look and
feel as well as in its weather patterns. It's a rough, raw place, a natural
wonderland and a haven for birds and other wildlife. Here the Lur-
Saluces owned a château dating from the fifteenth century.

These grapes show telltale signs of pourriture noble, *noble rot.*

Hainguerlot's father resigned from the navy after World War II and
returned to Brittany. He became a leading politician in the region.
Alexandre's family came and spent the summers there. The Lur-Saluces

and Hainguerlot families were best of friends. Their sons were even each other's witnesses at their weddings.

After earning his baccalaureat in Brittany, Hainguerlot went to Paris to continue his studies, graduating with a degree as an agricultural engineer from the prestigious Institut National Agronomique de Paris. In 1957 he completed his military service in the navy, a key coming-of-age ritual in the Lur-Saluces and Hainguerlot clans. The young, ambitious Louis needed a job. His father wrote to Marquis Bertrand de Lur-Saluces, the father's brother-in-law. "The timing is fortuitous," the marquis responded in a letter. Yquem's assistant manager was retiring and the post was open.

Hainguerlot moved to Bordeaux on November 1, 1957. He lived with his uncle Bertrand at the marquis's town house on the rue Saint-Laurent and studied enology at the university. Relations, at least initially, were good. The childless marquis, nearing seventy years old and in the throes of his struggle to keep Philippe de Rothschild from altering the 1855 classification, was an intimidating figure. Pictures of him show an older man, dressed fastidiously in a business suit, with wispy gray hair, spectacles, and a penetrating, severe expression. He impressed the young man with his elegance and taste. "His home was furnished in pure eighteenth-century style, as nice as in any museum," Hainguerlot recalled.

What happened next is a subject of dispute. Hainguerlot believes that just as he had warm feelings toward his uncle, so was the strict marquis grooming him as his protégé. Once Hainguerlot completed his enology studies, he was promoted from assistant manager to managing director of Yquem. Hainguerlot and his young wife moved into the second floor of the château in Sauternes. They conceived their first son, christened, naturally enough, Bertrand. Later, Alexandre de Lur-Saluces claimed that Hainguerlot never got along with the managing director and had him fired. Hainguerlot said the director resigned of his own accord when he saw a young protégé arrive.

Whatever the truth, both sides agree that the idyll faded. By the time Hainguerlot took over Yquem, sweet Sauternes faced a commercial crisis brought on by a series of events over the previous half century. The Russian Revolution dried up Yquem's best market and Prohibition removed the American consumer. After World War II, lakes of insipid, artificially sugared jug concoctions, such as Germany's Blue Nun, wrecked the reputation of the world's finest naturally sweet wines. While demand for Bordeaux's red wines began to recover in the 1960s, the market for its whites diminished. Prices and standards slumped.

During this time, in an effort to modernize, many Sauternes winemakers, notably the progressive Dubourdieu family at Château Doisy-Daëne, began producing dry white wines. In 1959 the marquis came up with the idea to release a strong, dry white wine called, simply, "Y," pronounced *ee-greck* in French. Unlike sweet Yquem, which is dominated by Sémillon grapes, "Y" has 50 percent Sauvignon Blanc. In Marquis Bertrand's mind, it was more an act of desperation than a real effort to expand Yquem's dwindling market. "Y" is not produced every year, just in those years when few of the grapes develop noble rot.

Hainguerlot was shocked to discover that Yquem still depended on horses and a mule to plow its fields. Fresh from his studies of agriculture and enology, the young director was eager to bring the estate into the modern age. But the aging and ailing marquis hesitated, because Yquem earned little money. He tried to steamroll his young nephew with his forbidding intelligence. "We would be having lunch and he would want to discuss the intricacies of a difficult mathematical formula," Hainguerlot recalled. The marquis would ask him to solve the algebraic equation. When Hainguerlot couldn't come up with the answer, the old man scowled.

Once, when the marquis was ill, his nephew represented Yquem during a tasting in London organized by a British importer. He did so with brio.

"You are lucky to have such a competent successor," the merchant reported back to the marquis.

Instead of applauding, the marquis was infuriated.

"Marquis Bertrand saw the praise as a sign of his own mortality and feared I would replace him," Hainguerlot recalled.

From that moment on, the slightest detail became a pretext for a quarrel. "I went from hero to villain," Hainguerlot said of that period.

The final break came in August 1963, when the marquis told his director to have a half bottle of Yquem prepared for tasting. Hainguerlot's assistant instead prepared a full bottle. When he discovered the error, the marquis fired his nephew.

"You are not ready to take over Yquem," he told Hainguerlot angrily, and sent him on his way. If he could have predicted the fate of his beloved château, the marquis might not have been so hasty.

Hainguerlot, though disappointed, seemed to take his dismissal in stride. He found another job, as a commercial director for the Champagne firm Moët & Chandon. With his wife and son, he moved first to the Champagne capital, Epernay, and later settled in Paris. Over the next thirty years he carved out a successful career, rising to top management in the firm, which expanded to sell a wide variety of alcoholic beverages. He learned from his six years at Yquem that the marquis would not give up power willingly in his own lifetime. Nor would the marquis accept someone as his eventual successor who didn't carry the name Lur-Saluces, or even a female Lur-Saluces. "My uncle didn't believe women were good except for preparing parties," he said.

Hainguerlot left just before the 1963 harvest, a particularly tough moment for Yquem. The marquis was already seventy-five years old, and despite his nephew's best efforts to polish it, the jewel's luster was fading. Wine critic Stephen Brook, author of *Sauternes and Other Sweet Wines of Bordeaux,* later wrote that Yquem's vintage that year "was rightly derided as a disgrace." In 1964 rain destroyed the entire crop. Not long after Louis Hainguerlot's departure, the marquis hired a new managing director from outside the family, Pierre Meslier. Meslier is a big, broad-shouldered man, well over six feet tall. He studied enology at the University of Montpellier, one of the best such schools in France. After graduating, he worked at Château Lascombes with the innovative American wine merchant Alexis Lichine. Lichine recommended him for the post.

Meslier struggled to restore Yquem to its rightful place at the top of the Bordeaux hierarchy. "Yquem wasn't making any money and the marquis kept telling me that it was only surviving thanks to funds from the family forests," Meslier said, referring to the vast acreage owned by the

Lur-Saluceses' clan. Like other noble Bordelais families, the Lur-Saluceses' real fortune at the time was tied up in both vines and timber in the Landes forest just south of Bordeaux. In the 1960s, they built a beachfront campground on their property, benefiting from the boom in tourism. "There was no question of distributing dividends to shareholders, no question of buying tractors or other modern equipment," Meslier recalled.

As much as the marquis resisted the idea, he realized he must prepare for his succession. If he wanted to install a male Lur-Saluces, only three potential candidates existed: his brother Amédée's sons, Eugène, Philippe, and Alexandre. None had any experience with wine. All three attended strict Catholic boarding schools far from Bordeaux. Amédée de Lur-Saluces, born in 1889, followed the Lur-Saluces tradition and was a career military officer. He was posted all over France before finally settling with his family in Burgundy. Unfortunately, the part of the region where he lived specialized in cattle grazing, not wine growing.

When World War II broke out in 1939, Eugène was eighteen years old and his brother Philippe was seventeen. Eugène was not a healthy teenager. He suffered from pleurisy and did not volunteer for army service. Alexandre was only six years old. "I have a family photo from 1940 and my brother is little more than a baby," Eugène said. In discussing the photo in Paris in 2001, he didn't mention his six sisters. The future of the Lur-Saluces name resided with the boys.

The war separated the three brothers, leaving a poisonous legacy. Eugène wanted to flee to England and join Charles de Gaulle's Free French resistance. His father forbade him. "My father was a strong believer that Marshal Pétain had saved the country," Eugène said. The senior Lur-Saluces wasn't just admiring of the marshal's valiant defense of Verdun during World War I that made him a hero. He felt that his accession to power in 1940 preaching a far-right agenda represented a "divine surprise."

Pétain's Vichy government agreed to send workers to Germany, at first to gain freedom for captured French prisoners of war and later out of shared ideological conviction. Eugène enrolled in a Vichy-sponsored work program. "It was a duty, and a Lur-Saluces sets the example," Eugène said when recalling his service. He was sent to Leipzig.

Before the war, Eugène had intended to attend college and study agriculture. "After what I had lived through, I gave up the idea," he said. Instead of undertaking a higher education, he went to work on a family farm in Burgundy, expecting one day to get a call from his childless uncle in Bordeaux that would lead to the logical conclusion of his taking over the family properties, including Château d'Yquem. During the long wartime years when the older and younger brothers were separated, they grew apart. When he returned home, Eugène felt he should be treated with the respect due an elder. Alexandre, in the meantime, had already entered puberty. "I never had time to gain authority over him before the war drove us apart," Eugène recalled.

The call from the marquis never came, and another sadder, more pressing mission intervened. Eugène's younger brother Philippe escaped World War II unscathed, only to suffer in France's subsequent colonial struggles. As a youth, Philippe was considered the most brilliant of the three brothers. He studied at the prestigious Saint-Cyr military academy, France's version of West Point, and then was dispatched for commando training in Algeria, in preparation for service fighting Ho Chi Minh in Indochina. Instead, the Algerian boot camp produced a nervous breakdown. Phillippe was admitted to a psychiatric hospital run by UNAFAM, an association to protect the mentally ill. Over the next several decades his brother's health, not Yquem or the family's other properties, preoccupied Eugène. He never married; he settled into a two-room family apartment in Paris and volunteered at the UNAFAM headquarters. "If you are the head of a family, your first obligation is to protect your family," he said.

The importance of being head of a family is rooted in a prerevolutionary tradition. In noble families such as the Lur-Saluces, the firstborn son becomes the marquis on the death of the previous one. Younger brothers and sisters are counts and countesses. Further down the chain of aristocratic honor are barons like Louis Hainguerlot.

A marquis receives a greater share of the family wealth, but in Eugène's mind, the inheritance comes at a stiff price, a responsibility to take care of the rest of the family. Eugène's father died in 1966. Since Bertrand was childless, the eldest Lur-Saluces would inherit the title on his death—Eugène. And Eugène planned to take his future responsibilities seriously. By the time Marquis Bertrand was ready to deal with the idea of a successor, however, Eugène was occupied taking care of Philippe. Instead, Bertrand called on the youngest brother, Alexandre. It was 1967 and Alexandre was overjoyed. He was thirty-six years old and believed he had been chosen to inherit the Lur-Saluces fortune.

Nothing in Alexandre de Lur-Saluces's childhood or education predestined him to play such a role. As a youngster, he never visited Yquem. He served as a parachutist in the army, including six months in 1962 at the end of the Algerian war. Pictures from that period show a trim, handsome young man in combat fatigues. His two army colleagues, smoking cigarettes, seem blasé, one looking down, away from the camera entirely, and the other looking absently askance. Only Alexandre stares straight into the camera, as if seeking the limelight.

Before his discharge, the young Lur-Saluces received a diploma from a business school in the northern French city of Lille. A cousin helped him land a job as a salesman in the north of France for the American multinational 3M. He hated the work. "It was oppressive," confirming his worst suspicions about giant multinationals, he told a French journalist later.

When his uncle called, Alexandre moved to Bordeaux immediately and rented a small apartment on the rue Chevalier near his uncle's town house. He passed a few courses in enology and watched how his uncle managed his businesses. At Yquem, Pierre Meslier ran the show. "Alexandre knew nothing about wine," Meslier recalled. "He just watched me do everything."

A year later, on December 19, 1968, Bertrand de Lur-Saluces went out for a walk. Within minutes the marquis was dead at age eighty, the victim of a heart attack.

"It was like a cement block falling on my shoulders," Alexandre later told one of his sisters. "I needed more time to become familiar with Yquem."

The marquis had not changed his will since it was drawn up in 1925. At the time, Eugène was only three years old. Under its terms, Eugène received the marquis's 47 percent of Yquem, in addition to the 1 percent he already had inherited from his father. Alexandre was stuck only with a small minority percentage. The rest of the château was split into small shareholdings among fifty other Lur Saluces, Hainguerlots, and various other family members. Eugène also inherited another Sauternes estate, Château de Fargues, forests, and the beachfront campground on the coast south of Bordeaux.

"My uncle had called me to his side because my brother had not shown proof of his abilities," Alexandre recalled. "He had taken his old will to revise it, but his death prevented him."

Not long after the funeral, Alexandre and Eugène went out to dine in a fashionable bistro across the street from the Grand Théâtre. Alexandre told his elder brother, now the marquis, that he had scheduled an appointment with the notary.

Soon afterward, the brothers went to the notary's office. In the United States a notary is just someone who witnesses the signing of documents and swears that the person signing a document is the person he says he is. In France, a notary is a powerful official, authorized by the state to draw up legal contracts. At the notary's office, Eugène signed a document dividing up half and half the Marquis's property and giving Alexandre the power of attorney. In return, Alexandre admitted that Eugène was the true inheritor of the marquis's title and remained Yquem's official owner.

Alexandre and Yquem prospered. He married Bérengère de Nattes, a young woman from a noble background in the west of France who soon earned a reputation as a superb hostess. A photo of the young couple shows Alexandre looking adoringly at his bride, prim and proper in a strict suit and bow-tied blouse as she sits on boxes of Yquem readied for shipping. In 1968, Yquem's annual sales came to a mere $150,000. "When I took over Yquem, the bank account was empty," Alexandre remembered.

The turning point came in 1983. It was a superb vintage and the American market, high on the Reagan recovery and a strong dollar, mopped up the elixir. Prices began to rise. Growers returned to the market. In 1976 Count Maximilien de Pontac of Château de Myrat, a second-growth Sauternes, uprooted his vines. In 1986 his children replanted. That same year, Yquem's last horses, a pair named Popaul and Pompon, retired, replaced by modern tractors.

As Yquem suddenly became prosperous, with annual sales reaching almost $15 million a year, a debate opened among the estate's shareholders about how much of this success was due to Alexandre. Did he just ride the increasing popularity of Bordeaux and Sauternes? The Hainguerlots certainly think this accounts for at least part of the success. Or did his efforts to preserve a high level of quality—not releasing any Yquem in poor harvest years, investing finally in tractors and modern presses—pay off? This is Alexandre's version of events.

Whatever the truth, the estate finally had money to pamper its vines. No chemical fertilizer is added, only animal manure. Although winter pruning is severe, Meslier and his boss Lur-Saluces avoided summer green harvesting, as practiced by Parker-influenced *garagistes*. They didn't consider it necessary. In the first few weeks of September, about twenty-five female employees thin the leaves around the clusters. Each woman is responsible for her own parcel throughout the year. Some of them have worked their vines for as long as thirty years and they treat them like their children, with a mixture of affection and respect.

Year-round, Yquem employs sixty-five workers, by far the most in all of Sauternes. During the harvest, a team of one hundred specially trained pickers is added. Most are hired year after year, for the entire six-week harvest season, and paid whether they work or not. A full-time Yquem employee accompanies each team. The foreman checks the contents of each basket before the grapes are taken by tractor to the cellar.

It takes years to develop the skills required to distinguish between bunches with noble rot and the ones with gray rot. And it is difficult to tell which fruit should be left for the next pass and which should be taken up. A few decades ago, local housewives took care of everything. They didn't ordinarily work outside the home and were happy to earn a little shopping money. Their delicate touch made them the ideal pickers.

But women's liberation and the automobile have encouraged these women to find better work outside of sleepy Sauternes, and replacements have proved hard to find. At Château Doisy-Daëne, the local unemployment office dispatches harvesters. "The workers we find now can't be trusted," said owner Pierre Dubourdieu. Dubourdieu came up with an innovative replacement: a freezer. Usually, skilled harvesters cut off small parts of bunches, just the right rotten parts, leaving the rest to reach optimum maturity. At Doisy-Daëne, workers are instructed instead to cut off the entire bunch, with fully rotten and less rotten fruit together. "Otherwise, they risk cutting off the wrong portion, releasing the best juice and turning everything else into vinegar," Dubourdieu said. Then, every evening, all the grapes harvested at Doisy-Daëne are frozen. When the grapes are pressed, the ice remains behind and the must is sweet and concentrated. Air contact is limited and oxidation becomes less of a risk. Flavors concentrate, fruitiness becomes accentuated.

The Dubourdieu technique has revolutionized white wine making. Pierre's son Denis is a renowned enologist, a professor at the University of Bordeaux and consultant to many estates throughout the region and the rest of France. For both dry and sweet white wines, he works hard to minimize oxidation to preserve every sip of freshness. Underripe Sauvignon Blanc, Denis Dubourdieu believes, gives dry Bordeaux whites their infamous cat's pee bouquet, and oxidation causes the color to brown prematurely, masking flavors. His dry whites, in contrast, are fruity and aromatic. Dubourdieu experiments, mixing different grape types, trying out different strains of yeast to start fermentation, fermenting in small oak barrels, stainless steel tanks, or in a combination of the two. A stocky bulldog of a man, Dubourdieu doesn't mince words and has few nice opinions about Alexandre de Lur-Saluces or Yquem's wine, which he finds overrated.

Not surprisingly, the feeling is mutual: Lur-Saluces rejected Dubourdieu's innovations. Although no sugar is artificially added in Doisy-Daëne's system, nature is manipulated and improved upon. That's against Lur-Saluces's philosophy. Modern Sauternes such as Doisy-Daëne are yellowy gold, fresh and full of fruit and finesse. Traditional Sauternes epitomized by Yquem are fat, rich, and unctuous. Their fruit is *"confit,"* almost jammy. Their color is copper gold. "Dubourdieu is an alchemist. He conjures up great wine no matter what the *terroir,"* says Florence Cathiard of Château Smith-Haut-Lafitte. "Alexandre respects tradition and *terroir*, perhaps too much."

This debate over winemaking generated little emotion among Yquem's shareholders. Even later when relations deteriorated, the Hainguerlots considered Alexandre's wine excellent, and most wine critics, with Parker disinterested, continued to praise the estate as the king of Sauternes. This success, along with Yquem's newfound profitability, allowed fraught family relations to enter a period of relative tranquillity. "Alexandre was doing quite well and I believed I had been mistaken to doubt his competence," said Louis Hainguerlot. In 1986 Alexandre's eldest son served as witness at Hainguerlot's eldest son Bertrand's wedding. As late as 1991, Alexandre sponsored Louis Hainguerlot's application to join the exclusive Jockey Club in Paris. Hainguerlot was happy away from Bordeaux. His career thrived. Moët & Chandon expanded into France's largest Champagne producer, part of one of the world's largest wine and spirits companies. Hainguerlot directed the part of the company's business that marketed Champagne and Cognac and Heineken beer.

At first Alexandre consulted his cousin Louis about Yquem's finances. "I had more commercial and financial experience than he did," Hainguerlot said. From his perch at Moët, he helped Alexandre gain entry for Yquem into the prestigious Comité Colbert luxury association. For most of the family members, the annual general assembly at Yquem was an enjoyable occasion. Alexandre paid for them to travel to Sauternes. He offered everyone a festive meal at the château, followed by a tasting of the best vintages of Yquem. "I became accustomed to our general assemblies '*si sympathiques,*'" Alexandre wrote to a sister at one point in the 1980s.

For Eugène, though, the bitter feelings persisted. Alexandre paid the bills for his brother's upkeep in the two-room apartment in Paris. When Eugène needed to buy a car in the early 1990s, he told Louis Hainguerlot he didn't have the money and was too scared to ask Alexandre. "I didn't want anything to do with that dragon," he said about Alexandre. During all this time, Eugène was still looking after his brother Philippe and volunteering at UNAFAM headquarters. At the same time, Alexandre insisted that he wasn't interested in money, only in protecting his family and safeguarding their inheritance.

The fraternal cold war represented a ticking time bomb and Yquem's sudden success triggered the mechanism. Shareholders began to look for dividends and worry about how their children would one day pay the inheritance taxes. At the end of the 1980s, Yquem needed to build a new cellar to ferment and age wine. It was to be located underneath the former stables, at the entrance to the château's courtyard. The shareholders agreed. Louis Hainguerlot suggested Alexandre take out a mortgage. "I said 'go ahead,' and showed him several possible ways to finance it efficiently," Hainguerlot said.

Despite his business school education, Alexandre hated the idea of debt and paid for the construction out of operating funds. Under French law, all shareholders are taxed on profits generated before investments. During the year of the heavy investments, Yquem, by all other measures a flourishing enterprise, suddenly saw its profits evaporate. "All of a sudden we ended up paying taxes without receiving any dividends, and on a business that was, by all accounts, not profitable," said Jean de Pouilly, a nephew of Alexandre's and the grandson of Isabelle de Lur-Saluces, Louis Hainguerlot's mother. Worse, the new cellar's cost escalated. A proposed $1 million investment soon soared close to $2 million.

A conflict between generations was fermenting. In 1990 Jean de Pouilly was thirty years old and was working for one of France's sharpest financial raiders, Vincent Bolloré. Bolloré Investissement is a $5 billion-a-year engineering and transportation firm which controls, among other things, almost all the cargo traffic between Africa and Europe. De Pouilly would soon be dispatched to Los Angeles to oversee the firm's American operations. Louis Hainguerlot's son Bertrand, also thirty, had just graduated from one of France's most prestigious business schools, INSEAD.

Their parents showed deference to Alexandre's authority. During their childhood, the Hainguerlots, de Pouillys, and Lur-Saluces gathered on the Brittany coast. Eugène sometimes came to go sailing. In the 1980s, they continued to socialize and invite each other to dinners. Alexandre always stayed away. When Jean de Pouilly criticized Yquem's management, Alexandre's aunt Anne de Chizelle interrupted him.

"I won't listen to any criticism of Alexandre," she said, ending the discussion.

But the younger shareholders refused to be silenced. At one general assembly, Jean de Pouilly asked for an explanation on a point in the accounts.

"If a boy who has a few shares begins to ask questions, where are we heading?" asked Alexandre, refusing to answer.

"I tried to calm the situation by saying that the young man's remark was interesting," says Louis Hainguerlot.

Alexandre wasn't accustomed to criticism—or to answering questions. His success at Yquem had catapulted him into a position of power and prestige among the people he cared about—his aristocratic peers and France's intellectual elite. By the 1990s, Alexandre settled into what appeared to be a comfortable middle age. His stomach expanded. His hair thinned. Instead of the sharp-looking young soldier, he epitomized the plump aristocrat. Bordeaux's nobility appreciated this hauteur. "Alexandre embodies a certain style and substance above the mere caprices of money," said Denis Mollat, who owns Bordeaux's largest bookstore and a small publishing house and who is a close friend, though himself not a noble.

Behind the glittering appearances, the count's autocratic instincts sparked a series of debilitating spats in the region. In 1971 the six hundred inhabitants of Sauternes elected Alexandre mayor. His first two six-year terms were unremarkable. During the third, the count decided to transform a municipal building, used for catechism classes and standing next to the village church, into a painting school. The plan infuriated Father Paul Salahun. When the next elections were held in 1989, Salahun campaigned against the count. Him or me, the priest inveighed from the pulpit. If Salahun left, a shortage of clerics in France meant that the church hierarchy wouldn't name a replacement. The clear choice prompted an over-whelming vote in the conservative village in favor of the church and cate-chism classes. "Neither the priest nor Alexandre likes listening to other opinions," said Jean-Michel Descamps, the mayor in 2001.

Alexandre continued to bulldoze anybody who threatened to share in Yquem's glory. At about the same time that he had the run-in with the local priest, he forced his cousin Henri de Vaucelles, owner of the second-growth Château Filhot, to remove the Lur-Saluces name from his label. The Lur-Saluces family had owned Filhot since the early nineteenth cen-tury and it had passed down through marriage to the de Vaucelles family. "For Alexandre, Yquem and himself came before anybody else," said a disappointed de Vaucelles.

Alexandre told no journalists or writers about the château's real own-ership. In 1985 the American food and wine writer Richard Olney pub-lished a coffee table book, a paean to the estate's glory, titled simply *Yquem*. No mention was made of Eugène or any of his brothers or sisters in the text, or even in the genealogical tree.

No mention was made, either, of Yquem's longtime managing direc-tor, Pierre Meslier, the man who arguably did more than anybody else to create the modern Yquem. Since the old marquis had hired Meslier back in 1963, he had lived on the estate, while Alexandre stayed in Bordeaux and visited just once or twice a week. Meslier took advantage of the absences. During the 1970s, he invited Jeffrey Davies, then an exchange student at the University of Bordeaux, to his home. The two would play Ping-Pong and savor the great vintages of Yquem. "Pierre gave me one of the sweetest introductions to Bordeaux anyone could hope for," said Davies with a smile. In the early 1970s, Meslier bought an estate called Château Raymond-Lafon, located just below Yquem. He used tractors and other material from Yquem to cultivate his fields, a common practice in the region. Meslier also bragged that his wine was as good as Yquem's, and some wine critics agreed.

For years Alexandre ignored these indiscretions. Then, in 1989, the count suddenly summoned Meslier to his office and, without warning, fired him, forcing Meslier to move out by the next day. "All of us in

Sauternes were shocked by Pierre's treatment," recalls Pierre Dubourdieu of Château Doisy-Daëne.

Instead of satisfying the Hainguerlots and other critics with his strong
action, Alexandre further angered them. He proposed taking Meslier's
salary himself, which was calculated at 2 percent of Yquem's revenues, or
some $300,000 a year. "I was very surprised that Alexandre wanted to
take such a large cut," Bertrand Hainguerlot remembered.

The young business school graduates began to sense that Alexandre's
virulent denials of interest in monetary gain were less than genuine. They
accepted that the count drove a BMW 7 series sedan. But they questioned
his $1 million-a-year budget for travel, ostensibly to promote Yquem. Was
this money well spent? The Young Turks doubted it. When Alexandre
visited Los Angeles regularly during the 1990s, he hosted invitation-only
tastings in restaurants. "There was no buzz, no one from Hollywood,"
recalls de Pouilly, who was living in the city at the time.

While the return on promotional events is always subjective, investments in buildings can be calculated, and Alexandre's inability to control
costs infuriated the young financiers Hainguerlot and de Pouilly. Not only
had the new cellar cost far more than expected; when two rooms in the
château were renovated, the budget surpassed $1 million. "Once the work
was all done, Alexandre came in and said, 'I don't like it,'" recalled de
Pouilly. "Everything had to be changed at great expense." In their opinion,
the worst misuse of money was spending $150,000 on a new bathroom for
the château. Admittedly, it was beautiful, featuring a running fountain of
warm water, but the young business school graduates with their eye on the
bottom line saw only extravagant waste. "Gold-plated toilets are not
exactly essential equipment," said Bertrand Hainguerlot.

These disagreements over commercial policy soon spiraled out of
control. Alexandre's refusal to sell his wine as a future in the spring following the harvest like Médoc's top growths, as well as his insistence on
waiting to sell it until it was bottled four years later, exasperated the
younger generation. They were also shocked to learn that he sold only
part of any given vintage, leaving thousands of unsold bottles of Yquem
backed up in the new cellar. Millions of dollars of unrealized sales slept

below ground. For M.B.A.'s, the huge inventory was a disaster waiting to happen. "If it were put on the market, the price of Yquem would collapse," worried Bertrand Hainguerlot.

The Young Turks proposed reducing the risk by creating a second label. Call it Demoiselle d'Yquem, Hainguerlot suggested. Château Margaux had its Pavillon Rouge and all the other first-growth reds bottled second wines. "It could be sold at half the price of Yquem and attract new customers to the brand," Hainguerlot said. Instead of just buying small parcels of vines and adding to Yquem's production, the critics wanted Alexandre to take over entire properties in Sauternes. "Yquem must not be an affair just about money," Alexandre told them.

Wherever they looked, the young dissidents saw missed opportunities. Marquis Bertrand's nemesis Baron Philippe de Rothschild, who died in 1988, had leveraged his first-growth Médoc into the multimillion-dollar mass-market Mouton Cadet business while maintaining the high sales prices for his cherished Mouton Rothschild. He had also expanded internationally, striking a profitable and prestigious joint venture with Robert Mondavi in the Napa Valley to produce Opus One, a robust red that won awards and set new records for California wine prices. "Alexandre should have been doing the same thing with Yquem, setting up joint ventures abroad and dominating the world's dessert wine market," said Jean de Pouilly. Several years after the fall of the Berlin Wall, Lur-Saluces did come up with a plan to buy a property in Hungary's Tokay region. By this time, though, he had lost the confidence of his relatives. "It was a pharaonic project, with little thought given to a real return on investment," complained de Pouilly.

Without such moves, the younger generation predicted Yquem would become fragile. Alexandre avoided the up-and-coming merchants like Jeffrey Davies. Instead of allocating Yquem to prestigious wine shops, the merchants Alexandre favored often unloaded it to lowbrow supermarkets. "When bottles of Yquem started appearing in Intermarché stores around France in the 1990s, we were horrified," remembered Bertrand Hainguerlot. What should have been an *haute couture* product was being sold like a pair of discount jeans. Alexandre didn't see any danger of diluting a premium brand if the supermarket carried the wine only on special occasions.

In his defense, Alexandre saw only ingratitude. He argued that he had taken a nearly bankrupt, worthless business and built it into a gem generating millions of dollars of cash each year. The value of the Lur-Saluces holdings had multiplied a hundredfold under his stewardship. Keeping a large stock in the cellar was only prudent, given the vagaries of Sauternes winemaking. It let him release a fixed amount of wine each year—even if an entire harvest was a washout. "It's my treasure chest," he told Hainguerlot.

A mass-market business in the Rothschild style only risked diluting Yquem's luster, and, Alexandre asked, who needed to take the risk? Yquem let him live a lifestyle befitting a count. He saw himself as protecting a national monument from overcommercialization. Business school theories disgusted him. Once Paris's prestigious Institut de Sciences Politiques invited him to give a speech. He planned to tell them about Yquem's rich historical tradition. But the students were bored. "What is your marketing plan?" one asked. "I don't have one," Alexandre replied. "I just want to preserve the fabulous inheritance I have received."

The count's main worry was the vexing weight of taxes, both income and inheritance. As the value of Yquem increased, Alexandre consulted a Paris-based auditor named Bernard Hinfray. In 1990 the auditor came up with a plan to create a holding company called a *société en commandite*. It would rent Yquem's land and own the growing inventory of bottled wine. This new company would reduce the shareholders' tax burden by keeping the profits before investments on its books. Better yet from Alexandre's point of view, the new company provided the director with almost unlimited powers to run Yquem as he saw fit. Alexandre would no longer need to listen to any unruly shareholders. He could start arranging for succession, preferably to his eldest son, Bertrand.

Also in 1990, Alexandre, usually a man who kept his own counsel, met a Bordeaux corporate psychologist named Marie-Odile Billé-Rode. Bérengère de Lur-Saluces told the Hainguerlots she had advised her husband to seek help.

"My husband often loses his temper," Bérengère told them.

"Be firm," Mme. Billet-Rode advised her.

Relations between the couple had been strained for some time and one divisive issue was what should happen to Yquem. The *comtesse* wanted Yquem split evenly among her three children. Her husband preferred to favor their eldest son. During the next general assembly at Yquem, Louis Hainguerlot noted that Bérengère was absent. In previous years, she had always been present at the head table. "We appreciated her," he remembered. "She had a calming influence on Alexandre." A few days later, Hainguerlot called Bérengère to inquire whether she was well.

"Thank you for asking," Bérengère replied. "But Dr. Billé-Rode advised Alexandre that my presence at Yquem is detrimental."

Without Bérengère as a soothing buffer, relations between the Hainguerlots and Alexandre deteriorated. "We saw Billé-Rode as the power behind the throne, pushing Alexandre to take full control of Yquem," said Bertrand Hainguerlot.

Alexandre soon demanded a divorce and, as usual, he got what he demanded. Bérengère eventually left Bordeaux for Paris, where the Hainguerlots lodged her for a while. She ended up resettling and remarrying in Belgium and will no longer speak about Alexandre or Yquem. Since her departure, the town house has been empty. Alexandre moved to Sauternes. He didn't take up residence in Yquem, but in nearby Château de Fargues, which he was also managing for Eugène. The difference was that while Eugène owned only 48 percent of Yquem, he owned 100 percent of Fargues, which also produced a well-respected Sauternes. "I think Alexandre saw danger coming with Yquem, but thought no one could touch him at Fargues," said Bertrand Hainguerlot.

Alexandre became isolated, not only from his own family but also from the wider world of Bordeaux wine. When the merchant and winemaker Jacques Thienpont and his wife, Fiona, visited Singapore on a marketing trip shortly after Alexandre's divorce, they spotted Yquem's owner eating alone in the hotel dining room and asked him to join them. The count refused. The following evenings, they saw Lur-Saluces eating alone again, but they didn't extend any more invitations. "Alexandre is such a sad, solitary figure," Thienpont said.

In November 1991, the count called an "extraordinary" shareholders' meeting in Paris, at the chic Royal Monceau hotel near the Champs Elysées. On the agenda was the auditor's plan to establish a *société en commandite* to manage Yquem's assets. Almost all of the shareholders attended. Jean de Pouilly flew back from Los Angeles. Hainguerlot father and son sat together. Alexandre's relatives filled the conference room. Eugène was absent, as usual. The count himself arrived with his auditor Hinfray, who proceeded to describe the structure of the new company. Behind the expressed purpose of setting up a *société en commandite* to reduce wealth taxes for shareholders, the Hainguerlots feared Alexandre had a secret agenda to wrest complete power.

"Let's take a few months to reflect on this proposal," said Louis Hainguerlot, once the auditor had finished speaking.

Alexandre was furious. In his view, Hainguerlot wasn't thinking of the estate's best interest, but reacting out of anger at his own unhappy, forced departure from Sauternes three decades earlier.

"Hainguerlot wants revenge on Yquem," he said as the meeting broke up.

It was a declaration of war. When the family reassembled two weeks later at the Hôtel Prince de Galles, also in Paris, a last-ditch attempt was made to arrange a cease-fire. Alexandre's aunt Anne de Chizelle, the leading representative still alive from Marquis Bertrand's generation, stood up. She had always defended her nephew. She had even donated part of her 9 percent share in Yquem to him in order to counterbalance Marquis Bertrand's exclusive choice of Eugène. Her moral authority was uncontested among the older generation of shareholders, including Louis Hainguerlot.

"Alexandre, you are about to take a decision that doesn't have unanimous approval," she warned. "Please take more time to reflect."

Alexandre went ahead anyhow and called for a vote.

The Hainguerlots were confident. They believed they needed only 25 percent of voting shares to block the project and they received 40 percent.

But when Alexandre announced the results, he smiled. "The project is accepted," he said.

The Hainguerlots were mystified. Then they looked at the order of the day prepared for the meeting, which they had received on entering the conference room, and discovered the explanation. Without their knowledge, Alexandre and Hinfray had changed the title of this shareholder meeting from "extraordinary" to "ordinary." At an "ordinary" shareholder meeting, a simple majority sufficed for approving the project of a new company.

An angry Bertrand Hainguerlot raised his hand and asked to see the official legal document authorizing Alexandre to vote Eugène's shares. Alexandre's face went pale from shock, one participant said later. The auditor intervened. Under the law, you have no right to see it, Hinfray said.

The shareholders' meeting adjourned. A few days later, Louis and Bertrand Hainguerlot obtained a court order and traveled to Bordeaux with a sheriff's officer. They drove up to Yquem's front entrance and demanded to see the count's power of attorney.

"Alexandre handed us a paper," Hainguerlot said.

It was from 1968—the same document drafted by the notary and signed by Alexandre and Eugène shortly after Marquis Bertrand's death. This paper merely authorized Alexandre to execute his uncle's will. No document signed by the old marquis's successor, Marquis Eugène, authorized Alexandre to create any *société en commandite*. In Alexandre's mind, the original paper sufficed to include representing Eugène in managing the affairs of Château d'Yquem. Under the law, however, it didn't.

—

CHAPTER 6

Right Bank Revenge

WHILE THE 1990S WOULD PROVE CONTENTIOUS FOR THE LUR-
Saluces clan, they were good to Saint-Emilion. The picturesque village
perched on a hillside with magnificent views over the Dordogne Valley
became a major attraction not only for its wines but for its history and
beauty. Parts of its medieval walls remain intact, along with a superb
fourteenth-century collegiate church and cloister. In 1999 the United
Nations Educational, Scientific and Cultural Organization selected the
entire ancient jurisdiction as a World Heritage Site, the first time it had so
classified a wine-growing region. Tourists love to stroll through the cob-
bled streets past the limestone buildings and drive the small roads around
the village gazing at the vistas of vines.

Where Sauternes is quiet, its grand palaces and villages almost emptied of life, with few hotels or restaurants to host visitors, Saint-Emilion
explodes with excitement: art galleries have sprouted next to wine shops
and bars, and the village hosts a highly regarded classical music festival.
At their châteaux, Gérard Perse and other nouveau riche immigrants
have built indoor swimming pools and private tennis courts. Celebrities
come for weekends. They stay in the newly renovated Hostellerie de Plai-

sance, owned by Perse, and eat at its ambitious gastronomic restaurant. "It's Saint Tropez in the vineyards," according to Daniel Cathiard of Château Smith-Haut-Lafitte.

Saint-Emilion wasn't always so chic. Although it flourished in the Middle Ages, religious wars of the thirteenth to fifteenth century rav-

Medieval Saint-Emilion has become the
wine world's center of innovation.

aged its vineyards. During the French Revolution, anticlerical revolutionaries defaced its Monolithic Church and Cardinal's Palace. Residents deserted the village's other historic buildings, fleeing for their lives. For more than a century the village and surrounding area were neglected. Hardly a soul was left.

Through the eighteenth century and well into the nineteenth, the Right Bank was cut off from the more fashionable Left Bank and from Bordeaux itself. Travelers from the city needed to cross two rivers, the Garonne and the Dordogne. Plans for bridges were published in 1782, but the Revolution interrupted construction: spans across the rivers were built in the first quarter of the nineteenth century.

Merchants didn't travel often to the Right Bank not only because the trip was arduous but because the wine there wasn't interesting. Most winemakers alternated vines with rows of grain. The grain required a lot of manure, and the manure pushed the vines to overproduce. Perhaps even worse, many of the vineyards best suited for producing red Merlot wines were planted with white Sémillon grapes. Until the 1850s, Pomerol, only a few miles from the village of Saint-Emilion, boasted one true château, the old estate of the de May family. A Paris banker bought it and gave it the pretentious name of Vieux-Château-Certan. Château Pétrus consisted of a modest house with a turreted gateway. Another great Pomerol named Château Trotanoy began its life under the discouraging name Trop-Ennuie, or Too Boring.

Saint-Emilion's only truly great wine was produced at Figeac, on the iron-rich clay and gravel plateau stretching north toward Pomerol. It belonged to the noble Vital Carles family, ministers under the Bourbons. After the Revolution, it went into decline. A small piece of land near the stables was broken off and sold to the Ducasse family. That's how the later-to-become-famous Château Cheval Blanc, or White Horse, received its name. "In the nineteenth century, most of Saint-Emilion was hunting land, more forest than vines," said Figeac's present owner, Thierry de Manoncourt.

Only in the twentieth century did the long-ignored Right Bank emerge as a serious challenger to the established Left Bank, largely as the result of the efforts of Jean-Pierre Moueix. In 1930 Moueix, then seventeen, arrived in Libourne, four miles to the west of Saint-Emilion, right on the Dordogne River. He came from the poor, mountainous Corrèze region more than a hundred miles to the east. Like many of his native region's inhabitants, he escaped poverty by loading all his possessions onto a boat, traveling down the Dordogne, and selling his belongings to get a start. Moueix, a big, theatrical man, was a consummate salesman, and once he arrived in Libourne he set his mind to selling wine.

The choice was natural. Saint-Emilion didn't have a port and what wine it was selling at the time was shipped through Libourne. Originally a fortress town, Libourne evokes none of the majesty and grandeur of

Bordeaux. Though there is a quay with wine merchants' offices, it is a sleepy midsize provincial market center that could be mistaken for a hundred others in France. Moueix settled there, far from the established merchants on the Quai des Chartrons in Bordeaux who neglected Saint-Emilion and Pomerol. The budding merchant originally avoided doing any business with England, because he spoke no English and the competition from the Médoc was too strong. Instead, Moueix traveled by train to northern France, Belgium, and Holland. There, to save money, he slept in train station waiting rooms. He sold wine door to door, by the case, or to neighborhood shops.

The strategy worked and Moueix's rise was meteoric. Even before World War II, he was rich enough to begin buying some estates in Pomerol, including Magdelaine and Trotanoy, then little revered but now considered icons. Moueix had a knack for spotting and seducing talent. During the war, he was in Belgium checking into a hotel and the man ahead of him couldn't find a working pen. Moueix lent him one, the two started talking, and Moueix found his Belgian sales agent. After the war, his business grew. Moueix still didn't speak a word of English, but in 1952 he made his first trip to the United States, where he managed to sell a good amount of wine. "He was the type of charismatic personality that attracted people to go out of their way for him," said Jean-Claude Berrouet, a talented enologist who has loyally worked with Moueix's firm for four decades.

By the end of the 1950s, Moueix owned twelve Pomerol properties. When he was unable to purchase an estate outright, he often became its exclusive agent. He became the sole distributor of Château Pétrus in 1945 and bought full control only in 1969. He was so successful that he had plenty of disposable income to support his habit as an art collector: he owned a brass dancer by Degas, a couple of Picassos, lots of Dufys, Warhols, and Rothkos. (When he bought Pétrus, he agonized because he needed to sell off a Monet to raise the money.)

In contrast to Saint-Emilion, Pomerol itself isn't grand. It is a collection of eight modest hamlets, clusters of undistinguished homes, strung along narrow country roads. The seven and a half square miles squeezed onto a plateau leave room for a mere 1,800 acres of vines. While a wine-maker such as Michel Gracia will stand up and announce, with pride, "I am from Saint-Emilion," Pomerol residents are more reticent. They are peasant farmers only a generation removed from near-total poverty. The village's few rich wine merchants don't even live there. The Moueix family members work and reside in Libourne. Their employees, mostly North African immigrants, remain behind in Pomerol.

Amazingly, the iconic Pétrus—whose vintages now sell at stratospheric prices—was almost unknown before World War II. The Loubat family acquired it in 1925. Since they couldn't make a living from the estate, they continued to run their Hôtel Loubat near the train station in Libourne. Edmond Loubat ran the hotel and left his wife to promote the wine. She was a "grande dame"—such a grande dame that to this day, everyone in Pomerol and books on the subject just call her Madame Loubat. Most journalists and merchants passed through Libourne, and many stayed at Hôtel Loubat. Madame Loubat made sure they drank Pétrus, and anyone with half a taste bud could tell that it was something special. The vineyards were located at the highest point on the rocky, clay-covered, iron-rich Pomerol plateau and planted with almost 100 percent Merlot, producing a wine that could be drunk young and was full of silky fruit.

When the future Queen Elizabeth married, Madame Loubat offered a magnum of Pétrus as a gift and received an invitation to the wedding. She went to London to deliver the wine. In Pomerol she was almost a queen herself. "Ah, Madame Loubat," recalled Geneviève Raynaud of Château La Croix de Gay. "Every Sunday, she would come a little late to church for mass, arriving after the service had begun. When she entered, everyone would watch as she advanced to take a seat in the front row."

After Madame Loubat died in 1961, her niece and nephew inherited Pétrus and sold it to Moueix. The merchant added eleven acres from the neighboring Château Gazin for a total of twenty-seven. Under French law, Pétrus or any other Pomerol estate can grow as large as the owner desires, provided the acquired vineyards are in Pomerol. But shrewd proprietors kept their wine scarce. Even after the expansion, Pétrus's annual production averaged only 36,000 bottles. No price was published. Only valued wholesalers who took cases of Moueix's less expensive wines from other estates were and still are offered cases.

By contrast, even Yquem sells an average of 110,000 bottles a year. Château Margaux makes up to 400,000 bottles a year, some of which, depending on the quality of the harvest, is sold as the cheaper Pavillon Rouge. That's a large amount of wine, far too much by definition to be considered scarce and in short supply.

Pétrus's relative rarity fueled demand, boosting prices, further increasing demand. During the 1980s and 1990s, the U.S. stock boom ignited a spiral. When Southeast Asia was flying high, new buyers arrived to the market. Tales of Chinese businessmen mixing Pétrus with Sprite or Coca-Cola circulated. In 2001 five British bankers from Barclays Capital lavished $62,700 on a celebration at a trendy London restaurant named, aptly, Pétrus. The restaurant didn't even bother charging for the cost of the food once the wine had been ordered. The bankers drank bottles of Château Pétrus from the 1945, 1946, and 1947 vintages. As bookends, they began and ended their meal with white wines, a Montrachet and a "hundred-year-old bottle" of Château d'Yquem. The restaurant charged $17,500 for the '47 Pétrus. The '45 cost $16,500 and the '46 another $13,400. The 1900 Yquem went for $13,100. After the extravagance was expense-accounted to the bank and widely reported in the press, the five were fired.

By this time, old man Moueix had long since retired, leaving his empire to his sons, Jean-François and Christian. Jean-François runs the mass-market merchant business based in Bordeaux. Christian took charge of the more prestigious luxury estates on the Right Bank. Since 1982 Christian has also directed a joint venture in California producing Dominus, a rich Napa Valley red that rivals the Mondavi and Rothschild Opus One for top California honors. Dominus is made in a striking, modern $8 million cellar near Yountville and sells for $90 or more a bottle.

Back in France, Christian Moueix's offices are located on the Quai de Priorat in Libourne. Since trucks now transport most wine, the riverside wharves and their grimy industrial buildings are mostly deserted. Only a small sign points to the Moueix headquarters, and from the outside it looks like just another dilapidated warehouse. When meeting a visiting journalist in 2001, Christian Moueix emerged to offer an Old World greeting.

"Dear sir," he began, "how welcome you are."

Moueix's own office is a windowless cubbyhole, more appropriate for an ascetic monk than a flamboyant wine salesman. Moueix is a tall, thin man and he had to stoop to fit through the door.

"Why not build something more comfortable?"

"It helps me concentrate," he replied.

As the Australians and Americans attack Bordeaux's bottom and middle end, Moueix is moving upscale. He is selling off mediocre estates and considering dropping his line of basic Christian Moueix Merlot. "A few years ago, I made wines that sold from $4 a bottle to $100 a bottle," he said. "We must concentrate on *grands vins* in which we are competitive."

Moueix seems an unhappy man. He complains about the high price of land around Pomerol. "People are asking $1 million for a hectare—it's ridiculous," he moaned.

Many former peasant winemakers in Pomerol no longer want him to market their wine exclusively. Instead, they prefer to use the *place de Bordeaux* to spread out their limited and suddenly in-demand supply. "We merchants are treated like garbage," said an angry Moueix.

Even though he could have doubled his prices for the magical millennium harvest of 2000, he kept them stable. "Crazy" was his comment about others who had raised their prices so high. "The wine was good, but not as good as everyone says."

As a young man, Moueix was open to new ideas. Before almost anyone else, he tore leaves off the vines during the summer in an effort to increase the body of his wines. In 1973 his workers cut bunches of unripe grapes from the vines during the middle of the night in order to avoid scandalizing their neighbors, who would have considered it a sacrilege to reduce the number of grapes on a vine. The local Pomerol priest condemned him.

But the former innovator doesn't like the way Michel Gracia and his friends are reducing yields. The new style of jammy, plush wines turns him off. He displays a particular disdain for Robert Parker and Parker's friends in Pomerol. Parker has always rated Moueix's top growths well. Nonetheless, Moueix can't stand the American critic. In his *Atlantic Monthly* profile, William Langewiesche describes meeting "one of the most powerful producers in the trade, a businessman with formal manners, who did not want me to use his name." Parker later said this was Moueix. With Langewiesche, Moueix closed the door of his office for privacy and suggested that Parker was part of a grand conspiracy to destroy France.

"Was he going to tell me that Parker was in it for the money after all?" asked Langewiesche. "That he had hidden allies? Secret meetings? Understandings with governments?"

No. Moueix picked up a fax that someone had just sent him. It was a page from a recent issue of the *Wine Advocate,* a survey of Australian wines, many of which Parker had rated in the 90s.

"Bob is a big, dramatic man, with big, dramatic tastes," Moueix continued. "But our wines are supposed to be red, not black." He held up his pen, a shiny black Mont Blanc, to demonstrate the color of the wines that he thinks Parker favors. "I have known him for twenty years, but I will no longer read what he writes. He wants to lead us down a path to destruction."

PERHAPS THE GARAGE phenomenon is so painful to Moueix because it draws in part from Pétrus's own success and is rooted in his home village of Pomerol and nearby Saint-Emilion. Like Moueix, the first true *garagiste* was not a penniless worker. He was a leading member of a distinguished Belgian wine merchant family, Jacques Thienpont.

The Thienponts had owned châteaux in Bordeaux since the 1920s. Their best-known property was Vieux-Château-Certan, which Jacques's cousin Alexandre ran for the family. Alexandre lived full-time in France. Jacques spent most of his time in Belgium managing his merchant business. He had grown up in Brussels, the son of a prominent banker. Like many Belgians, he spoke three languages perfectly—French, Dutch, and

English. In 1996, at the age of fifty, he met Fiona Morrison, a bubbly Brit who is a master of wine, worked for Seagram's in New York and Paris, and then moved to Bordeaux for a position on the region's marketing board. The couple soon had two young children and they now live most of the year near Ghent in a grand hilltop château that has been in Jacques's family for several centuries.

Jacques Thienpont comes to Bordeaux for a few months a year. His home there is a simple worker's cottage, a modest box in the part of Pomerol called Catusseau. It is the hamlet in Pomerol closest to Libourne, built at the beginning of the century as the last stop on the Libourne tramway. In American terms, it is a suburb. In 2001 Pomerol's mayor— owner of Catusseau's bakery—lobbied to reattach the village to Libourne.

In 1979 Thienpont bought a five-acre plot behind his Catusseau cottage for about $150,000. The previous owners were poor, and until Thienpont bought the plot it produced a generic Pomerol sold in bulk to local merchants. The land was on the plateau, only a few hundred yards away from his family's older property, and Thienpont thought at first about extending Vieux-Château-Certan. But while Pétrus and Vieux-Château-Certan were on thick clay soil, iron-enriched limestone lay below the clay and fine gravel on Thienpont's new vineyard. And while Vieux-Château-Certan included a large percentage of Cabernet Franc and Cabernet Sauvignon, the new plot was planted almost entirely with Merlot. "Our soil was special, different," he said. A separate wine was justified. Attached to the plot was one of Catusseau's ugly concrete-box houses. The property's only redeeming feature was a pine tree, which gave gentle shade. Originally it was called Clos du Pin. Thienpont dubbed his new wine Le Pin, literally, the pine tree.

How was he going to produce it? The vineyard was too small to require a full-time worker. His cousin Alexandre subcontracted him workers from Vieux-Château-Certan to cultivate and prune the vines. Seeking further help, he contacted a Dutch friend named Antoine van Gorp, who ran a pub near Antwerp. Antoine didn't speak any French, only a minimum of English, and he had never made wine before. Jacques didn't care. He knew Antoine was meticulous, a fanatic for hygiene, and he believed that an outsider would bring needed new ideas. A few weeks before the first harvest, he and Antoine transformed the cottage's garage into a basic cellar. It was simple. There were no computers or high-tech measuring or pumping equipment, only a few small fermentation tanks and some new barrels.

The winemaking formula was just as straightforward: severe selection of hand-harvested grapes aged 100 percent in new French oak barrels. Before harvesting, Thienpont waited, waited, and waited until the grapes were superripe. Because the vineyard was so small, everything could be harvested in a single day. That represented a significant advantage over large estates, which had to plan out their picking and would often have to make compromises. Thienpont installed a sorting table in the cellar, allowing him to choose, berry by berry, the ripest and healthiest fruit, discarding all stems and leaves, and all berries with gray rot.

While the rich, plummy wines produced by Thienpont were considered "modern" and would soon be championed by Parker, he argues that small yields and ripe grapes represent a return to the preindustrial winemaking methods. In his view, the new resistant rootstocks and the fertilizer- and pesticide-driven race of the 1960s and 1970s to increase production represented the dark side of "modern" techniques that resulted in weak and weedy wines. By returning to the "traditional" and "natural" way of growing grapes, the new wavers argued, their fresh, fruity wines were actually made in the spirit of their grandfathers. Their rich wines respected the true *terroir*.

If there was innovation, it came in the cellar. When making any red wine, continual contact is necessary between the juice of the crushed grapes and their skins to impart color. Crushed grapes are transferred to a fermentation tank, which can be fashioned out of wood, stainless steel, or cement, depending on the winemaker's preference. As the "primary," or alcoholic, fermentation ensues, the sugar in the juice is converted into alcohol and carbon dioxide by the action of the indigenous yeasts that are found on the skins of the grapes and, to a certain extent, in the cellars themselves. (Some New World winemakers, in particular, prefer to kill the naturally occurring yeasts by adding sulfur dioxide along with selected yeast strains.) The grape skins rise to the top of the tank. This thick "cap" of skins floating on the surface needs to be immersed in the juice in order to favor extraction of color, flavor, and tannins. This is done in one of two ways: by pumping the juice up and over the cap or by punching down the cap, breaking it up, and allowing the juice to flow more freely in and around the solids in the tank. The first technique is called *pigeage* and the latter is called *remontage*.

After primary fermentation is finished, the wine retains a hard edge. A "secondary" fermentation—the malolactic fermentation, generated not by yeast but by a bacterium—transforms the tart malic acid into lactic acid. The wine becomes softer and creamier. Until recently, most Bordeaux winemakers preferred to work with big, easy-to-monitor tanks, running the new wine off into barrels for aging only once the malolactic fermentation finishes, as late as February of the following year.

Thienpont broke with this idea. Just after the yeast finished turning grape sugar into alcohol, usually in ten days, he removed the young wine from the steel tanks and put it right into new oak barrels. The technique didn't stem from any ideological preference, at least not at first. It was a practical matter, chosen because Thienpont had no other space to store the wine. In the barrels, the wine underwent its malolactic fermentation. Today, advocates of this approach argue that it produces a better marriage between the wine and the wood. That premise is debatable. One result, though, is clear. The wine takes on its oak much earlier than in a big tank and is much flashier and complex in time for the all-important March tastings.

Traditionalists such as Christian Moueix scoff. At Pétrus, newly crushed grapes are placed in concrete tanks and the wine is only transferred to barrels three months later. Moueix favors keeping the wine in large receptacles ranging from 1,825 gallons to 4,900 gallons. Transferring the wine into barrels for the malolactic fermentation is a labor-intensive undertaking. Each individual barrel must be monitored for infection and that is difficult for large estates. Temperatures must be maintained at around 22 to 25 degrees Celsius or fermentation may stop. It is easier to control temperatures in one large tank than a hundred smaller barrels.

Le Pin is produced in limited quantities. At first Thienpont made only about 3,000 bottles a year. In 1985 he acquired another two and a half acres from the local blacksmith. Later, he bought a vegetable garden and planted a few more vines. And yet the maximum production never rises above 9,000 bottles a year. In most vintages, only 6,000 bottles are produced.

Almost as soon as the first bottle of Le Pin reached the marketplace, word began to spread concerning an astonishing Pomerol, rich, full-bodied, smoky, exotic, and exuberant. One French writer dubbed it the Romanée-Conti of Bordeaux, after the famed Burgundy microestate. Le Pin began to surpass all other Pomerols in blind tastings, and it became even harder to find than Pétrus. The price at auction began to rise. A case of 1982 Le Pin was sold two decades later for $2,500 a bottle. During the 1990s, investment bankers bragged about the cases of Le Pin in their cellars, just as they did about their Lamborghinis or their new Swan yachts. No matter that few could appreciate the wine—or even that its producer considered the cult status ridiculous. "No wine is worth that much," Thienpont said.

He himself has not cashed in. For the first ten years, he sold Le Pin for a mere $40 a bottle. He finally raised the price to about $250 a bottle for his original, faithful buyers, and about $400 for the few others who could get on his buyers' list. "One of my British friends told me he had auctioned all his Le Pin and been able to pay for a marvelous new house," he said. There was no bitterness in his voice. To the contrary, the story pleased and amused him.

In 2001 no sign pointed to Le Pin's cellar. It remains the garage under the unadorned concrete two-story worker's house in the middle of Pomerol's plateau. The worker who lives there receives free rent in return for keeping watch over the treasure below. The contrast between this setting and that of a grand Bordeaux estate couldn't be starker.

Jacques Thienpont didn't set out to create a cult wine. He just wanted to make a good drink. "Life is like a river," he reflected. "You follow it and it takes you on a strange course."

Soon after its first appearance, someone used the term garage wine to describe Le Pin. No one's sure who invented the phrase. Some say French wine writer Michel Bettane coined *vins de garage*. Others credit another French writer, Nicholas Baby, who called Thienpont a *garagiste* in an article about Le Pin at the end of the 1980s. And yet others point to Florence Cathiard, who, upon seeing one winemaker's cellar, compared it to her own palatial Château Smith-Haut-Lafitte and asked, "Just a garage?" Whoever minted the moniker, the Thienponts don't appreciate it. "We are not *garagistes*," says Fiona Thienpont. "We're just winemakers."

DESPITE THEIR LACK of pretension, the Thienponts can't hide their pedigree: they are not "new" winemakers forcing open the closed Bordeaux establishment. The real *garagiste* is an outsider and proud to be one, like Michel Gracia. When Gracia went looking for inspiration, he didn't turn to Thienpont. He looked to his neighbor, Jean-Luc Thunevin, who lived just around the corner from his garage on a narrow Saint-Emilion back street. "Jean-Luc's been a buddy for years and he showed me how to do everything," said Gracia.

Thunevin is an unlikely winemaker. Born in Algeria in 1951 to French settlers, he moved to Libourne in his teens, when his parents sent him there to attend boarding school. The French somewhat derisively call people like him—any Frenchman born in North Africa—a *pied noir*, literally black foot. He never did well in school—his only diploma was in cabinetry. In his early twenties, he was delighted to land a job as a bank teller at a small Crédit Agricole branch in the nondescript Dordogne village of Villeneuve-de-Lonchat. He made a little more than $1,000 a month and lived without any worries other than boredom. In 1982, after a decade at the bank, Thunevin was passed over to become branch director. If he stayed at Crédit Agricole, he would have to remain a teller, he was told. Instead, he quit.

His wife, Murielle, is from Libourne, so the couple decided to move there from the Dordogne, settling in a small apartment in a public housing block. They opened a postcard shop in Saint-Emilion that doubled as a *salon de thé*. The seats were made of plastic. The next year, they opened a wine bar. It was one of more than fifty such establishments in Saint-

Emilion and the Thunevins struggled. They made ends meet only because Murielle worked as a nurse's aide at the hospital in Libourne and Jean-Luc as a part-time disc jockey.

Even though their bar didn't thrive, the couple learned about wine. Thienpont's Le Pin inspired them. "The cellar was so ordinary, but the wine was so fantastic," Thunevin said. In 1990 they took their savings of $65,000 and bought a minuscule parcel, a mere two acres, just a few rows of vines. It was poorly located, north of the village on a shady valley hillside, where it was cooler than in other parts of Saint-Emilion. They dubbed their project Valandraud—combining *val* for valley with Murielle's surname, Andraud. From April to September, the couple spent every spare moment pruning their vines and tilling the soil. Murielle's parents had been professional gardeners, specializing in growing chrysanthemums for All Saints' Day. All the flowers they grew had to be harvested in a single day. Why not treat the vineyard like a flower patch? The Thunevins limited yield, leaving only four to six bunches of grapes on each vine, far less than average in Saint-Emilion. And they left the fruit to ripen until the last possible moment.

After the harvest, the couple spent hours destemming each cluster by hand. Other winemakers thought they were crazy to sort berry by berry in an effort to save only the ripest, cleanest grapes. "It wasn't an ideological thing," Thunevin said. "We just didn't use a mechanical destemmer because we didn't have the money to buy one." Instead of a mechanical press, the Thunevins pressed their wine with their bare feet. They had heard about Burgundy winemakers who used a stick to punch down the cap when it was in the tank and picked up the habit rather than the more traditional Bordeaux *pigeage*. By this time, the Thunevins were living in a small run-down house on a street at the bottom of Saint-Emilion's hill. Their cellar was, literally, in their garage.

In 1991, their first harvest, they produced a mere 1,280 bottles. Parker scored it 83. "Exceptionally oaky, with the wood dominating the moderate quantities of sweet ripe fruit," he wrote. The breakthrough came the next year. Nineteen ninety-two was a mediocre vintage for most Bordeaux wines, but not for Valandraud. Jeffrey Davies saw it on a broker's future offering, for a high price, and he ws intrigued—he knew most wines being offered as futures, but had never heard of this one. He met the audacious Thunevin. They spent several hours tasting the different barrels and discussing the project. While stretched financially, Davies offered to buy the entire crop, 3,600 bottles, on futures. Thunevin was amazed at the offer. He agreed to sell Davies half the production—and Valandraud was off and running. The wine drew a more than respectable 88 points from Parker—among the highest scores in that mediocre, rain-drenched vintage. The next year, Thunevin added another few acres of vines. The Parker scores continued to rise: 93 in 1993, 94+ in 1994, and 95 in 1995. "The wine exhibits an opaque purple color and a sensational note of roasted herbs, black fruits (cherries, currants and blackberries), and high-class toasty oak," Parker wrote about the 1995 Valandraud. "The finish lasts for over 30 seconds."

Valandraud soon achieved cult status. At Sotheby's in 2001, six-bottle lots of 1992, 1993, and 1994 Valandraud sold for $5,285, $6,138, and again $6,138—more than twelve-bottle cases of 1982 Latour, 1986 Lafite Rothschild, and 1989 Mouton. Journalists started flocking to Thunevin's garage. The popular French television weekly *Capital* featured him. And the Gallic equivalent of *60 Minutes, Envoyé Spécial,* devoted a long feature to him.

The Thunevins sold their *salon de thé* and *bar à vin* and focused on making wine. They bought more land and added it to Valandraud. Unlike traditional estates, none of the parcels were connected. Some sat atop the excellent limestone plateau east of Saint-Emilion. But many were planted on damper, heavier clay soil below the village, on the plain extending toward the Dordogne River. By the end of the 1990s, the Thunevins had assembled almost fifty acres and were making 55,000 bottles a year. They produced 20,000 bottles of a second wine, Virginie de Valandraud, named after their daughter. While Thunevin never rejected the *garagiste* label as the Thienponts did, he had outgrown it.

Alongside Valandraud, Thunevin built a merchant business. He emulated Jeffrey Davies's model, searching out passionate producers. He didn't care if they had an 1855 classification. He just cared if they produced good wine. If someone had good land in Saint-Emilion, he was ready to supervise the work on their vines and make the wine for them. By 2000 Etablissements Thunevin distributed four hundred different wines and generated $12 million a year in sales. With a partner, Murielle started her own garage winery in the Médoc called Marojallia. In the process, she gained a reputation as one of the best vine pruners in all of Bordeaux— and one of the best chefs. Invitations to her home-cooked meals were sought after. In October 2001, *Food & Wine* devoted an eight-page feature to her cooking.

As the Thunevins' businesses grew and they became wealthy, they renovated their house. A nondescript garden became a Japanese-style oasis of calm, complete with a small fountain. An indoor swimming pool was built next to the original garage. The garage itself was transformed into an immaculate modern winery. Jean-Luc drove a black Mercedes S-500 salon. Murielle scooted about in a silver BMW Z class convertible. Only a few sentimental vestiges of the rural past remained: a chicken coop in the garden with clucking birds ready to be plucked. And a ferocious work ethic. The Thunevins still went out into the fields and pruned the vines themselves with their workers. In the evenings, Murielle prepared meals for twelve, fourteen, even sixteen guests without flinching.

In Saint-Emilion, Thunevin's hard-driving success attracted admirers. His best friend was Alain Vauthier, owner of Château Ausone, one of Saint-Emilion's historically most renowned wines. Vauthier was a coinvestor in the Thunevin wine bar. He helped Thunevin with his experiments because he couldn't try anything out at traditional Ausone, where he shared control with his cousin. "Jean-Luc is always questioning, trying to improve," he said. When Vauthier finally gained full ownership of Ausone at the end of the 1990s, he adopted many of the Valandraud methods. Ausone, an under-achiever in the postwar years, suddenly began winning top scores.

But most of Saint-Emilion disliked the feisty Thunevin and his follow-ers. Angry holders of established estates came up with a nickname, *Tue-le-vin*—kill the wine. They criticized the upstart for his loud mouth and all the attention it was attracting. They didn't like his nouveau riche tastes. And they said they didn't like his brash, fleshy wines. "They should

148 · *William Echikson*

be made in California, not in France," complained one of his most vocal critics, François de Ligneris, owner of Château Soutard and of Saint-Emilion's most popular wine bar and bistro, L'Envers du Décor, the one who dreamt up the anti-Parker poster.

The ambitious Thunevin also managed to grate on many of his early admirers—including Jeffrey Davies. In retrospect, the conflict was inevitable. Thunevin was a natural showman who grabbed the limelight. Davies believed, with reason, that he had discovered Valandraud. After all, it was he who presented the wine to Parker and first distributed it in America. But soon Thunevin become more famous than Davies and didn't need outside help to distribute his wines. As Thunevin's merchant business grew, the two became competitors.

A major rupture occurred over a case of spilled wine. In 1995 a Dane named Peter Sisseck began producing a garage wine in Spain called Pingus. After Davies presented it to him, Parker called the first vintage "one of the greatest young red wines I have ever tasted" with "an opaque purple color, followed by a magnificent nose of jammy blackberries, truffles, smoke and subtle notes of *pain grillé*." He gave it a 98, the first time a Spanish wine ever received such an accolade.

Both Thunevin and Davies distributed Pingus. In 1995 only 325 cases were produced. The initial futures price was about $20 a bottle. Davies's allocation was 125 cases. In 1997, when the wine was bottled, a truck brought the cases to Bilbao, where it was loaded onto the MS *Cristina* freighter for shipment to the United States. In a storm near the Azore islands, the ship ran aground and fractured. The precious Pingus plunged to the bottom of the sea. Tens of thousands of dollars were lost.

An argument ensued. Sisseck had insured the wine at the original $20 price, though by the time of the accident Parker's scores and the fast-rising notoriety meant the wine's futures were selling for $250 a bottle. Davies claims he sent a fax insisting that the wine be insured at this higher price. When Sisseck came to Bordeaux to discuss the disaster, he and Davies met at the Dane's lawyer's office. Thunevin also showed up and he took Sisseck's side, loudly and vehemently arguing with Davies. "The price was going up so fast that between the time Jeffrey bought his insurance and the time we declared the wine lost, we were underinsured," Thunevin later explained.

Davies contended that Thunevin should be doubly happy: with all Davies's Pingus gone, he still had a lot left for his European customers. "Since there was even less to go around, the price would only go even higher and Thunevin would make even more profit," Davies recalled. "I still don't understand why he was so upset." With Thunevin maintaining that Davies should have insured the wine at a higher price and Davies claiming that he tried to get Sisseck to do so, they separated at an impasse.

Not long afterward, Thunevin took away Davies's consignment of Valandraud and Davies stopped talking to him. "Jeff and Jean-Luc—it's like two chickens in a cockfight," concluded Michel Gracia. The disputes were the natural outgrowth of success. Competition and emulation spurred advances in winemaking. In Saint-Emilion and Pomerol, everybody knew everybody else. They drank coffee together in the morning at the local café. They ate lunch at L'Envers du Décor. Saint-Emilion winemaking represents a perfect example of the phenomenon Harvard Business School guru Michael Porter calls "cluster," the economic vitality that comes from a combination of close proximity and competition.

—

CHAPTER 7

Luxury on the Block

BY 1994 THE DISSIDENT HAINGUERLOTS WERE FURIOUS. THEY were sickened by the discovery that Alexandre de Lur-Saluces had been managing Yquem for more than two decades, solely on the basis of a power of attorney signed in 1968.

When Alexandre transferred Yquem's inventory to his new company, a *société en commandite,* in 1992, he did so at one-seventh the regular wholesale price. The Hainguerlots examined Yquem's accounts and were shocked to find tens of thousands of dollars billed to Marie-Odile Billé-Rode. Alexandre told them that she was collecting an oral history of Yquem and provided indispensable management support. "We never saw any of the results of Madame Billé-Rode's project," said Bertrand Hainguerlot. "She was becoming a de facto regent—and we were paying the bill," he said.

In November 1994, three years after the back-to-back shareholders' meetings in Paris, the Hainguerlots wrote to Alexandre and asked him to dissolve the new company. It was a last-ditch effort to find a compromise. But Alexandre refused all negotiations.

The Hainguerlots felt they had no choice: they decided to sell. They asked other relatives to join them. Almost all agreed. Even Alexandre's two youngest children, Isabeau and Philippe, decided to part with their 4 percent share. With their father wanting to leave almost all of his holdings to their older brother, they feared losing everything unless they

Bertrand Hainguerlot led the younger generation's revolt against Yquem's longtime director.

cashed out. The aging Anne de Chizelle, Alexandre's aunt, also agreed to part with her shares, under one condition: "Don't sell to a Japanese."

Curiously, throughout this period no one considered consulting with the Marquis Eugène, who owned 48 percent of the estate. Little was known about Alexandre's reclusive older brother. The Hainguerlots believed he supported Alexandre and Alexandre believed the Hainguerlots could never sell Yquem without the marquis's approval.

Nonetheless, by the end of 1994 the Hainguerlots had assembled a group of family members representing a 37 percent stake. They gave Pierre d'Harcourt, who worked for the Paris investment bank Eurofin, a mandate to locate a buyer. D'Harcourt had helped the Martell family sell its Cognac business and was a specialist in dealing with family-owned companies. Bertrand Hainguerlot knew and admired him. D'Harcourt was only thirty-four years old at the time, a thin curly-haired man with bookish glasses who liked to drive around Paris in a tiny British-made Mini.

The banker first contacted AXA, the French insurance giant that had already invested heavily in prestigious Bordeaux châteaux. But the insurers weren't interested. They had purchased a Sauternes château called Sudiraut and it had proven to be "our worst investment," recalled Jean-Michel Cazes, AXA's director in Bordeaux as well as the owner of Château Lynch-Bages. The beverage companies and conglomerates weren't interested, either. Coca-Cola, Nestlé, Philip Morris, and RJR Nabisco had all dabbled in wine in the 1980s only to end up selling out.

Wine is not an easy business for bottom-line companies. Thousands of producers fight for sales, and markets are fragmented, making it difficult to obtain a dominant position. Worse, as any farmer anywhere knows, supply can never be guaranteed. Wine is particularly subject to boom-and-bust cycles. Giant alcoholic-beverage companies such as Seagram's and Diageo are more interested in selling whiskey, rum, and vodka that can be made almost anywhere and aren't dependent on a sense of place, or on the mystique imparted by hundreds of years of history. One manager at a major food company once told *The Economist*: "Two thousand years ago, Jesus achieved the first wine miracle by turning water into wine. We're still waiting for the second miracle, which is to turn wine into profit."

D'Harcourt next targeted supermarket magnates. During the past few decades, high taxes have made it hard for all except a few Frenchmen to accumulate fortunes. Supermarket magnates are the glaring exceptions. Although France invented the department store way back in 1852 when the first Bon Marché opened, large grocery stores came late. In one leap after World War II, the country went from dependence on the little local shop to reliance on supermarkets and the biggest hypermarkets in

Europe, huge emporiums selling everything from lawn mowers and cashmere sweaters to fresh salmon and produce. Originally, their low prices won them a warm welcome from the government and the public.

More recently, the hypermarkets have generated hypercriticism. They have been blamed for causing urban sprawl, for pushing down prices of farm goods, and, above all, for killing off family-owned neighborhood shops. In 1973 the government passed a law limiting expansion of large stores. A second law in 1995 went further, banning construction of almost all new hypermarkets of more than 30,000 square feet. As the noose tightened, the only way for ambitious retailers to grow became to buy out others. Prices for such properties rose. Many regional owners sold out and began looking for ways to spend their money both profitably and enjoyably.

Daniel and Florence Cathiard of Château Smith-Haut-Lafitte were the first hypermarket magnates to settle in Bordeaux. Daniel is a former member of the French Olympic ski team and teammate of skiing legend Jean-Claude Killy. After the Grenoble Olympics in 1968, he returned to work at his family's small group of markets, turning it into one of the largest supermarket chains in France. He also created Go Sport, a chain of sporting goods stores, with distribution across western Europe and California and an annual turnover of around $1 billion. His auburn-haired wife, Florence, was also a champion skier and just as ambitious and dynamic as her husband. She launched her own advertising and marketing firm. In 1989 he sold their retailing business to Carrefour and she unloaded her agency to McCann-Erickson. Together they took a cruise around the world in celebration, and even ran in the New York marathon.

The next year, they began prospecting for wine properties. Daniel considered settling in the Napa Valley but Florence wanted to stay in France. They looked at Burgundy. "It was too cold and all the properties were too small," Daniel recalled. In Bordeaux, just south of the city, they found the magnificent property in Graves called Smith-Haut-Lafitte and paid $40 million for it. "We can get to the city center or the airport from here in fifteen minutes," Daniel boasted.

Although d'Harcourt hoped the Cathiards would want to extend their empire, and Yquem was only fifteen minutes south of their Smith-Haut-Lafitte, the couple didn't like Sauternes and their entrepreneurial methods jarred with those of Alexandre de Lur-Saluces. When the count invited Florence Cathiard to give a presentation to a Bordeaux wine association on marketing wine, she shocked him by using jargon such as "the ultimate cocoon" in reference to consumers' attachment to individual personal values. The count looked on, befuddled by the marketing talk.

Sleepy Sauternes would never seduce this dynamic couple. When the Bordeaux regional wine association's marketing committee rejected her ideas, Florence Cathiard turned her energy to promoting a club of five châteaux called "Les Cinq" to organize joint tastings and publicity ventures. The five included two Médocs, one Saint-Emilion, one Pomerol, one Pessac-Leognon—and no Sauternes. "It's like a rock and roll band—there's no room for anyone else," she says.

Nor could d'Harcourt interest Saint-Emilion's Gérard Perse, who had started out in his youth as a housepainter and eventually found his way into the grocery business. He made his millions selling his Continent hypermarkets and his Champion supermarkets located in the Paris region and settled in Saint-Emilion in 1993, buying Château Montbousquet. After modernizing its wines, he purchased Château Pavie-Decesse in 1997 and Château Pavie, a prestigious *premier grand cru classé*, in early 1998. All soon became Parker favorites. But Perse was no fan of sweet wines. "I drink only one bottle of Sauternes a year, so why would I bother to live there?" he asked. Plus, "you can't even buy a newspaper in Sauternes, while here in Saint-Emilion, we have twenty-five restaurants."

Having failed to tempt the nouveau riche supermarket magnates, a desperate d'Harcourt sent out feelers beyond France. He tried Fiat's owner, Giovanni Agnelli, who, with the Mentzelopoulos family, had taken over Château Margaux. "Agnelli wasn't interested in inserting himself in the middle of a family feud," d'Harcourt said. He even contacted Microsoft's Bill Gates. "I didn't have much hope," d'Harcourt admitted. But the banker's telephone rang late one evening. His secretary had gone home, so d'Harcourt answered himself. It was the software magnate. He would consider Yquem as a wedding gift for his fiancée, Melinda French, and asked for more information. D'Harcourt dispatched a copy of Richard Olney's *Yquem* to Seattle.

The next day, a fax arrived. Gates wouldn't make a bid. "Although the property is interesting, it is not too practical for me," Gates wrote. "But if you have anything else, please don't hesitate to contact me."

No one, it seemed, wanted to buy the myth called Yquem.

PIERRE D'HARCOURT decided to change strategy. He would no longer focus on selling Yquem as a wine estate. Sauternes and its noble rot simply weren't powerful enough to draw an attractive price. Instead, he would repackage Yquem as a fashion item, a symbol of Old World luxury. He approached Louis Vuitton Moët Hennessy, or LVMH, the successor company to the firm where Louis Hainguerlot had spent his career and from which he had since retired. A huge company with billions in sales every year, LVMH owned the high-fashion leather-goods purveyor Louis Vuitton and *haute couture* icons such as Christian Lacroix and Christian Dior.

LVMH's owner, Bernard Arnault, craves publicity and prestige. His conglomerate, formed in 1989, could swallow up the Sauternes château without the smallest risk of financial indigestion. And if someone wanted to be accepted within the upper echelons of Old France, as Arnault did, little could be more impressive than winning control over one of its ultimate symbols. In a country that frowns on capitalists, Arnault generated controversy. When he studied at the Ecole Polytechnique, he started an investment club. It was 1968 and most French students were storming the streets or occupying their university buildings. Almost all Polytechnique graduates went into the top echelons of the civil service. Arnault instead chose to join his family's construction firm.

In 1981 socialist François Mitterrand was elected president and began nationalizing companies. Arnault fled France and settled in America. The thirty-year-old real estate developer built seaside apartments in Palm Beach, Florida. But he never thought about staying forever. Meanwhile, across the Atlantic, Arnault asked his family lawyer, Pierre Gode, to be on the lookout for an investment opportunity back in France.

Gode was a six-foot-six-inch former basketball player: he was smooth, elegant, and diplomatic. Arnault was a trim, dapper six-footer, and a fanatic for physical fitness. He was charming in private, but cold and calculating in public. His angular features would later add to his reputation as a capitalist shark.

Gode called in 1984. He had found a poorly run textile company called Boussac that was on the verge of collapse. Boussac caught Arnault and Gode's fancy because amid its money-losing manufacturing operations, it also owned the globally recognized brand Christian Dior. Arnault and Gode realized that it was a neglected treasure. Once in control and with Gode at his side, Arnault slashed jobs and sold off all of the textile factories. They focused on Christian Dior, creating a recipe that would later be copied at luxury businesses around the world. Licenses for everything from watches to cigarette holders that devalued the brand were discontinued. Arnault and only Arnault controlled Dior products and sold almost all of them in exclusive Dior boutiques. Margins improved and sales soared. Within a decade, the near-bankrupt Dior was worth more than $1 billion on the Paris bourse.

In 1989 Arnault wielded the Dior stock as currency to make a run at LVMH. An epic takeover battle ensued, the French version of the RJR Nabisco saga chronicled in *Barbarians at the Gate*. Arnault first forged an alliance with LVMH's chief, Henry Racamier, a fixture of the Parisian establishment. In mid-negotiation, Arnault turned traitor. He enlisted the British distiller Guinness to attack Racamier. Together, Guinness and Arnault bought enough shares of LVMH on the market to gain control. In Manhattan, the aggressive Arnault's audacity may be admired. But in the polite, somewhat ossified world of French capitalism, his behavior wasn't appreciated. When Arnault, backed by the Guinness company, gained control of LVMH later that year, he celebrated in front of press photographers by drinking a glass of Moët & Chandon Champagne. France was shocked. The Parisian press derided the luxury magnate as "the Raider."

Arnault isn't a teetotaler, but he isn't much of an enophile, either. No wine is served at his lunch table, he admitted, because "I couldn't think straight afterwards." When Jean-Michel Cazes attended a gala dinner, he sat next to Arnault and his wife. "My other neighbor told them, 'Here is one of Bordeaux's best-known winemakers and his wine is excellent,'" Cazes recalls. But Arnault wasn't interested in sampling Cazes's Château Lynch-Bages.

If wine didn't interest Arnault, Yquem's aristocratic image did. At another dinner with Cazes and AXA insurance magnate Claude Bébéar, Arnault said he wanted to buy a Bordeaux first growth. Cazes told him that Saint-Emilion's famed Cheval Blanc was for sale. As with Yquem, Cheval's ownership had splintered among family members—in this case twenty-nine—over several generations.

"But it is not Lafite, Mouton, or a real first growth" from 1855, Arnault replied.

"It's equal to or even better than a first growth," Cazes told him. Arnault was never fixed in his ideas or closed-minded. He listened and in 1998 ended up buying Cheval Blanc with Belgian billionaire Albert Frère for $156 million.

Once Arnault was offered Yquem, he sent an emissary to talk with Alexandre de Lur-Saluces. Even though he believed Alexandre could not stop him from buying the estate, he thought he could reach an amicable agreement. "Between Alexandre and me, everything existed for an intelligent solution," Arnault said. "We would ensure the future of Yquem, eliminating the problem of inheritance and division of capital. In return, we would love to see Alexandre continue to make the wine." But the count refused to discuss any solution. "Yquem is not for sale," he informed the LVMH representative.

Neither the rebuff nor the family feud frightened the corporate raider. "Alexandre de Lur-Saluces owned less than 10 percent of Yquem's capital and only the real owners of the property could decide to sell or not," Arnault said. If he could outmaneuver the world's most sophisticated businessmen, a count of limited business experience didn't seem like serious opposition. "Arnault figured he was much more clever than Alexandre," said Pierre d'Harcourt.

Arnault's interest gratified those who did want to sell their 37 percent share in Yquem. The relatives of Louis Hainguerlot's generation felt comfortable not only because Louis had worked for LVMH but because the company was French. In April 1996, LVMH sent Pierre d'Harcourt a letter of intention to buy their shares. D'Harcourt went to Sauternes. Alexandre welcomed him into the château and served coffee. "The minority shareholders have decided to sell and we have found a buyer," he told Alexandre. "No one will want to buy a minority share of a château," a confident Alexandre replied. After an hour, d'Harcourt left without visiting the cellars or tasting any wine.

LVMH valued Yquem at a total of $160 million, or about $666,000 an acre. For a business that made an average of $3 million in profits each year, "we considered it a dream price," d'Harcourt said. This dream price was contingent on Arnault's receiving a majority share. For a minority, he would pay less. That decision rested with neither the Hainguerlots nor Alexandre de Lur-Saluces. Only Eugène, with his 48 percent share, could decide. And no one had been in touch with him for years. In May 1996, just after the family reached an agreement with Arnault, Eugène called Louis Hainguerlot and invited him to visit. "I wasn't sure what he wanted," Hainguerlot said. "Our relationship was so rare and distant. I feared he thought we were conspiring against him."

Eugène's modest apartment on the Avenue de Ségur, where he has lived most of his adult life, is a short walk from Hainguerlot's own luxurious apartment on the Boulevard Saint-Germain. When he arrived, Hainguerlot thought he would be leaving in a quarter of an hour. Instead, Eugène offered him an aperitif, a glass of J&B whiskey, the same product that Hainguerlot had once sold for Moët Hennessy. The two men talked. After a half hour, Eugène asked if Hainguerlot had any lunch plans.

"No."

"Let's go to a bistro and have a bite," he proposed.

Hainguerlot agreed. Eugène surprised him. Instead of a recluse, he discovered a courteous, polite host. Eugène asked about the psychotherapist Billé-Rode. He believed that she was bewitching his brother and stealing the family fortune. He listened to Hainguerlot's plan to sell to LVMH. Eugène said he would prefer the family to stay united as owners. By the time the two men separated, it was almost evening.

Eugène moved to head off the crisis. He instructed his lawyer to meet with Alexandre's representatives. She asked Alexandre to distribute larger dividends to Eugène and the other shareholders in order to avoid a sale. He refused.

During the summer, Eugène made other last-ditch attempts to contact Alexandre. If Alexandre had responded with "just a small gesture," Bertrand Hainguerlot believed the whole project to sell Yquem could have collapsed. "We felt fragile," he admitted.

But Alexandre wouldn't change anything. He knew, of course, that the Hainguerlots and other family members were attempting to sell their stakes. He wasn't worried because he didn't think anybody would be interested in buying such a minority shareholding, and even if they did, he believed he could stay in control. He never imagined that his older brother would sell out.

The Hainguerlots agreed anyhow to sell their minority stake, even though without Eugène they would receive an inferior price from LVMH. Louis Hainguerlot decided that he should tell Eugène of their decision personally. While the final papers for the sale of Yquem were being drawn up, he invited the marquis to the family seaside home in Brittany, where the two had spent many happy summers as children. They took walks together along the seashore. One day, Eugène turned to Hainguerlot and asked about Yquem.

"I am sorry, we are close to an agreement," Hainguerlot told him.

"Very close?"

"Yes."

Eugène paused. For a full minute, he didn't say anything.

"What will happen to me when you sell?" he finally asked.

"You will still be the largest single shareholder," Hainguerlot responded. "You will need to discuss that with your brother and the representative of LVMH."

Eugène seemed lost in reflection.

"I am sorry, but our decision is irreversible," Hainguerlot said.

The two men started walking again. Eugène remained silent. Then, suddenly, he turned to his cousin.

"And what if I also sold?"

Hainguerlot was both staggered and delighted. With Eugène adding part of his shares to those of the Hainguerlot group, suddenly a minority became the majority. Arnault would pay a premium and in return would win full control of Yquem.

Eugène ended up selling only 18 percent of Yquem to LVMH, keeping 30 percent. The Hainguerlots and other family members retained another 5 percent. All wanted to preserve their ties to Yquem. In the sales contract, Eugène made LVMH promise "to preserve the estate's identity." That meant keeping the château's period furniture and paintings. Eugène also fought to retain control of the voluminous archives. "My actions were ensuring the family's legacy," he said.

When Agence France Presse published the news on November 28, 1996, Alexandre was scheduled to travel to Tokyo. He knew that Bernard Arnault was going there.

Vowing to fight back, Alexandre canceled his Japanese trip. "This is a jewel that must be constantly polished and protected," he said at the time. "For thirty years I've fought against diluting the name of Yquem. Arnault buys brands and does just about anything with them."

"What would Arnault do with Yquem?" a journalist asked Lur-Saluces.

"If he gets hold of the château," the count warned, "he will install fashion models and start producing a perfume called Yquem."

—

CHAPTER 8

Riding the New Wave

ALMOST AS SOON AS THE 2000 FUTURES SEASON FINISHED WITH a bang at the end of June 2001, millennium madness subsided. The stock market bubble had burst, and the world began to look more precarious. Bordeaux's mandarins knew they couldn't shield themselves eternally from the global economy.

The 2001 vintage loomed as a turning point. Everyone accepted the fact that prices needed to fall. The debate centered on whether the drop would be gentle or precipitous. Poor weather added to the stress. It rained throughout much of June, just at the critical moment when the vines burst forth with buds after their winter hibernation. The irregular flowering meant that many bunches of grapes emerged stillborn. Mildew was also a problem and large amounts of fungicidal spray were deployed to fight it. Superb quality had propelled the 2000 vintage to record prices. A poor-quality 2001 might provoke an implosion, just as in the financial markets.

During July, the rain continued. Winegrowers removed excess leaves from the vines in order to allow the sun to better shine on the maturing fruit. At Yquem, for example, workers on tractors trimmed the vines' leafy tops. Others bent down and thinned the leaves off the east side of each plant in order to maximize sunlight and air circulation. The west side of the plant was left in place to protect the grapes from sunburn. In Saint-Emilion, *garagistes* went even further, redoubling their "green harvesting," eliminating the bunches that flowered improperly in hopes that the remaining clusters would ripen completely.

By August, the hard manual labor in the vineyards was nearly done. The weather turned hot and sunny, giving growers hope that the vintage

*Dr. Alain Raynaud brought an exuberant personality and
public relations savvy to the Lascombes project.*

could be saved. "June makes the quantity and August makes the quality," goes one of the Bordeaux winemakers' favorite sayings. A couple more dry weeks followed by a hot September could transform the green grapes into deep purple fruit.

In good times or bad, the Bordeaux wine trade converges in summertime on the shores of Cap Ferret on the Bay of Arcachon, where many have villas. Alexandre de Lur-Saluces took off the entire month of

August. Only a few workers remained on call at Yquem, watching the weather and checking, if it rained, whether mildew or some other unwanted disease had set in and more spraying and leaf thinning were required. Since the 2000 vintage was virtually all sold, the merchants had little work. Jeffrey Davies took his family on their annual pilgrimage to the United States.

Yves Vatelot vacationed on the Riviera in Saint-Tropez, his wife's hometown, but by mid-August he was back at work in Bordeaux. Only a few weeks were left to ready Château Lascombes before the harvest. Since the sale of the estate had gone through in April, he had rushed to improve the vineyards, pruning severely the way *garagistes* do, and he was busy overseeing the construction of the new $5 million winery and aging cellar. Another step was bringing on board Dr. Alain Raynaud, Parker's friend and the former president of the Union des Grands Crus. The fifty-three-year-old Raynaud is a portly, imposing man who puffs on a pipe as he speaks. He was hired as Lascombes's public face, the man who would explain the makeover to the wine world. Even before Colony Capital's purchase of Lascombes, Vatelot had enlisted Raynaud in his search for a property in the Médoc. When the duo heard that Lascombes was for sale, Vatelot wanted first to check the state of the vineyards. Luckily, Raynaud had inside information. A patient of his was Lascombes's vineyard manager and he took them to look at the property in secret. "We saw a lot of good potential there," Raynaud said.

Born in Pomerol, Alain is the elder of two children. Growing up, he understood that his family's Château La Croix de Gay did not bring in a great deal of income. Since Alain was a fast learner and excelled in school, his parents, Noël and Geneviève, wanted him to leave the estate and, as he says, "earn a living with my mind." His sister, Chantal, a perfectionist, anguished over homework. When she was only eighteen, she married a military doctor named Michel Lebreton. After several assignments away from Pomerol, Michel managed to get a post at Libourne's hospital. The couple bought a house down the road in Saint-Emilion and Chantal joined her parents at La Croix de Gay in 1982. Alain was working full-time as a doctor in Bordeaux, though he would take off for two weeks each year to participate in the harvest. In 1983 Alain persuaded his father to take one special parcel of old Merlot vines next to Pétrus out of La Croix de Gay, cut yields, vinify it apart, rename it La Fleur de Gay, and create a garage-style wine.

Brother and sister couldn't be more different. A gifted talker in English as well as French, Alain moves in the wine world's high society. Chantal is reserved and hands-on. He wears designer clothes. She dresses in jeans and work boots and spends more time in the vineyards than in the office. Alain has a baroque desk and prefers the activity in the cellar and the tasting room. Chantal is a worrier. Alain is exuberant. Chantal questions every centime of investment. Alain goes to the banks, borrows millions, and worries less about expenses, only about buying the best.

After Noël Raynaud died in 1997, Chantal took over the family properties, backed by her mother. Not long afterward, Alain sold his medical practice and decided to work full-time in wine, but he preferred to go out on his own. Besides running his own Château Quinault L'Enclos, Raynaud went to work as a consultant for other winemakers. Gérard Perse retained him as his public relations director. The salary was more than $100,000 a year and the work was only part-time. "Alain has a golden tongue," Perse said. This "golden tongue" generates controversy, though. When he was president of the Union des Grands Crus, Left Bank mandarins criticized him for favoring Right Bank wines. When he became friendly with Robert Parker, the criticism increased. "Alain likes to shake things up and that annoys the establishment," says a friend, Jean-Noël Hervé, a winemaker in the Right Bank village of Fronsac.

Vatelot met Raynaud in 1997. The go-between was Jeffrey Davies. The American was a friend of both men and took them on a promotional tour to California. When Raynaud bought Quinault later that year, Vatelot lent him some equipment. Raynaud introduced Vatelot to the local movers and shakers. "Alain opened Bordeaux's doors for me," Vatelot admitted. At Lascombes, Vatelot was the man with access to Goldman Sachs and big-time finance. He could invest millions on his own account and was the hard-driving entrepreneur who set goals and ran fast after them. Raynaud was the insider who picked up the pieces, made sure the operation ticked, and explained it all to the outside world. He was hired as a consultant but his role would be more like a partner and alter ego to Vatelot.

On a hot August 2001 morning, Raynaud geared his Toyota Land Cruiser and guided it, slowly and surely, west along the highway connecting Libourne to Bordeaux. About halfway there, he pulled off onto a small country road that winds up and down gentle hills, punctuated by rustic farmhouses, suburban housing developments, and vineyards. Raynaud soon pulled up in front of a wrought-iron gate, with the intertwined letters Y and S, for Yves and his wife, Stéphanie. He punched the intercom and announced himself.

The gates opened to reveal a tree-lined avenue to a magnificent turreted château resembling the famous Château de Cheverny in the Loire Valley. Although the bucolic setting suggests the eighteenth century, instead of a horse and carriage, a silver BMW Z3 convertible stood ready at the front door. Out back, there is a swimming pool, a tennis court, and a helicopter landing pad. This is the Vatelots' Château de Reignac.

Yves Vatelot emerged, dressed in jeans and a polo shirt, followed by Stéphanie, a trim, athletic young woman, dressed much the same way. Their two-year-old son Balthazar, a small boy with curly blond hair, stood beside her. He had come down with the flu, and Vatelot asked Raynaud to examine him before they left for the day.

Stéphanie is a professional interior designer, and the château is decorated in an airy, eclectic mix of modern Italian and elegant antiques. The front door opens onto a grand marble staircase. To the right is the living room, with an imposing wide-screen television. To the left, a large dining room contains four tables of elegant whitewashed wood. Modern abstract paintings hang from the limestone walls. In back of the dining room, at the end of this wing is an open-plan kitchen, complete with a professional stove and rotisserie, two stainless steel refrigerators, and copper pots and pans hanging above a countertop of hand-painted antique Mediterranean tiles.

Raynaud propped Balthazar up on a chair and opened his mouth to look at his throat. "It's a little red, but nothing serious," he pronounced, writing out a prescription.

The two men climbed into Raynaud's Land Cruiser and headed across the Garonne River to Château Lascombes, where they planned to spend the day checking on the construction of the new wine cellar. Traveling from the Right to the Left Bank is time-consuming. Once off the Bordeaux ring road, only a few two-lane country roads lead north to the Médoc peninsula. Industrial parks dominate the area bordering the city, then give way to suburban housing estates dotting the pine forests. Eventually the vineyards appear, stretching to the horizon, punctuated by grand manors and modest villages. While the castles are used for receptions and offices, modest limestone houses dominate even the most famous villages—and even on sunny days, their shutters are drawn closed.

The Médoc middle class has fled in recent years. The biggest blow came when Shell closed a refinery in Pauillac in 1989. The ugly round structure with its huge red and white chimney was built in 1927. It spoiled the view of the Gironde River estuary from the vineyards. For decades, Philippe de Rothschild fought to get it razed. He died just the year before his effort succeeded and it was shut down. Several hundred workers were laid off. Dozens of small shopkeepers in Pauillac went belly-up. "The refinery employed well-educated engineers and technicians, and when they left, the entire middle class here was decimated," said Jean-Michel Cazes of Château Lynch-Bages. "Even our tennis club closed."

Most Médoc owners live in Paris and even their managers commute to their properties. Château Cos d'Estournel's general manager, Jean-Guillaume Prats, drives almost an hour and a half each way to work so that his children can attend school in Bordeaux. Prats received an M.B.A. in Paris and worked as an investment banker in London before succeeding his father at the highly regarded second growth. He wears snappy suits and preaches free-market economics. In Saint-Estèphe, he plunged into the middle of what he felt was Marx's class struggle, his workers ready at almost any moment to rise up in protest. Each harvest, he hires Spaniards; he thinks they work harder than French locals, and with fewer complaints. "The social atmosphere here is rotten," he complained. Young singles with ambition prefer to stay in the city, because there is so little to do in the Médoc after leaving the vineyards and cellars.

Leaders of the older generation see little hope of stemming the exodus. "I'm the last of the Mohicans," said a wistful Cazes, who lives at his family-owned Lynch-Bages just outside Pauillac.

Vatelot and Raynaud, by contrast, are confirmed Right Bankers. Since the takeover of Lascombes a few months before, they had been visiting once or twice a week in order to supervise the grand plan. In his BMW roadster, Vatelot can make the journey from Reignac to the Margaux château in a mere twenty-five minutes. When still in his twenties, Vatelot drove race cars, becoming a professional Formula 3 driver. "It was just a hobby," he says, but now he likes to go fast in everything. When he arrived at Reignac, he hired 150 workers and pushed them twelve hours a day to finish rebuilding the cellar in just two months—and not any two months, but July and August, when most of France is on vacation. Vatelot was determined to achieve similar results at Lascombes.

In contrast, Raynaud is a prudent driver and the trip from the Right Bank to Lascombes took him close to an hour. Raynaud loves to sit and chat. Though sometimes a risk taker, he can also be cautious when it comes to major decisions. After he bought Quinault in 1997, he waited two full years before selling his medical practice. He first wanted to make sure his new wine venture was going to succeed. "Sometimes I fear that Yves tries to cut corners," Raynaud later admitted.

Now the unlikely pair was nervous. Their first few months at Lascombes had proved more difficult than expected. Traditionally, the Margaux *appellation* is famous for producing polished and perfumed wines. The soil has the deepest concentration of small white gravel of any part of the entire Médoc, draining well. This facilitates the ripening of Cabernet Sauvignon grapes and gives wines a special perfumed fragrance.

In recent years, underachievers had dragged down the *appellation*. Over the years, plots were sold or exchanged higgledy-piggledy, erasing much of the historical continuity. At Lascombes, many of the vineyards acquired by a previous owner in the 1960s and 1970s were located far inland, on heavier clay soil. While many good plots were located next to Château Margaux, many others were on poor land near the Garonne River. Worse, many areas were planted with what Raynaud and Vatelot considered the wrong grape variety. "We have Cabernet Sauvignon on clay soil where there should be Merlot, and we have Cabernet Franc on gravelly soil where there should be Cabernet Sauvignon," said Vatelot. Raynaud and Vatelot began regrafting and replanting, placing what they considered the right fruit types in the right places. Twenty-five acres and seventy thousand rootstocks were replanted.

The biggest difficulties, however, weren't with the vineyard. They were with the employees. The incumbent general manager resisted changing the methods he put in place when he arrived in 1998, when the British brewing conglomerate Bass Charrington owned Lascombes. Before then, the manager had run a respected estate in Saint-Estèphe. At Lascombes, he figured he was producing a reasonably priced, drinkable wine, good enough to sell for a comfortable profit. But Vatelot, Raynaud, and Colony Capital didn't want just decent quality and comfortable profits. They were on a mission in search of excellence, resurrecting a reputation—and searching for giant capital gains.

During the first week of May, Vatelot and Raynaud ordered the entire staff out into the vineyard. Some of the cellar workers refused. They had never worked in the vineyards before and considered it below their station in life. The manager refused to force them. When Vatelot and Raynaud learned about the slowdown among workers and the boss's unwillingness to push them, they decided on a drastic course of action. They fired the general manager.

AT THE BEGINNING of June, Vatelot and Raynaud hired a new general manager named Dominique Befve. The forty-four-year-old Befve worked for the Lafite-Rothschild company and could only start full-time at Lascombes at the end of July. Until then, he went to Lascombes two days a week to check on progress. Befve is a thin, handsome man, but unlike his predecessor, he doesn't wear ties and jackets. He favors khaki pants and Shetland wool sweaters. A head of elegant silver hair completes the Brahmin look. A true professional, he knows both the Right and Left Banks.

At Lafite-Rothschild, he had learned how a large Médoc estate was managed and became imbued with the Left Bank belief in *terroir*. As at Lascombes, parcels had been added to Lafite over time. Many of these were used to produce the estate's less expensive second wine, Carruades de Lafite. About 20,000 cases of the first wine were produced each year and the same number of cases of the second. The first wine sold for four to five times the price of the second. Why not produce more of the first? Befve was assigned the task of taking a parcel that regularly produced grapes for the second wine and transforming it into one that could produce grapes worthy of the first. He slashed yields. He practiced drastic deleafing. Harvest times were pushed back two or more weeks to the end of September. And what happened? "We still couldn't produce first-growth fruit," recalls Befve. "The wine wasn't as long in the mouth." He became convinced that "the human being was only 10 percent of the equation."

In 1999 the Rothschilds took control of a well-regarded Pomerol property called Château L'Evangile and named Befve as its new technical director. L'Evangile is equidistant between Pétrus and Cheval Blanc and the potential was unlimited. But L'Evangile has only 35.8 acres of vines compared to 247 acres at Lafite. It produces an average of 40,000 bottles of wine per year compared to 440,000 bottles of first and second wine at Lafite. In Pomerol, Befve learned about garage techniques and got a chance to employ them. He renovated the cellar and installed expensive winemaking equipment. More important, he added workers to practice green harvesting and lowered yields from 55 hectoliters per hectare to between 35 and 40. The estate soon became one of the Right Bank's shining stars. "At L'Evangile we had great *terroir*," Befve said. "When we added great technology, we produced great wine."

When Raynaud's Land Cruiser rolled into Lascombes's long gravel driveway around noon, Befve greeted Vatelot and Raynaud, and the three men began walking around the property. The château itself is a wedding cake concoction, topped with ornate turrets and covered with vines. A low-slung concrete office building marred the garden. Vatelot planned eventually to convert the castle into a sparkling new Napa Valley–style visitors' center. He was convinced guests would pay $300 a night to stay there. There wasn't much competition for the tourist dollar in the Médoc. Unlike in the Napa Valley, where wineries were set up to receive visitors, Bordeaux châteaux required reservations far in advance— and even then only opened their doors to a privileged few. The first growths led by Latour and Lafite were the snootiest of all. Philippe de Rothschild, true to his rebel spirit, built an American-style visitors' center at Mouton Rothschild. Otherwise, Jean-Michel Cazes of Lynch-Bages was the only Médoc owner to appreciate the value of tourism. He transformed a neighboring estate in Pauillac into a Relais & Châteaux hotel called Cordeillan-Bages. Cazes also hired a prizewinning chef named Thierry Marx. The hotel restaurant soon established itself as the best in the Médoc, winning two stars from the Michelin Guide, the only restaurant so honored in the Bordeaux region. Vatelot planned to have Cordeillan-Bages cater a dinner at Lascombes during next March's spring tasting week.

Before tourism or tastings could take place, though, the cellar needed to be completed. In the former marshlands of the Médoc, most cellars are built above ground, and so is the one at Lascombes. The dilapidated old building had been gutted. Welders now burned steel pylons into the ceiling and screwed shiny stainless steel tanks into the floor. Electricians sprawled out across the floor, laying down miles of wires. Others climbed up ladders to install light fixtures. The innovative new cargo elevator for moving the freshly harvested grapes squeaked up to the second and third floors. It still needed to be oiled. Huge conveyor belts were being installed so the grapes could be sorted berry by berry. The grapes would then be deposited in the stainless steel and French oak tanks by gravity rather than pumping so the fruit wouldn't be bruised, as Vatelot had promised visitors during the spring tasting. Then the fresh must would be treated with dry ice before fermentation, concentrating flavors and softening tannins. Architects and contractors pored over plans for the ultramodern new winery.

Vatelot was worried about whether the builders would finish in time for the harvest. A perfectionist and a hard taskmaster, he didn't like some of the work he saw being done. The electrician had installed an emergency generator that could deliver only 150 kilowatts per hour.

"We need twice as much power," Vatelot bellowed. "Otherwise, we won't be able to run the sorting tables at the same time as all the stemmers, crushers, and temperature controls in the tanks."

"It won't be ready in time for the harvest," the electrician protested.

"Yes it will," Vatelot insisted. He didn't argue or cajole. He gave the order, expecting it to be followed, and departed with Raynaud. And indeed the additional power source was installed for the harvest.

A FEW WEEKS LATER, around one o'clock on a clear, dry September afternoon, a black Mercedes sedan glided into Château Lascombes's front courtyard. Out stepped Michel Rolland. The dapper fifty-three-year-old Rolland wore a double-breasted blue suit, set off by a ready smile behind his trimmed beard. Rolland was Lascombes's consulting enologist—and not just any enologist. When Colony Capital bought the estate, the purchase was conditional upon Vatelot hiring Rolland. The enologist was being paid $50,000 for making fewer than a dozen visits in a year. If Robert Parker is the leading fan of new wave winemakers, Rolland is their guru. This was the first of his visits before the harvest.

Rolland follows in a long French tradition of enology. The word derives from *oinos*, the Greek word for wine, and the French invented the scientific study of wine and winemaking. Louis Pasteur of pasteurization fame was the first real scientist to work on winemaking, discovering how fermentation occurs and how yeast transforms grape juice into wine. In the 1850s many French wines were still turning sour or vinegary. Putting the bad wine under his microscope alongside samples of healthy wine, Pasteur identified the bacteria responsible for the various wine diseases.

In 1880 a student of Pasteur named Ulysse Gayon set up an enology school in Bordeaux, the world's first. It was attached to the University of Bordeaux in 1916. From the 1950s to the 1970s, the enology school's star professor was Emile Peynaud, who was born in 1912. Peynaud started out as a simple worker in the cellars of the Calvet merchants. He studied at night and moved on to the university, getting his doctorate only in 1946.

Peynaud never became the dean of the enology school. He remained a simple professor. But he wrote the definitive book about making wine, called simply *Knowing and Making Wine,* and the definitive professional book, published in 1983, about tasting and enjoying wine, *The Taste of Wine: The Art and Science of Wine Appreciation.* In 2001 Peynaud was still alive and lived near the university just outside Bordeaux, but he was too ill to work anymore.

In addition to teaching, Peynaud consulted. His clients included Cheval Blanc, Lafite Rothschild, and Margaux. When he started visiting estates in the 1950s, he was shocked to discover that the cellars of Bordeaux's most prestigious names weren't cleaned regularly, which allowed dangerous bacteria to form. Temperature controls didn't exist, causing fermentation to start, stop, and accelerate, almost at will.

The professor-consultant battled to modernize the cellars. He helped introduce new stainless steel, temperature-controlled fermentation tanks. The steel was easier to clean than the old concrete or wood tanks. At the University of Bordeaux, Peynaud worked with his colleagues to decipher and harness the process of malolactic fermentation. Instead of putting the new wine into barrels early, Peynaud advocated leaving the new wine in tanks where the secondary fermentation could be closely monitored. If the temperatures became too cold, the cellars would be heated to induce the bacteria to start working. Only after malolactic fermentation was finished would the wine be run off into barrels, usually between late December and early February. His success led to a vast improvement in quality and less spoiled wine.

Peynaud became legendary not just for his academic talents but because of his winning personality. A stocky man with a square, craggy face and an easygoing manner, he had a down-to-earth style that went over well with vineyard workers. Until the 1990s, most cellar masters were technicians. Their position was often handed down from father to son for generations. The idea of an important professor coming from Bordeaux to tell them what to do was frightening. Peynaud understood. When he first visited Lynch-Bages in the 1970s, he drove up in his battered car and asked first to speak with the cellar master, not the owner. He listened to what the cellar master was trying to do. He suggested a few improvements, most to do with temperature control. When he left, the cellar master went to owner Jean-Michel Cazes and said, "That guy is a real man, he knows what he's talking about." Over the following months, Peynaud encouraged the cellar master to make a series of other changes which slowly revolutionized how Lynch-Bages produced its wine. "In several years, Peynaud managed to get most everyone who could afford it to switch to stainless steel fermentation tanks and to clean up their cellars," said Cazes.

Peynaud preached harvesting ripe and healthy grapes, but he had so much to do in the cellar that he didn't concentrate as much on the vineyards. That task was left to the next generation, led by Michel Rolland. The enologist was born into a simple Pomerol family that owned one of the village's least-known estates, Bon Pasteur. The most exalted wines, such as Pétrus and even the Thienponts' new Le Pin, came from vines on the top of the clay plateau. Bon Pasteur was two miles away, on a plot of lower-quality soil. Like the Raynauds at La Croix de Gay at mid-century, the Rollands knew their Pomerol estate couldn't assure a livelihood for their two children. Both families sold almost all of their wine in bulk to merchants. Even with the name Pomerol on the label, it was too hard to bottle and market the wine. "When I was growing up, I thought Pomerol was a rattrap—people were always saying bad things about everyone else," Rolland recalled.

The Rolland and Raynaud families were friendly and their two firstborn children were good friends. "Michel and I met in the baby carriage," says a smiling Alain Raynaud. After high school, when Raynaud went to medical school, Rolland's brother, Daniel, went to law school. Rolland was a poor student. He didn't make it into the regular *lycée,* instead attending a technical school for future farmers. But when he graduated, his father couldn't afford to take him on at the family estate. So Rolland went to study at the University of Bordeaux's enology school.

"I wasn't a star student," Rolland admitted. Only three women were enrolled at the school. The prettiest was named Dany Bleyne. She was svelte, with a long mane of auburn hair. Her father had succeeded as an entrepreneur in the building business in the nearby Dordogne. Dany came to Bordeaux to study medicine. But it was 1968 and in May striking students shut the universities in protest. Her exams were pushed off to the fall. Over the summer, she didn't study. When she took the tests to continue her medical studies, she failed. So she enrolled in enology. In those studies, she soared to the top of the class. She also met the handsome Rolland.

The two soon married, the brainy, beautiful wife and the charming but struggling student of a husband. When they graduated in 1973, the Rollands bought a small enological laboratory in Libourne. Winemakers were beginning to bring samples to a lab for tests to make sure the wine was healthy and stable, that it had the proper level of alcohol and volatile acidity to be sold under the *appellation* rules. "We were only making sure no faults existed in the wine and that the product could be labeled, as we said, 'honest and salesworthy,'" Dany said, echoing the "loyal and without any defaults" saying of the fourteenth century.

Michel hated being penned up in a lab. He left the work to Dany and began driving out to the properties to pick up samples. When he arrived, he often saw how poorly kept the cellars were. He learned to give advice. Many of the growers with small Right Bank properties hesitated to invest in the stainless-steel tanks fitted with temperature controls to manage fermentation. Rolland convinced them, ever so gently. He would taste the wine.

"Do you have a little piece of ham to go with it?" he would ask.

A dinner invitation often followed. The charm kept flowing and his customer base mushroomed. Soon Rolland was a full-fledged consultant, though the real money earner remained Dany's laboratory. Rolland often gave away his services as a loss leader to win loyalty from customers for the lab tests.

Only one problem remained: even after cellars were cleaned up, the wine often remained poor. Throughout the 1970s, Bordeaux was cursed with a series of poor vintages. "We kept asking ourselves, 'Why is the wine not better?'" Dany said.

In 1981 Robert Parker rang one day at their lab. He was looking for wines to taste and he thought an enologist would be able to help him get appointments. "I have lots of samples," Rolland responded. Once they met, the two men hit it off. They were the same age. Both were unpretentious and fun-loving gourmands. Both were hard workers who spent twelve hours a day or more at their labors, tasting and judging more than two hundred wines daily without losing their senses. They even looked alike—broad-shouldered, stocky men with rugged, round faces. Not surprisingly, they decided to keep in touch. Angry Bordeaux traditionalists would later complain that hiring Rolland as a consultant was an effective shortcut to a good rating from Parker. "I realized Rolland was a smart guy who knew good wine, and over the years, like me, he has been pigeonholed, criticized for only making black and white wines that mask individual differences, something that is totally untrue," Parker later said.

The timing was fortunate. In 1982 Rolland saw right away that the vintage was exceptional and told Parker about the breakthrough, helping to convince the American. The grapes were full of sugar with ripe tannins. Even though yields remained high, the resulting wine was round and rich. "What had happened?" Rolland asked. Since the cellars hadn't changed, he realized that the raw material—the fruit—must have made the difference. "How can we get the same kind of maturity in the fruit every year?" he asked. His answer was simple: most Bordeaux vines were producing too much and most Bordeaux growers were picking their fruit too early.

If 1982's success was going to be repeated, Rolland realized he couldn't just stay in the cellar like his professors. He needed to get out into the vineyards and preach to growers that "great wine begins with great grapes." For him *terroir* counted, but great *terroir* could be found in surprising places. Before buying Château de Reignac in 1990, in addition to consulting a geologist, Vatelot asked Rolland whether the property had any promise. Reignac's vineyard sat atop two prominent gravel-rich plateaus. Rolland was impressed. "I looked at the soil and saw it was well exposed and well drained and stored the sun's heat during the cool evenings to accelerate ripening," the enologist recalled. Ironically, Vatelot didn't believe that such an eminent enologist would want to work on a simple Bordeaux *supérieur,* so he didn't hire Rolland to consult with him until 1995. When he called, Rolland responded, "I've been waiting five years for you to ask."

Good *terroir* can be found in many places, so what counted was the willingness to work hard and take risks. During the 1980s, Rolland encouraged the drastic *garagiste* treatment: severe pruning in the winter months, "green harvesting" to reduce the number of grape bunches left on each vine, and leaf pulling in the late summer to better expose the grapes to direct sunlight and air circulation, all of which served to produce riper, healthier grapes and, by extension, deeper, richer, more concentrated wines. But his real innovation comes later in the cycle. When others begin harvesting, Rolland waits. And waits. More than any other person, he convinced new wavers to pick—by hand—only at the last possible moment before the fruit, now lusciously ripe, starts rotting.

For many in Bordeaux, waiting for that optimal moment is frightening. In good years, the cool Atlantic Ocean breezes bring to the region a pleasant autumn climate like that of South Carolina. In bad years, though, danger lurks. In 1999, just before the harvest, a vicious hailstorm swept through Saint-Emilion. It lasted only a few minutes, but Alain Raynaud remembers that it hailed so hard that he was forced to pull his Land Cruiser off the road and wait it out. When the sky cleared, a swath of great Saint-Emilion estates that had courageously played the waiting game before bringing in their fruit, including Angélus, lost much of the harvest.

The burning question in September 2001 was when to pick. Just as it is important not to harvest too early, it is also crucial to avoid waiting too long. Grapes become overcooked and dry out if they stay too long on the vine. The optimal moment doesn't last long. One year, Rolland

and his friend Christian Dauriac of Château Destieux, a Saint-Emilion *grand cru,* went out to play a round of golf. Both thought they still had a week before beginning to harvest. The weather was hot, though, and they began to worry. On the sixth hole, Dauriac telephoned his vineyard worker from his mobile phone and asked him to go out and taste some grapes in the field.

"You need to harvest in three days," the worker reported.

On the twelfth hole, Dauriac called again.

"Go to another parcel and check the fruit," he ordered.

On the fifteenth hole, the worker called back.

"I think you have to harvest the day after tomorrow."

After finishing the round, Dauriac and Rolland decided to check for themselves. They drove to the vineyard and Rolland sampled a few grapes.

"You better start tomorrow," he said.

While grapes can be tested for sugar, acid, and extract levels in laboratories, judging optimum ripeness remains an inexact science. Despite positive lab analyses, tannins contained in the skins of the grapes can still be bitter. The only sure way to know the right moment is to taste and chew the grape. It takes an experienced taster to judge the perfect level of maturity. And without a doubt, Bordeaux's foremost taster is Michel Rolland.

WHEN ROLLAND ARRIVED at Lascombes on this sunny day in September 2001, it was lunchtime. Vatelot invited him into the gaudy reception room, where a table was set. He uncorked a bottle of 1995 Lascombes, poured it into a decanter, then into glasses. Alain Raynaud and Dominique Befve joined them for the meal. Everyone sipped and stayed silent. The wine was drinkable, pleasant, but with little body or punch. A great wine inspired conversation. This wine did not. No doubt that was Vatelot's point.

A dish of country pâté was served as an appetizer, followed by roast chicken for the main course, and the conversation moved right to work.

Most estates in the region had already started harvesting their white wine grapes. Lascombes makes no white wine and Rolland specializes in red. He had no opinion about that part of the Bordeaux harvest. Elsewhere, he thought more time was needed before the red grapes were ready to be harvested. He still wasn't sure how the vintage would turn out. Despite the poor spring and early summer, Rolland judged that if the hot sunny weather continued, "it still could be very, very good."

The conversation moved on to the differences in winemaking between the United States and France. The University of California at Davis boasts a fine enology department. But Rolland was skeptical. In his opinion, Davis-trained enologists preach risk avoidance. They want to make sure nothing goes wrong with the wine. Grapes can be harvested before full maturity provided they are well treated in the cellar. American-trained enologists depend on cultivated yeast strains to avoid risk during fermentation, add tartaric acid to keep wines stable, and subject the wine to flash pasteurization to avoid spoilage in the bottle. The philosophy pained Rolland. "If you don't take risks, you won't make exceptional wines," he said.

Rolland knows the United States well. He told everybody at the table about his first visit there. It was in 1986. Zelma Long, winemaker of Sonoma Valley's Simi Vineyard, had visited Bordeaux and asked some merchants who were the region's best enologists. "I hardly could speak any English when she called," Rolland admitted.

"Can you come to California?" she asked.

"What date?" Rolland inquired.

Long suggested the following month. Rolland didn't yet have too many clients and was excited about the prospect. But he didn't want to appear too excited. He opened his calendar and frowned, making it seem like a visit was going to be tough to fit in.

"Oh, I think I can make it," he said after a long pause.

Despite language difficulties, Rolland and Long hit it off and Simi's wines improved. Another call came in 1988, this time from Argentina. Rolland didn't speak Spanish; he responded in broken English. The Argentinean wanted to sell his wine in the States, and his potential American importer told him that he needed to sign up Michel Rolland before he would take on his wine. Intrigued, the French enologist traveled to Argentina at the end of Bordeaux's winter, the slow season in Europe but the busy one for winemaking in the Southern Hemisphere, since the seasons are reversed. Rolland fell in love with South America and would later buy his own property there. The contracts kept pouring in, more from California and Argentina, but also from Morocco, Chile, South Africa, and even India. By now, he worked in twelve different countries and even made kosher wine for some clients. Though he received offers from Australia, he refused them, saying it was too far away. In Europe, he consulted in Portugal, Spain, and Italy. Rolland's well-earned nickname was the Flying Winemaker.

"How many estates do you consult?" Vatelot asked.

"Two hundred," Rolland answered. "Tomorrow I'll be in Italy, then Friday in Portugal."

"You must make a fortune," Vatelot said.

In France, few people dare discuss their earnings, out of a Catholic aversion to moneymaking and a fear of the tax man. But Rolland didn't hesitate.

"Oh, about $2 million this year," he said.

But money wasn't his only motivation. He gave many of his friends from Pomerol advice free of charge. When Christian Dauriac needed space to make his wine from a new vineyard there, Rolland offered it to him in his own family's cellar at Bon Pasteur.

At Château Lascombes the clock was ticking and Rolland had already finished his cheese course. He took a last bite of his dessert, a bowl of strawberries and raspberries floating in cassis, and looked at his watch. "My flight to Italy is at 4 P.M.," he announced. Everyone immediately left the table, headed outside, and piled into Raynaud's Land Cruiser, which could navigate the tractor trails between the vineyards. The road led through a neighbor's vineyards that had not been plowed or tended. The vines plumped down on the ground, a mass of leaves shading thick bunches of fruit. "What a jungle," said Rolland, disgusted.

When they arrived at the parcel where Vatelot wanted Rolland to taste, everyone jumped out to inspect. A tractor had turned up the soil, revealing a rich bluish clay. Rolland poked down below and hit on sandy gravel. Most leaves were cut away. Only six bunches remained per vine. The enologist plucked off a few berries. He tasted. They were delicious, full of sweet juice, but still with a slightly bitter aftertaste. "It needs two more weeks of hot, dry weather," he pronounced.

Within a few minutes of delivering his judgment, the Flying Winemaker was off to the airport and the team back at Lascombes was left to hope and pray for dry weather.

CHAPTER 9

A Garage Dinner

BEHIND THE WHEEL OF HIS SILVER BMW SUV, JEFFREY DAVIES sped down a narrow country road toward Saint-Emilion, his wife Françoise at his side. Davies wasn't outfitted in his typical work uniform of jeans and blue Ralph Lauren Oxford shirt. Tonight he was dressed in a smart blue blazer and sported a bright blue and yellow silk tie. Françoise looked resplendent in a shimmering evening gown. Their destination was Davies's latest "baby," a wannabe garage winery called Château La Fleur Morange, owned by Jean-François and Véronique Julien. The invitation was for 7 P.M. "Come celebrate the inauguration of our new cellar," it read.

It was only a week after the terrifying terrorist attacks of September 11 and everyone in Bordeaux was tense. The immediate reaction was sympathy. "We are all Americans" ran the headline of an editorial on *Le Monde*'s September 12 front page. Many Bordeaux winemakers' largest market was the United States and they had spent a lot of time there. Jean-Michel Cazes had a son-in-law living in New York, and although he was spared, the collapse of the World Trade Center terrified him. Cazes remembered eating at Windows on the World. He also remembered how U.S. soldiers had liberated France in 1944.

But just as Robert Parker evoked mixed emotions, anger and criticism about overweening American power soon emerged. On September 12 on the front page of *Sud Ouest*, editorialist Paul Meunier wrote, "The world's first power must ask itself about its political and economic vul-

WILLIAM ECHIKSON

Jean-François Julien aimed to join the ranks of the successful garagistes.

nerability. Isn't it a result of the domination that it imposes on others?" He and others in France feared a new global conflict in which they would be unable to control their own destiny. They remembered how disastrous the last world war was for their country and overlooked the fact that Americans helped free them from tyranny.

Within the wine world, fears of recession mounted. Davies's business was already suffering. One of his best customers was a wine shop in lower Manhattan. It had closed, and the owners had no plans to reopen. American friends told Davies how restaurants over the city were empty and cocktail bars were being visited only for quick, stiff drinks. The restaurant Montrachet in SoHo, a good customer, reopened after the first few days but served few diners. New Yorkers were reeling in the wake of the tragedy, just trying to cope. "Americans are drinking less wine and more hard liquor these days," Davies observed, worried not only for his countrymen but for his own business.

Davies's angst also focused on Gérard Perse. He had second thoughts about his decision to purchase Perse's 2000 vintage Château Pavie at $110 a bottle. Davies already had a large stock of the unsold 1999 vintage. "My customers say it's too expensive," he explained. "This could break me." When Davies called Perse to see whether he could forgo some of his 1999 allotment, the uncompromising supermarket magnate said no. Alain Raynaud attempted to intervene but Perse rebuffed him, telling him Davies was just "a jerk." He soon calmed down, however, and since he knew Davies had long been a staunch supporter, took back the wine.

Aside from this specific concern, Davies was generally pessimistic about the marketing prospects for the upcoming Bordeaux vintage. Even if the quality was superb, he predicted "a tough year." Prices needed to come down from their 2000 Olympian heights. He was lobbying for a drop of as much as 50 percent. Otherwise, he feared Parker would explode in a tirade, just as he had when he found out how owners and merchants were using his ratings to extract more money for their wines. "People don't need to buy any more wine—they already have a lot—and Parker won't recommend they buy anything as a future unless the quality is as good or better than 2000 and unless the prices are much lower," Davies said.

Davies vowed to take a tough line during the upcoming futures campaign. In the past, he did Perse and Raynaud diplomatic favors, unloading some of the substandard wine they inherited when they bought their properties. "If Alain or Gérard try to dump stuff on me, I won't just be able do it this year," he said. At the same time, he feared being black-balled. "You won't want to buy much, but you'll be scared not to buy out of fear of losing your place on their list of allocated merchants," he explained. "Worst of all, you will have only a few minutes to make your decision."

He hoped tonight's party would lift his spirits. The Juliens, both in their thirties, live next door to her parents almost five miles east of the village of Saint-Emilion in the hamlet of Saint-Pey-d'Armens. The family belongs to the local cooperative, the Union des Producteurs de Saint-Emilion, and their vineyards border the eastern edge of the Saint-Emilion *appellation*. A few yards further east and the wines become only Côtes de Castillon *appellation* and sell for half the price or less. Most of the family's grapes are harvested by machine, and the co-op produces a less than memorable concoction from them called Château du Basque, the name of the parent's property. Jean-François, the son-in-law, used to work as a carpenter, but now both he and his wife help her parents with their vineyards.

In 1999 the Juliens became frustrated with the cooperative and, with the blessing of Véronique's parents, decided to try their hand at making a garage wine. Among ambitious locals, Saint-Emilion's co-op was known as one of the least progressive in all of Bordeaux. The Union produced 4.5 million cases each year. They sold because they were labeled Saint-Emilion, even if many were poor examples of that hallowed *appellation*. Until recently, the wine was offered in two varieties. An ordinary batch had a blue label with gold type and sold for $8 retail in French supermarkets. Few U.S. importers would even bother to stock it. The *grand cru* version had a red label with gold type, and cost $10.

The Union's large concrete hangar of a headquarters was built in the 1930s on the plain below the village, and didn't look as if it had changed since then. In 1994 the co-op made a costly error by buying a once flourishing but then bankrupt merchant house called Eschenauer, the business of one of the most notorious World War II collaborators on the *place de Bordeaux*. Until then, almost all of the co-op's wines were sold in France. The new merchant house was supposed to begin exporting them. It turned out that in addition to the sorry wartime legacy, Eschenauer came with a bundle of unexpected debts. The co-op closed the merchant business in 1998 and sued the former owners, but only after taking a $3.5 million hit.

While the co-op was embroiled in the messy legal dispute, needed investments were postponed and quality deteriorated. Count Stephan von Neipperg's well-respected estate, Canon-La-Gaffelière, is located next door to the co-op headquarters. "During harvesttime, I'd watch tractors with huge tanks of grapes park outside and wait for hours under the boiling sun," he said. "The premature oxidation that took place killed the wine."

Belatedly, improvements were undertaken. A hard-charging president named Alain Naulet was elected in January 2000. He sensed the Parker revolution and pushed co-op members to cut yields and harvest riper fruit. He was revamping the cellar and covering the reception area so the grapes wouldn't "fry" before they were crushed and pumped into the fermentation tanks. He even launched the co-op's own limited-production "garage" wine using the fruit from several of the co-op's best growers to produce a high-quality wine called Aurélius. Other special "château" bottlings produced by the co-op were pitched to various market niches. "The winds of change are blowing in Saint-Emilion, and if we don't do something, they will just blow us away," Naulet said.

But the Juliens remained dissatisfied. "There are more than three hundred members, and each time we suggested a necessary investment, somebody ended up voting to block the needed change," complained Véronique Julien. Like Michel Gracia, the couple saw how Jean-Luc `Thunevin was breaking all the traditional rules and prospering. Véronique's parents gave them a four-acre parcel, and they decided to call their wine Château La Fleur Morange. Friends helped out with the harvest. In 1999 they made a mere 900 bottles. They produced the wine in a rented garage and stored it in an abandoned warehouse.

In mid-2000, the Juliens met Davies through a broker familiar with Davies's interest in new garage wines. While the couple's enthusiasm and dedication impressed him, he felt they lacked guidance and he didn't like their wine. It was too coarse, too rustic for Davies's taste, and he turned down an offer to buy any of the 1999 vintage. In his opinion, the Juliens were rushing the vinification process. Their enologist told them to complete the first fermentation in steel vats in four days. Davies wanted to lengthen the process to a full month. "Let me find you an enologist who can help you realize your ambition," Davies said.

Davies called Claude Gros, a leading enologist in the Languedoc region of southern France, and introduced him to the Juliens. Gros helped the Juliens determine the right time to begin harvesting. He fine-tuned their winemaking techniques. Sure enough, Parker fever struck: armed with an impressive score of 89–91 and a glowing commentary for the 2000 vintage, the Juliens aimed this year to up production to 6,000 bottles. Davies had agreed to buy a fifth of the total. The Juliens had received $35 a bottle for their 2000 vintage and hoped to get more for the 2001.

Davies pulled his SUV into the parking lot in front of the new cellar. This was no makeshift Gracia-style garage. The Juliens had built a new state-of-the-art winery by themselves. A sorting table was installed for the upcoming harvest. There were also new truncated dual-walled stainless steel fermenters and, up on a balcony, dozens of new oak barrels. Not just any barrels either. These came from a small cooperage in Pomerol called Darnajou where every barrel is crafted by hand, the wood toasted to perfection over embers rather than an open flame. Monsieur Darnajou learned his craft working for the Moueix family and still makes the barrels for Pétrus. During the past decade, more and more *garagistes* and other new wavers demanded new French oak barrels and the price of them more than doubled, to $600 or more apiece. It requires dedication to insist on new oak. The Darnajou barrels were of just the right "toast" and they smelled like roasted cherries. The American was impressed.

"Wow!" exclaimed Davies. "These are the Rolls-Royces of barrels." Although he had helped choose them, seeing and touching them gave him a feeling of immense pleasure. But the new cellar didn't please all of the French guests.

"I miss the garage," said one partygoer.

"Why?" asked a surprised Jean-François.

"It was folklore."

Julien was wearing a tie and jacket, not his customary informal attire.

But unlike Davies, he looked less than comfortable. His shirt collar hung open unbuttoned and his tie was loose at the neck. Instead of half a dozen merchants wearing the Bordeaux uniform of blue blazers and gray flannels, there were about one hundred partygoers—locals, construction workers, office clerks, and peasant farmers. "This is my harvest crew," Julien explained. "They're volunteers and tonight's party is my way of thanking them."

The American was surprised. Although he had been involved in the creation and launch of La Fleur Morange, he thought the reception would be for merchants. But only two other merchants attended and one of them was Jean-Luc Thunevin, accompanied by his wife, Murielle.

"*Ooh la la,*" Davies muttered under his breath when he first saw Thunevin, adding, only half in jest, "My archnemesis!" The two had rarely spoken since their falling-out in 1997 over the cases of Pingus that went to the bottom of the sea. They tended to give each other a wide berth at events where they were likely to meet. Tonight, though, a meeting was unavoidable. The Juliens gave Thunevin, Davies, and their wives a tour of the new winery. The two men were less than talkative. Françoise broke the ice, striking up a conversation with Murielle. The women are about the same age and are steady voices calming their more volatile husbands. "Loosen up, Jeff—she's being quite pleasant," Françoise whispered.

IT WAS A BALMY EVENING and Champagne was served outdoors as an aperitif. At about 9 P.M., the guests headed to a tent where tables were set with white linen tablecloths and napkins and silver cutlery.

For the Juliens, Thunevin promised to become a perfect complement to Davies. The Frenchman would sell in Europe. The American would stick to North America. While the young winemaking couple had heard a little about the bad blood between the two merchants, they went ahead anyhow and seated them together at the head table. Davies and Thunevin gave each other a stiff smile, finally shook hands, and sat down.

The meal was a tasty, hearty affair, not *haute cuisine* but rustic and filling. Grilled salmon appeared as the first course, accompanied by a Portuguese white wine. "Some friends make it," Julien said, hoping to sound sophisticated with his international contacts. The next course was duck *confit.* The 1999 and 2000 vintages of La Fleur Morange were decanted and then poured into glasses. Everyone tasted. The 1999 lacked punch. The 2000 exploded with flavor. Both Thunevin and Davies smiled. "You're improving," Thunevin said.

The dinner table conversation turned to the upcoming harvest. In Bordeaux as in other winemaking regions, young people from all over Europe used to come for the two weeks of grape-picking. They would live at the estate. But successive socialist governments had introduced ever stricter labor laws. The authorities demanded separate rooms for women and men. They insisted on high-level hygiene. It became too expensive to keep up dormitories that were occupied only two weeks a year. Most workers these days own cars and want to go home to their families in the evenings. Many Bordeaux estates depend on temporary workers hired by agencies. It was becoming too risky to hire students or foreigners. "The police use helicopters to fly over the vineyards during the harvest and check the number of people working," Thunevin complained. "Then they come and ask to see labor records for all the pickers. It's a real pain in the ass."

Thunevin and Davies found common ground lambasting complicated, cumbersome French regulations. One handicap was the rules for buying vineyards and selling them. Authorities determine who can grow what and where. Thunevin himself had just gone through a nasty run-in with the Institut National des Appellations d'Origine (INAO). Before Valandraud's last harvest, he had spread plastic sheeting on the ground to prevent rain from soaking through to the vines' roots and swelling the grapes with water, which dilutes the juice. INAO reacted by declassifying that portion of Valandraud's production. The authorities said that covering the land with plastic sheeting "stresses the vines" and would "change the landscape." "They meant, 'It doesn't look nice,'" Thunevin argued. "It wasn't like we were trying to add some chemical to the wine." Instead of being able to sell Valandraud as Saint-Emilion *grand cru,* he had to sell the declassified part as table wine.

Thunevin was just as critical about Saint-Emilion's own wine authorities and specifically the village's attempt to compete with the Médoc. On the centennial of the 1855 classification, the Saint-Emilion wine union decided to publish its own classification. Promoters argued that the new classification would add to their prestige. An attempt was also made to avoid Médoc-style ossification. Rankings were not permanent. They would be updated every ten years.

It didn't work as intended. In order not to offend anybody, Saint-Emilion's classifications were complicated, framed in terms of various versions of wonderful. Cheval Blanc and Ausone were placed on top as *premier grand cru classé A*. They were followed by ten *premier grand cru classé B*, seventy-two *grand cru classé*, dozens more *grands crus*, and several hundred marked as simple Saint-Emilion. The rankings were no sure indicator of quality, either. Through the 1990s, famed *premier grand cru classé B* such as Châteaux Figeac, Belair, La Gaffelière, and Trottevieille were consistent underachievers but retained their exalted positions anyhow, while up-and-comers such as Valandraud never surpassed the *grand cru* level.

The good idea of revisions every decade provoked nasty battles. In 1965 the committee of winemakers, brokers, and merchants couldn't agree on changes and none were made. The concept of regular grade checks was kept alive, but the execution was variable. The next changes came out in 1969. They made almost no alterations. When they were made, they often weren't done for reasons of quality. In 1985 a *premier grand cru classé* named Beau-Séjour Bécot was demoted. The Bécot family had added some extra acres of vineyards from a *grand cru* château called La Carte. When the committee demanded that they be removed, the Bécots refused. "My father was stubborn and said, 'If I'm going to be declassified, there are twenty others in Saint-Emilion who should also be declassified,'" recalled Gérard Bécot, a present owner. "It was more about politics than wine quality."

The dispute did produce a beneficial side effect. When Gérard and his two siblings inherited the estate, they paid a much lower inheritance tax. "The irony was that the whole story helped us to keep the estate in the family," Gérard said. In 1996, Beau-Séjour Bécot's higher ranking was restored. The younger Bécots agreed to divert the grapes from the contested vineyard parcels to another wine and not use them for the classed growth.

Otherwise, Saint-Emilion classifications became a way of preserving the status quo. Since brokers and merchants sat on the evaluation committee, they insisted that all *grands crus* that desired a higher classification pass through the traditional Bordeaux commercial system, with each player taking a markup. Christian Dauriac initially resisted and continued to sell wine direct from his Saint-Emilion *grand cru* Château Destieux. It cost the consumer $30 a bottle and he had no trouble selling it. But then he decided that he wanted the prestige of a higher *grand cru classé* ranking. He began to work with merchants, who paid him only $15 a bottle. "It was a giant economic sacrifice in the short term," he acknowledged. "My hope is to create more value long-term for my estate."

From the beginning Thunevin decided he didn't want *grand cru classé* status for Valandraud. In part, he wasn't eligible, since Valandraud's vineyards were scattered around Saint-Emilion and he vinified the grapes kilometers away in his garage. The de facto criteria for a *grand cru classé* required one contiguous set of vineyards and a cellar at the same location. But Thunevin had no regrets. If Valandraud became a *grand cru classé*, his daughter Virginie would have to pay much higher inheritance taxes. And because they were complicated and lacked credibility, he believed the rankings weren't worth so much in determining commercial success. "When a portion of Valandraud was declassified and sold as a simple table wine in 2000, I had the last laugh," Thunevin said. "It fetched prices higher than any Saint-Emilion *grand cru classé*."

Davies agreed with Thunevin: the contradictions infecting France's bureaucracy were impossible to fathom. It is permissible to add sugar to wine to increase the alcohol level. But out of a fear of "altering the *terroir*," French law forbids taking measures to prevent rainwater from diluting the wine. "Adding sugar is called tradition, while naturally concentrating the wine is considered heretical," Davies observed with a chuckle.

Dessert was served and a band geared up. All the musicians looked older than fifty. There were two accordions, one electric organ, and one guitar. They sang some old-fashioned Charles Aznavour–style crooners, intermingled with a few American rock and roll and Motown classics.

One of the grape pickers, a retiree surely in his seventies, grabbed the microphone and launched into a sentimental ballad by France's answer to Frank Sinatra, Corsican Tino Rossi.

Davies and Thunevin didn't dance. They huddled and discussed selling the Juliens' La Fleur Morange. Their arguments seemed forgotten. They agreed that the Portuguese white wine served with the first course was bitter, green. "I'm worried," Thunevin said. "Anybody who could serve such a bad wine at a party may not be capable of making truly terrific stuff." Davies was also worried. "This party was pure Deep France, *la France Profonde,*" he said. "The Juliens are peasants, doing a lot of the right things. They are now working with a top enologist and marketing their wine in an attractive package. The elements of the puzzle are all there. But they have to be put together."

The two merchants fretted together about selling the upcoming 2001 vintage. The dot-com bubble had burst. The United States was falling into a recession. Would the market for fine wine plummet? "Then there's the big question: Will Americans continue to pay $100 a bottle for wines that are still virtually unknown outside a small circle of merchants and writers?" Davies asked. By the time the Juliens' wine got to the American consumer, it would cost almost that much. Thunevin didn't answer.

By now, it was 2 A.M. and Françoise was ready to go home. The party was still going strong. Davies sat down in his BMW SUV and roared off back to Bordeaux, speeding at 100 miles per hour. His pleasant evening underscored rising tensions in successful Saint-Emilion. Michel Gracia, Jacques Thienpont, and most other *garagistes* were not attending the dinner at La Fleur Morange. They considered the Juliens upstarts attempting to cash in on a movement they had begun, and they didn't socialize with them. Davies, who enjoyed discovering and promoting garage wines, was beginning to worry about oversupply. As long as the garage movement remained small-scale, it needed to appeal only to a few dedicated connoisseurs. If large numbers of *garagistes* emerged, they might flood the market.

CHAPTER 10

—

Paysan Promises

T HE MORNING OF JULY 6, 2001, DAWNED WITH A SOFT SUMMER sun. Rémi Garuz and his wife, Nathalie, began pruning and cleaning the vines at their family farm near the town of Sauveterre de Guyenne. At around ten-thirty, the sky suddenly turned black. Garuz thought a short thundershower was brewing. Instead of rain, though, golf-ball-size hailstones pelted the earth.

The storm lasted only a few minutes, but by the time the sky brightened, almost two-thirds of Garuz's vineyards were hit. The nature of the damage was hard to comprehend. Budding grapes on one side of the vines were shriveled, while the fruit on the other side emerged unscathed. "What God gives, he sometimes takes away," Garuz noted philosophically.

Garuz lives east of Bordeaux, inland from the sea, about twenty miles south of Saint-Emilion and twenty miles north of Sauternes and Château d'Yquem. This rolling landscape of woods, pastures, and vineyards is the Entre-Deux-Mers, so called because of its position "between two seas," actually rivers, the Dordogne to the north and the Garonne to the south. Romanesque churches, forests, castles, and small fortified towns, or *bastides,* throughout the area are reminders of the wars fought here for centuries. The English founded Sauveterre in 1281 as a fortress. During the Hundred Years War, it changed hands ten times before finally being retaken by the French in 1453. To this day, the *bastide* has preserved four of its original gateways, along with its central square ringed by gently curved arcades.

.*Sauveterre co-op president Rémi Garuz is proud to be a peasant.*

For Garuz, life moves to different rhythms and expectations than for the owners of the grand châteaux, whether old-line or nouveau riche, or for the makers of the garage wines. The grapes he grows become bottom-level Bordeaux wine. Such wine, which accounts for 95 percent of the entire region's production, sells to French consumers for less than $5 a bottle in supermarkets. While sales of the high-end château and garage bottlings were rising both in France and abroad, prices and sales of simple Bordeaux were plummeting. Over the summer, growers in southern France had blockaded supermarkets and overturned trucks carrying cheap wine from Spain into France. Though Garuz was not among them, he sympathized with their cause. "I understand their frustrations, even if I don't agree with their methods," he said.

Sauveterre and the rest of the Entre-Deux-Mers historically have produced dry white wine. Once the French ousted the British in 1453 and reclaimed the region, Dutch traders came to dominate the local commerce. They sought quantity over quality, at the lowest possible price, and this tradition has persisted. When Garuz was growing up, wine was cheaper than bottled water and one of the few commodities in France that was not taxed because, like bread, it was considered a staple. The average Frenchman downed his *p'tite bouteille* at lunch and again at dinner. Many even started right after breakfast at the local café. In the 1960s, the government launched an anti-alcohol campaign. Cafés and restaurants could no longer serve alcoholic drinks to minors, and it has become rare to see babies two or three years old being given glasses of diluted wine, as was common in the past. In the 1990s, most advertising of alcoholic drinks was banned.

As France became richer and its population moved from the land to the cities, wine became, as in Anglo-Saxon countries, a festive treat. Since 1960 consumption has fallen by more than half, from about forty gallons per person per year to about fifteen gallons. While that is still far more than the average two gallons a year drunk by Americans, consumption of more expensive, higher-quality wines has increased in both countries. "We're drinking less but better" is a common phrase heard these days. Mass-market consumers around the globe have shown with their pocketbooks that they like the cheap, fruity flavors and the consistency of the New World brands. Generic Bordeaux white often has a green, bitter taste. At best, Garuz and his fellow growers produced a fruity, pleasant drink. At worst, they made what smelled to many wine critics like cat's pee.

New World upstarts were cleaning up in the markets that count: North America, northern Europe, and Asia, where wine consumption was growing, particularly in wines selling for $5 to $15 a bottle, the same markets where the generic Bordeaux were losing sales. Overall, French wine exports fell by 5.4 percent to $4.6 billion in value from 1999 to 2000, and millions of liters of unsold wine were still sitting in cellars in 2001.

France's market share in the United States slipped from 7 percent in 1998 to 5 percent in 2001, while sales of Australian wine almost tripled. For Garuz, this competition proved calamitous. Since 1998 the price of his white wines plummeted by an average of 40 percent. He and his fellow farmers were growing grapes at a loss. Prices for basic Merlot and Cabernet Sauvignon, on the other hand, had remained steady and were keeping many out of bankruptcy. "We are in the front lines of the fight against Australian and American wines," he said.

The forty-year-old Garuz usually dressed in Levi's. He spoke in a gruff voice and called himself a *paysan*—a peasant. In France, the term has no pejorative resonance, whereas in America, it connotes a country hick. Until recently, the majority of France's agrarian population was spread out across the countryside, working a mass of archaic small plots. Peasants such as Garuz were proud to call themselves by that name. For them, the ultimate badge of honor was to say that they have always lived in the same house on the same piece of land. Garuz's grandfather fled poverty in Spain in 1914, and eventually married a Frenchwoman whose family owned the farm, which produced milk and grains as well as grapes. "I was born here and I intend to stay here," Garuz liked to repeat. "For me, a peasant is the true noble of the land."

In order to survive, the growers of Sauveterre needed to improve the quality of the wine they produce. Garuz was the general in charge of the effort. Since 1990 he had served as president of Sauveterre's cooperative, Cellier de la Bastide, or the Bastide's Cellar, its logo featuring a drawing of Sauveterre's medieval turrets. But the drawing didn't resemble the reality: the co-op itself was located in a large concrete block of a building just south of the village, outside the medieval stone walls. This was a factory, not a garage or a château. Sauveterre's co-op was founded in 1934, two years after Saint-Emilion's, but it faced many more handicaps. Saint-Emilion is a recognized brand name. Its co-op wines, even if of poor quality and difficult to export, command $8 a bottle in most French supermarkets. Over the past decade, as the *garagistes* expanded Saint-Emilion's reputation, the co-op tripled its prices. "How can those guys in Saint-Emilion justify such price rises?" asked an angry Garuz. "They're making

70 percent margins." In contrast, Sauveterre was not a household name and it produced much more wine than the relatively small Saint-Emilion co-op. Over the years, Cellier de la Bastide grew into one of Bordeaux's largest co-ops. By 2001 it counted 130 members and $15 million in annual sales. It sold most of its production in bulk to Bordeaux merchants.

The cooperative continued to grow, even as times became more difficult in the Entre-Deux-Mers. Three new members had joined in 2000, signing up to deliver all their grapes for the next twenty years. The contract was renewable every five years after that, and it was expensive to withdraw. Overall, the co-op's volume had ballooned by 50 percent in the 1990s. Garuz was worried about where he would sell the extra wine and at what price. But he couldn't turn down the growers who wanted to join. "When people knock at your door, you have a responsibility to help them," he said.

The co-op was now investing about $10 million to keep up with the mounting volumes. Alongside the old concrete headquarters, a new steel frame was rising. It contained a dozen shiny stainless steel tanks. Each stood about fifty feet high and was big enough to hold almost 15,000 gallons. Workers were installing computerized temperature controls and hundreds of oak barrels for aging. Garuz also wanted to become a marketer rather than a simple producer of wines. His co-op owned part of a merchant house called Producta. It sold about 10 percent of the co-op's production. In the coming year, Garuz hoped to launch a brand for the first time under the co-op label, something that could compete against the likes of Kendall-Jackson from California and Lindemans from Australia.

The most important changes were not going to cost money, however. Garuz's most pressing priority was to transform the mentality of his co-op growers. Traditionally, members were paid according to the quantity of fruit they delivered. That encouraged high yields. In order to make more competitive wine, they needed to reduce quantity and bring in riper fruit. So when others began harvesting, Garuz wanted his members to wait. Picking would begin only at the last possible moment, when the fruit had achieved maximum ripeness.

Garuz installed a Danish-made computer control system called a GrapeScan at the co-op. It measures the sugar and acid levels and the amount of ignoble gray rot in the harvested grapes. Instead of all members receiving the same amount per ton of grapes, farmers bringing in ripe and healthy fruit would receive a premium. Those who harvested poor fruit would be penalized. But resistance to the plan ran deep. Some growers were just lazy and wanted to bring their grapes in as early as possible in order to go out bird hunting—and they didn't seem to care that they would be penalized for bringing in unripe fruit. Others were frightened by the possibility of rain and feared losing their harvest to rot by waiting. What might happen if he insisted on a long delay? "I could be lynched," Garuz admitted.

ON SEPTEMBER 19, GARUZ stood in front of sixty members of the Sauveterre cooperative in the co-op's meeting room. All were men. Many women are prominent as winemakers in Saint-Emilion and other prestigious *appellations*. But wives stay in the home in this part of Bordeaux, while their husbands work in the vineyards.

The annual general assembly was taking place to decide when to begin harvesting. For the past few weeks, all of the members had brought in samples of their grapes for testing. July's hailstorm had proved more of a fright than a real danger. It hit only a five-mile-wide swath, sparing most of Sauveterre. Though Garuz had not emerged unscathed financially, his insurance company reimbursed him about $80,000 toward his losses.

At Sauveterre, no enologist went out into the vineyards and tasted the members' grapes. Co-op members depended on laboratory analyses, and although tests often showed perfect ripeness, harvested grapes were far less ripe. "We have only one technician to go out and check, and he can't do it for 1,800 hectares," Garuz acknowledged. Technician Christian Caviole joined the co-op two decades before as a manual worker. He learned about wine on the job and lacked contacts with the larger wine world. A thin, balding man with metal-framed spectacles, he wore a distinctive Gallic beard, a triangle of stubble that stayed below his mouth and left a clean line above it. "We are close, very close to the right moment," Caviole told the assembly. "Let's just wait a few more days so that everything is perfect." He proposed starting to harvest on Monday, September 24.

"What if it rains before then?" one member asked. He wanted to begin on Friday.

"The forecast is dry, so let's take the chance," Caviole responded.

Garuz called for a vote. Even though he was president, he could not decide the harvest date alone. The co-op is a democracy. Members must approve all major decisions.

"Let's see a show of hands for starting on Monday," Garuz called.

Almost the entire roomful of arms shot up in the air.

"For Friday," Garuz asked.

Only a few hands rose.

"Monday it is," he announced.

Garuz won the first round, but several more remained to be fought. A young man in the back of the room asked for the floor. He was wearing a New York Yankees cap and seemed agitated.

"How many tons of fruit can we bring in on a single trip?" he asked.

"Three tons," Garuz answered.

"Why not seven?" the young grower asked. "We could fill our bins and save 50 percent on fuel costs."

"If you bring so much in at the same time, you'll crush the grapes," explained Garuz.

Murmurs of protest swept about the room. Garuz knew the sound. The discontent wasn't really about the amount of fruit delivered on each trip to the co-op. It was about the speed of the harvest. If he let members bring in seven tons on each trip, they would rush to finish. Ripe parcels would be mixed with unripe ones and it would be almost impossible to control quality.

Another unspoken concern hung over the meeting: the hunting season. Sauveterre stands in the middle of one of France's largest hunting regions. Each fall, migratory pigeons fly south, away from the winter. Locals construct little fortresses in the forests called *palombières*, cabins they stock with enough food and wine to keep a group of hunters happy. Rope ladders are hung from trees and wooden outposts built on the treetops. Hunters wait there, up in the sky, one hand attached to a shotgun, the other to a string tied to the leg of a pigeon. When migrating birds fly over, the hunters jerk on the string and the trapped pigeons let out a cry to attract their fellow birds. The targets settle on the treetops, and the hunters open fire.

Animal rights activists led by Brigitte Bardot oppose this carnage. Each year, she leads massive demonstrations around Bordeaux. "She's our bin Laden," said the co-op's most fervent hunter, Didier Dezon.

For locals, the hunt is the year's highlight. It begins on October 1 and runs for only two weeks. If harvesting was to start on September 24 and only three tons could be brought in at a time, then it risked delaying the departure for the woods. Garuz hates hunting. He isn't squeamish about killing animals. His farm is full of chickens and rabbits that he eats for dinner. But he detests how the rush to the forests takes precedence for many co-op members over the quality of their work.

"If we allow seven tons of fruit to be delivered, I will resign," Garuz told the assembly.

A murmur of concern swept the room. Everybody understood the stakes. The hunters needed to decide whether to forgo a few days of their pleasure or lose their co-op's president. Garuz called for a show of hands.

"Seven tons?" he asked. Only a few hands shot up, led by the young-ster in the Yankees cap.

"Three tons?" he asked. A clear majority of hands rose.

The meeting broke up after about two hours of heated discussion, around 11 P.M. Afterward, Garuz was satisfied with his victory, though angry that the divisive issue had once again provoked a row. "Every year we have the same debate and every year my authority is chal-lenged," he said.

GARUZ'S FARM SITS on a hill about four miles west of Sauveterre itself. A two-lane country road knifes through a series of no-name villages, mere clusters of limestone houses. In Saint-Brice, population 310, a smaller road turns off to the left, then runs down toward the railroad track linking

Bordeaux with Sauveterre. The trains stopped running a few years ago and the track has been turned into a recreational bicycle path.

The Garuz farm stands a few hundred yards further alongside the path. There is no tidy, American-style red barn and silo, but a complex of several squat stone buildings dating back a century and a half. Official documents list the Garuz farm as "La Pombrède." Since its vines cover a specific piece of land, the grapes grown there can be sold under the grand label of Château Pombrède, even if the wine produced from them is made in the cooperative several miles away in Sauveterre. No marble columns or grand entryway exists at Château Pombrède, of course. Simple stucco envelops the buildings, and the passages between them are covered only with dirt. But the co-op was careful to keep track of the vines associated with the location in order sometimes to bottle its wine with a label picturing an impressive castle.

In one dwelling, Garuz's parents live, along with two elderly aunts. Jean Garuz, Rémi's father, was going on eighty in 2001. He is a small, squat man. But he still works full-time on the farm, driving the tractor and stacking hay. Rémi's mother, also short, stocky, and dark-haired, does lighter chores and cares for the rabbits and chickens.

When Garuz was growing up, the farm raised sheep for slaughter and cattle for milk, along with a wide variety of vegetables and grains. But one by one, all of these products lost their profitability. Argentinean beef and New Zealand lamb were much cheaper. Luckily, the wine industry filled the gap. It turned the Entre-Deux-Mers's farms into small businesses and almost all of the acreage is now covered with vines. Farmers, including Garuz, still cultivate some wheat in fields where grapes cannot prosper. "It's more a hobby than a serious money-earner," Garuz admitted. The rabbits and chickens are only for home consumption.

Rémi and Nathalie Garuz live in one house on the compound with their two daughters, aged six and nine. Even though their dwelling was renovated and boasts all the modern conveniences—no outhouses here, thank you—the rooms remain small, a relic from the time when heating was expensive and difficult. Rustic, heavy pieces of mahogany dominate the furnishings. "I would prefer to live in Bordeaux," Nathalie confided.

A sultry, dark-haired woman with a resemblance to Natalie Wood, she grew up in the city, the daughter of shopkeepers. She works as a secretary in a local office and doesn't like farm tasks. She thinks the city where their children would attend top-ranked schools would be better than the countryside. "But Rémi would never move away," she said. "He doesn't care too much about studying."

Garuz admits he never finished high school and that books bore him. "I learned by doing," he replied to his wife's reproach. Behind his informal manner, however, the *paysan* is a street-smart, hardworking, and ambitious man. In 1982, after running the family farm for a decade, he applied to join the co-op's board. He liked the administration and politicking. The president, Robert Bonneau, a friend of his father's, took an immediate liking to him. Garuz was a third-generation member of the co-op and his family had not been involved in any disputes. "Rémi's got the common touch," Bonneau said. "Plus he can be tough as nails when he needs to be." When Bonneau retired, he recommended Garuz as his successor.

Presidency of Sauveterre's co-op propelled Garuz up the rural Entre-Deux-Mers hierarchy. In 1999 local politicians asked him to consider running during the next election for the municipal council. He thought hard about the offer, since he resented the socialists who were governing France. The socialists had imposed a thirty-five-hour workweek the year before that was supposed to force companies to hire new workers. Garuz thought this was crazy. At the co-op, he wasn't going to hire new workers. There just wasn't any money. Work would have to go undone. That wasn't the only problem. "Taxes are too high," he railed. "Everybody looks to the state to support them. We're becoming a welfare nation."

After long deliberation, Garuz turned down the chance to run for municipal office. Just as he is uncomfortable with socialism, he is impatient with the region's paternalistic conservatism. Farmers working in the co-ops often look at their jobs like bureaucrats: they don't have to care much about quality because they only grow grapes. They don't make or market the wine made from their grapes. That is left for somebody else. And if their product can't be sold, they expect the government to step in and save them.

202 · *William Echikson*

The co-op's payment system hides the danger of declining consumption and the increase in production from New World wineries. Growers cash in only two years after the harvest, so in the fall of 2001 they had just received their checks from 1999 when the price of generic Bordeaux remained healthy. During the late 1990s, a resurgence of the phylloxera louse dried up supply from California just as demand from Asia expanded, and Bordeaux's overall image was boosted by the success of its most famous châteaux. The co-op's main problem at this time was producing enough wine. More vines were planted and growers pushed for high yields. Stocks expanded just as competition intensified from Australia, Chile, and other New World producers.

The excellent 2000 harvest, the same that made fortunes for established estates such as Margaux, ambitious new wavers such as Vatelot, and up-and-coming *garagistes* such as Gracia, proved poisonous for the bulk producers. "Consumers got the idea that a bottle of Bordeaux needed to cost a fortune," Garuz complained. When the economy proceeded to fall into a recession, prices of generic Bordeaux plummeted and threatened to go even lower in 2001. "A few years ago, we sold 200,000 bottles to Danish or Dutch supermarkets in the blink of an eye," Garuz remembered. Sales were falling fast, yet the co-op's members wouldn't feel the pinch for two years.

Garuz was caught between the conservatism of his co-op's membership and his realization that the world was changing fast. He himself is a curious mix of traditional and modern, Slow and Fast France. His life on the farm is tied to unchanging rhythms that cannot be accelerated. Patience is needed for his vines to flower. If his fellow farmers are hunters, it is because they enjoy nothing more than going off into the forests and holing up in their *palombières* for hours on end.

Just as Garuz can't imagine anything more boring than hunting, he also identifies with the country of the TGV bullet train and the supersonic Concorde jet. As a child, he had dreamed of becoming a professional automobile racer. When he was a teenager, he raced go-carts. After he quit high school, he applied to a professional racing school on the Côte d'Azur. He went away for a week and took the tryout. Although he wasn't quite fast or bold enough, his love of fast cars lingers. With his visitor in tow, he walked out of the house and over to a barn. When he opened the door Garuz pulled off a sheet to reveal a bright red Ferrari. The $250,000 car is shared with two other friends. "We take it out on the weekends and burn up the roads," he said. Accidents are common. Only a few days before, Garuz was going so fast that he swung off the road and came to an abrupt stop. Except for the shock, he emerged unscathed, but the bumper was broken. It would cost $1,500 to repair.

For everyday use, Garuz drives a silver BMW 316, a sporty sedan that does 130 miles per hour on the narrow country roads. Garuz makes it to Bordeaux in twenty-five minutes; drivers observing the posted speed limits take a full hour.

"With two children, you should slow down," Nathalie protests, presumably for the thousandth time.

"Speed is a virus," Rémi insists. "You're born with it and there's no medicine to get rid of it."

FOR DINNER ON the Saturday night after the co-op's general assembly, Garuz's mother slaughtered a hen from the farm's own chicken coop. Some friends were invited for the evening and the occasion merited a special wine. Garuz opened a Mouton Rothschild, 1989. He bought two cases of it for his wedding and he still had some left. At the time, the price was a mere $30 a bottle.

The guests brought a new wave bottle from Saint-Emilion from 1998. It wasn't a named growth and it wasn't expensive. Garuz decanted both wines and let them sit for about half an hour before serving. The Mouton emerged watercolor pink, while the Saint-Emilion came out oil purple.

A debate erupted with the first sips. To the guests, the mature Mouton seemed tired, while the Saint-Emilion burst with youthful vigor. Garuz disagreed. When it came to wine, he was a traditionalist. He discerned a lingering perfume in the Mouton. In his opinion, the Saint-Emilion lacked finesse. It was too strong, too full of alcohol and fruit. "When you harvest that late, your wine tastes like strawberry jam," he com-

plained. In his opinion, the goal of the cooperative wasn't to make concentrated garage-type concoctions. It was to take out the bitterness that
came from harvesting unripe grapes. "We need well-made wines, ones
that the consumer can drink with pleasure on a daily basis," he said.

A few years before, Garuz visited Argentina with a group of Bordeaux winemakers to see how wine was made in the New World. Christian Moueix's chief winemaker, Jean-Claude Berrouet, traveled on the
same trip. He and Garuz became fast friends and agreed on the goal of
improving traditional techniques in small steps. When they saw the
immense Argentinean estates, all mechanized, producing a homogenized, standardized product of high quality, they were shocked.

Surprisingly, the Parker and Rolland system disgusts Garuz. Whereas
Parker sees himself as the great democratizer of Bordeaux—remember
"I don't care about whether your château has hundreds of years of history in the same family"—Garuz spots a dangerous elitist. Parker deals
only with the top 5 percent of the Bordeaux production. "He ignores all
the commercial wines," Garuz complained. In his opinion, garage wines
don't obey the normal laws of economics. Since supply is limited, even a
minimum of demand drives prices up. The American guru won't even
consider production from Sauveterre. And Garuz doesn't see how anyone can taste two hundred or more wines a day and do so accurately. So
much liquid, even when spit out, makes the mouth pucker up and
fatigues the palate. Everything begins to taste astringent.

The Parker-Rolland garage recipe is easy to duplicate, Garuz insisted.
Plant Merlot vines. Keep the plot small. Slash yields. Put all the harvest in
new oak barrels. Pay Michel Rolland $100,000 a year. And presto, get a
good Parker score and sell it for $100 or more a bottle. "There's nothing
mysterious about it," Garuz said. Even if Garuz disliked the wine produced by such methods, he believed the formula worked only on small
plots producing small quantities of wine, not at a huge co-op with millions of gallons to sell. Sauveterre's co-op produces so much wine that a
good Parker score in a given year might not suffice. The co-op needs big
clients. Baron Philippe de Rothschild's "La Baronnie" was a loyal customer. Sauveterre provided much of its basic Bordeaux blends, the Mou-

ton Cadet red and white. But in the past few years Rothschild was cutting its purchases. "They're suffering in the U.S.," Garuz explained.

In place of the struggling merchant, the co-op's biggest client now was Carrefour. France's biggest, best-run hypermarket chain triumphed with stores that make some of Wal-Mart's superstores seem small. The chain sells everything from computers and TVs to foie gras and Roquefort cheese. Hypermarkets distribute about 60 percent of all the wine sold in France. Attitudes toward the chains divide Bordeaux. Saint-Emilion's *garagistes* do everything in their power to ignore them. They forbid their merchants from selling to them, and if they find their wines on the shelves, they discover who betrayed them and strike them off their list for supplies the next year. But Garuz has no qualms. The supermarkets place individual orders of up to 2 million bottles. "They are the biggest buyers, so I have no choice except to deal with them," he said, taking a final sip of his 1989 Mouton Rothschild.

The two bottles of wine soon were empty. It was near midnight and Garuz bade good night to his guests. Instead of heading toward his bedroom, he went to the barn, opened the door, and jumped up on his tractor. "I'm going to harvest a little wheat," he said. "Just for fun."

IT RAINED ON Monday morning, September 24, the harvest's opening day, so Garuz decided to postpone picking. He made appointments instead in Bordeaux. His BMW rolled out onto the country road and began picking up speed until the hills faded into a blur. West of the city, at the entrance to the highway, he stopped off at a Carrefour. He filled up his BMW. This and other hypermarkets sell gas practically at cost, up to 20 percent less than at normal gas stations.

Garuz proceeded on his way, ignoring the large banner outside the store blaring FOIRE AUX VINS. Twice a year, in the spring and at harvesttime in September, the hypermarkets and supermarkets hold two-week-long wine fairs, offering the best bottles at unbeatable prices. At this fair, the wines came from dozens of prominent estates, such as Carbonnieux, a well-known white Pessac-Léognan, and the Cathiards' red Smith-Haut-

Lafitte. While many small Parkerized Right Bank creations can ignore the supermarkets, most of the larger Pessac-Léognan and Médoc estates can't be so picky. They had a lot of wine to unload and few independent wine shops remain in France.

Even cases of Yquem lined racks and filled wooden cases, offered at cut-rate prices. Carbonnieux went for a mere $18. The Cathiards' second wine, Les Hauts de Smith, was even less, $12. "The prices are better here than at the châteaux themselves," reported salesman Jean-François Clemenceau. Bottles from the 1997 vintage filled the shelves. In 1997 merchants had, against their better judgment, stocked up at high prices. "The 1997s are being dumped," Clemenceau said, smacking his lips with gratification. Business was good. During the two weeks of the fair, he said, more than 20 percent of the branch's yearly wine sales took place and almost half of its prestige bottles were sold.

The big grocers revel in their power. "We can make or destroy anybody we want," said Charles Burke, Carrefour's chief wine buyer at the time. Outside of the wine fairs, the supermarkets and hypermarkets offer only a few of the top estates and concentrate instead on basic Bordeaux bought from co-ops, including Garuz's Sauveterre. Much of the production is sold under their own house label. "Otherwise, we would have fifty thousand château labels fighting it out among themselves," Burke explained.

Carrefour's arrival in a city often provokes the same kind of unrest a new Wal-Mart's opening does in the United States, with shopkeepers screaming that they are going to be killed by the powerful, aggressive retailer. In recent years, Carrefour has begun to diversify its wine offerings away from its traditional French wine suppliers, selling Australia's Rosemount and Lindemans, and America's Gallo. The quantities are still small. In 2001 less than 2 percent of the total wine drunk in France was imported. French wine drinkers remained chauvinistic. But the foreign wine companies were willing to mount large marketing campaigns, and their arrival gave the chains additional leverage over local suppliers, forcing them to lower prices to compete. "We need the supermarkets but we also fear the supermarkets," Garuz admitted.

Since dozens of co-ops are spread out over Bordeaux, Garuz knew the only way to claw back some bargaining power from the merchants and the big chains was for the co-ops to combine. Saint-Emilion was staying aloof because its name recognition meant it didn't need help from the others. Elsewhere, though, mergers were already taking place. Neighboring Rauzan had taken over the large Luchon co-op in the Fronsac region. Sauveterre wanted to remain independent and decided on another formula: a marketing marriage. Its marketing company, Producta, represents seventeen co-ops throughout Bordeaux. In 2001 the world's largest winery, Gallo, generated four hundred times larger sales, more than $1.5 billion a year. Garuz knows that Producta can never compete on such a scale but that it needs to grow larger to be able to afford decent marketing budgets and to supply supermarkets and other large customers with branded, affordable wine in large quantities.

Producta's headquarters are in downtown Bordeaux in the historical Chartrons quarter, near the broad Place des Quinconces—the largest square in Europe—and only a few blocks from the Grand Théâtre. They occupy the first floor of a suitably grand building that was erected in the middle of Bordeaux's eighteenth-century boom. Two years before, Garuz was named Producta's president. Though he was one of the founders, his position is more honorific than hands-on. Professional managers take care of the details. Garuz represents the co-op members and sets broad strategic guidelines. His goal is to double sales within five years. He spends a day a week there and enjoys a large office overlooking the splendid square. It is ornate, a little staid in its Old World furnishings, high ceilings, and decorative moldings with a flower motif. The stocky peasant Garuz looks out of place.

Today, his first appointment was lunch. The guest was the president of the co-op in Bergerac, east of Bordeaux at the entryway to the Dordogne Valley. It produces robust reds, dry whites, and some sweet whites, the best known of which is Monbazillac. This is no Sauternes. A bottle of Monbazillac sells for half as much as a "run-of-the-mill" Sauternes. If Sauveterre's co-op faced challenges, Bergerac, enjoying even less fame, confronted a crisis. The restaurant Les Caves de Bigoudy served local specialties—grilled duck breasts and hearty cassoulet. Garuz loved the food and washed it down with a Sauveterre red. Dessert was a fruit tart. A Monbazillac was poured. While Sauternes's sweetness lingers on the lips, the cheaper wine attacks the mouth like penny candy. Producta's professional managers had worked out the basic outlines of the deal. Lunch was more a formality and Garuz's presence was diplomatic. "When the papers are signed, they want to see the president there," he said.

After eating, everyone returned to the office and the serious work began. Economies of scale achieved by joining forces with other co-ops were necessary. The real solution, though, was to make better wine and to sell it more effectively. In order to sell its wine, Sauveterre needed to become more than just a supplier of huge vats of bulk wine to the Rothschilds and Carrefour. It aimed to bottle its own wine and sell it by itself.

The name Sauveterre or even Producta elicits little excitement among consumers and Garuz wanted to create an attractive brand. At the beginning of 2001, he hired a bilingual marketer named Giles O'Connolly to do the job, and today was O'Connolly's chance to present his ideas. Blond and ruddy, the forty-four-year-old O'Connolly has a French mother and an Irish father. He was born and raised in Vancouver. At school, he spoke English. At the dinner table, he spoke French. "We were allowed to speak English only with dessert," he said. When he was in his teens, his parents moved to southern France. Once he graduated from college, he settled in Paris and became a marketing manager in the fashion industry for such illustrious names as Karl Lagerfeld and Jean Paul Gaultier. For those jobs, he traveled often to Australia and New Zealand.

After fashion, what could be more appealing than wine? O'Connolly took a winemaking degree in Mâcon but decided he didn't want to shed his tie and jacket for farmer's boots. He took another course in wine marketing at a business school and joined a small Bordeaux merchant house. When Garuz went searching for someone to create a new brand and found O'Connolly, it was too good an opportunity to pass up.

O'Connolly and Garuz headed into a meeting room with a few other colleagues. Dozens of bottles of the co-op's wines were arrayed about the room. They represented a bewildering assortment of offerings from different villages, ranging from the celebrated Saint-Estèphe to the unknown Sainte-Foy-La-Grande. The labels were all similarly red and black with Old World typefaces.

WILLIAM ECHIKSON

*Giles O'Connolly, of French-Irish heritage, aimed to
create a brand for one of Bordeaux's biggest co-ops.*

"Bordeaux's image is too old, too masculine, too snobbish," O'Connolly began. "We need to appeal to younger buyers and to women, who are buying and drinking New World wines."

He opened a large portfolio and took out several drawings. Under his guidance, an English design firm created the proposed labels for the new brand. A large red heart dominated the images, drawn with what looked like lipstick.

"We need something feminine, romantic, even sexy," O'Connolly said.

The mention of femininity made Garuz cringe. He thought it was wimpy.

"We can't be as simple as the Australians," Garuz interrupted. "We have to be more sophisticated."

O'Connolly defended his idea. "I was in the fashion industry and I saw that women love hearts. They have them on their necklaces, on their T-shirts. We can't continue with pictures of intimidating châteaux," he said. "We can't be snobs."

"No snobs," Garuz agreed. "No hearts, either."

THE NEXT DAY, GARUZ arrived at the co-op at 8:30 A.M. He still wasn't going to start picking himself. If he rolled out his own giant harvesting machine, it risked getting caught in the wet ground. The forecast was for sun over the next few days. More time on the vines would help. "If I wait another day, I have a better chance of harvesting dry grapes, and dry grapes are better grapes," he said.

At 9 A.M., Sauveterre stirred. Farmers gathered in cafés under the arcades in the village's central square, where they downed thick black espressos. Just outside the medieval walls, the cooperative bathed in the early morning peace. Its wide cement loading dock was empty. In the middle of the dock sat a glass-walled booth. This was the harvest control center.

Before 10 A.M., tractor-trailers containing up to three tons of grapes, as agreed, began lining up in the co-op's driveway. They first headed to a testing station in front of the main building. A robot arm shot out and grabbed a bunch of grapes. It took the fruit and passed it through the GrapeScan, which measured the sugar and acid content—and determined whether the fruit was rotten. A grade was given from 1 to 10. The smallest numbers represented ripe fruit. The higher the number, the more unripe or rotten. The members' premium would be about 20 percent if they brought in ripe fruit, and the penalty would be about 20 percent if their fruit was underripe or rotten.

After receiving his "report card," the farmer parked his tractor to one side of the reception center, where his load was weighed, and a deep horn sounded, followed by a clanging bell. A young woman in the control center shot her hand up into the air to indicate the bins for receiving the grapes were clear and ready for a new load. The horn blared again. A flashing light hanging in front of the control center turned yellow. The young woman gave a thumbs-up sign and the farmer pushed a button in his tractor.

His trailer lifted up and swiveled downward, freeing a mass of grapes that thundered down a chute into a large steel receptacle inside the building. The grapes sloshed along, pushed by a huge metal screw that turned slowly, stripping the berries from the stalks and crushing the fruit into pulp. The system had been computerized for this harvest, in order to separate loads and allow more careful vinification. But a problem emerged: while the new GrapeScan worked well, the computer software in the main reception room was malfunctioning, printing out the wrong weights and sending grapes down the wrong chutes. Everything had to be corrected and done manually. This slowed the process and led to a traffic jam in the driveway. It took an hour or more for the farmers to unload their fruit. Engines idled. Men with lined, grimy faces talked in small groups. Cigarettes were lit; tempers flared.

"I need to get back to the harvest," one yelled.

"You see, you should have let us bring in seven tons at a time," yelled the Yankees-capped youngster who had caused so much trouble at the harvest meeting a few days before.

Garuz walked away without saying anything. He had a terrible headache. Luckily, Caviole the technician emerged wearing his blue lab coat and carrying a pitcher and a few wineglasses. A cloudy white juice bubbled inside.

"It's been fermenting since this morning," he said. He poured Garuz a glass. The warm juice gave off heat on the tongue, moderated by a lemony, refreshing sweetness.

"Pretty good," Garuz said, his morale lifted.

It took until almost 10 P.M. to clear up the backlog of tractor-trailers waiting to unload their grapes. But the mood improved as the night turned long. The growers knew this was their last run of the day.

The next day the sun came out. "It's going to be a hot one," Garuz said, jumping up into the driver's seat of his twelve-year-old harvesting

During the 2001 harvest, tractors queued up to unload their grapes at the Sauveterre cooperative.

machine. It was blue and built like a tank on top of a tractor chassis and it rumbled down the small road. High off the ground, it straddled the vines. Deep inside the machine, two large rubber belts vibrated, shaking the berries from their stems. The fruit fell onto a conveyor belt, which carried it to holding bins. The machine produced a jarring, rattling noise. It was ugly but efficient. "A machine like this lets you harvest twenty-five acres in a day," Garuz said proudly.

All of Sauveterre's co-op members depended on harvest machines. Even in prestigious *appellations*, many growers had resorted to them. In Pomerol, Noël Raynaud at Château La Croix de Gay became so fed up with harvest workers that he used a mechanical harvester beginning in 1982, one of the main reasons why Robert Parker was so critical of the resulting wine. When his children took over, Alain and Chantal restored manual harvesting. A delicate hand could bring in unbruised fruit with few stems or leaves.

But manual harvesting was expensive and complicated the logistics. Pickers were difficult to find and needed to be fed and housed. And perhaps worst of all, they were slow. "If I used manual workers, it would take me three weeks to harvest my vineyards, and some of the fruit would go bad," Garuz said. The big advantage of the machines was that the grower could pick the moment when the grapes were ripest and bring them in fast, before they rotted. Over the years the machines had improved: new models treated the fruit more delicately and removed unwanted leaves.

The temperature increased and soon could be mistaken for midsummer, hitting 95 degrees Fahrenheit. Garuz had to work fast or his grapes would rot. Before mechanization, harvesting might have been a festive event that brought the community together. "We would have Basques from Spain who would come harvest and they became part of the family," Garuz recalled. That camaraderie was now lost. The harvest had become a chore, something to be finished as fast as possible. In Sauveterre, all shops and offices shut for two hours at midday. But for Garuz, there would be no lunchtime siesta. He would harvest all day, stopping only to eat a sandwich. "It's true, the machine has broken the human equilibrium," he said.

Suddenly Garuz's mobile phone rang. He whipped it out from his shirt and responded, perched in the driver's seat in his high harvest machine. An angry grower was on the line. His grapes had only 11 percent alcohol and Christian Caviole was forbidding him from harvesting. But he feared forecasts of rain for the next day.

"My grapes are ripe, and if I don't get them in, they will rot," he insisted.

"No," Garuz said firmly, supporting the technician. "At only 11 percent alcohol, they cannot be ripe."

He returned to his own work. It took him only about half an hour to collect about three tons of grapes. It would have taken a team of twenty pickers an entire day from dawn to dusk to bring in the same amount. Garuz's father drove up in a tractor and the trailer full of fruit was hooked up. The senior Garuz took the load the five miles to the co-op. When he returned, he reported that the grapes had measured 13 percent alcohol, which was quite good. But the hailstorm had bruised much of the fruit and some of the berries were rotten. On the 1-to-10 scale, they rated 4.5, too low to rate any bonus. The two Garuzes continued to work until 6 P.M.

When they returned to the co-op, tractors again lined up in the driveway. After the farmers had spent several hours sitting in the sun waiting to unload their harvest, their fruit had begun to bubble. Yeast clinging to the grape skins had been released and fermentation was set off prematurely. The young grower in the baseball cap again seethed at the wait. When he finally arrived in the test pad area, he became even madder. His Muscadelle grapes rated 7.

"Your fruit is rotten," Garuz said. "It should be thrown out."

"That's against the rules," the young man said. He was right. Co-op regulations require all grapes, rotten or not, to be accepted.

"It's not my fault," the young grower said. "It rained a lot. The Muscadelle grape is sensitive."

Garuz walked away.

"Sure, it's particularly sensitive when you grow too much and your fruit rots," he whispered to himself.

Cleaning up Sauveterre's mess was going to be a slog. If Garuz were in Australia or America, he would be the CEO of a company and could just fire the lazy young employee. In a co-op of equal members, that was impossible. Garuz could hope, with some reason, that he could continue to scrape by, thanks to Bordeaux's continuing positive image, the product of centuries of glorious tradition and, more recently, the revolution wrought by Robert Parker and the Saint-Emilion *garagistes*.

CHAPTER 11

Battle Royal

IN THE FALL OF 2001, PERFECT CONDITIONS CONVERGED ON
Sauternes: severe heat followed by light rains. Almost every day in September began with a humid mist, which burned off by midmorning. The vines reacted on cue. Speckles of brown appeared on the grapes' yellow-green skin. "They're going chocolate," locals said. Water evaporated and the fruit shriveled and shrank. While growers of red wine still feared that the poor June and July weather would lead to a mediocre vintage, Alexandre de Lur-Saluces was delighted. Yquem's berries were not becoming bloated. They were drying out and showing the telltale signs of noble rot.

For Lur-Saluces, pleasant prospects for the upcoming harvest represented a welcome respite from the past five years of legal battles. The November 1996 sale of Yquem to LVMH had appeared all over France's front pages, on radio, on television, and in magazines. "The King of Luxury Offers Himself the Greatest Wine in the World," the weekly *VSD* proclaimed in its headline. Bernard Arnault was pictured smiling in *Paris Match*, a decanter full of Yquem in one hand, a glass of the wine in the other, and a look of satisfaction on his face. In interviews, Arnault admitted that Yquem earned only about 2 percent a year on its capital, far from enough for an ambitious publicly traded company. He didn't care. "This is a jewel, the best-known, most prestigious, best wine in the world," he said. "When we found it was for sale, we could not resist." By buying Château d'Yquem, Arnault argued, he was acquiring a rare symbol of real luxury.

CIVB

Yquem's cellars are home to more than 700,000 bottles
of luscious, golden Sauternes.

Back in Bordeaux, Alexandre and his defenders perceived Arnault not as a benefactor but as a predator. They decided to fight LVMH, but feared being steamrollered by the company's $200 million-a-year advertising budget. LVMH even owned one media outlet, the influential financial daily *La Tribune Desfossés*. According to one of the count's early supporters, philosopher Alain Etchegoyen, the press didn't even want to hear Alexandre's side of the story. "The count tried to obtain the right to respond in those newspapers that had been so quick to announce the news," Etchegoyen said. "Most refused. One weekly even admitted to him explicitly that it didn't want to anger LVMH."

Stubborn Alexandre began to organize his defense. He hired two of Bordeaux's best-known lawyers.

The media counterattack centered on portraying the count as an everyman David fighting off the Goliath Arnault. Lur-Saluces was a crusader for eternal French values of land and family. Interviews were arranged with journalists who might be sympathetic. Surprisingly, the left rallied to the count's defense, latching on to his cause as a battle against capitalism, defining the enemy as an American-style marketer making war on individualistic France.

It didn't matter that Bernard Arnault was French, or that Yquem's minority shareholders had made an effort to avoid an American buyer. "Better LVMH than Coca-Cola," Louis Hainguerlot had said. *Le Monde* journalist Jean-Yves Nau didn't hide his view that the sellers had betrayed France. His front-page story was headlined "The Battle for Yquem." "Weakened by tax laws, family enterprises are becoming the food for voracious multinationals," he concluded.

The Bordelais nobility didn't like an outsider taking one of its jewels and rallied around one of their own. Writers, restaurateurs, wine merchants, and journalists were enlisted to portray capitalist greed as ready to destroy French tradition. In particular, Dennis Mollat, the prominent Bordeaux publisher and bookseller, assembled a group of writers to put out a tome called *For Yquem,* full of expressions of support for Lur-Saluces. "One cannot replace the prestige of a signature with the weight of capitalization on the stock exchange; the heart of Sauternes does not beat to the rhythm of Wall Street," wrote the combative philosopher Etchegoyen.

Mollat identified personally with the count's struggle. His great-grandfather founded the Librairie Mollat in 1876 on the rue Vital Carles in downtown Bordeaux. In the 1980s, Virgin Megastore, the European version of Barnes & Noble or Borders, opened a branch in Bordeaux and the venerable independent bookstore veered toward bankruptcy. Mollat himself was working as a physician in 1989 when his family persuaded him to quit and try to save the *librairie*. He is a small, meticulous man, always dressed in dapper business suits, even on sweltering summer days. Visitors are received in a formal office, complete with ornate Louis XV furniture, chandeliers, and wall engravings. By expanding and modernizing his bookstore, by organizing authors' readings and offering a large selection of works by local writers, Mollat resisted the arrival of the chains and thrived. "My fight was the same as Alexandre's, to save a small independent family enterprise from a giant capitalist bulldozer," Mollat said.

Another of Alexandre's top cheerleaders was Bernard Ginestet, the aging scion of the once great Bordelais merchant and winemaking family. Ginestet had inherited and then been forced to sell Château Margaux. Under his family's direction, Margaux had fallen far from its Olympian heights because the Ginestets had lost a lot of money as merchants and didn't have the funds to invest in quality. And yet when they sold the château in 1977 to the Franco-Greek supermarket magnate Mentzelopoulos family, old-line Bordelais were horrified. Even after the new owners restored Margaux to its former glory, it took years for the Mentzelopouloses to feel at home. Ginestet himself was left with almost nothing after honoring the family debts. He was elected mayor of the village of Margaux and turned to writing in order to make a living. Over two decades he produced a series of wine books concentrating on Bordeaux's individual *appellations* before passing away in the fall of 2001.

To Bernard Ginestet, upholding the sanctity of these *appellations* and their *terroir* represented a sacred cause—one that pitted the count and old-line Bordelais against heathens such as Bernard Arnault and, by extension, Robert Parker. When the American journalist William Langewiesche asked Ginestet about Parker, the Frenchman was scathing. "Standardized," he said of Parker. "Price-conscious. Unsubtle. Square." Why? "Americans like certainty," Ginestet answered. "If wine contains a truth, it is the absence of certainty. One of the reasons Bob has succeeded is that he knows no doubts. Today, there is globalization. Bob is an artisan in the globalization of wine."

Not surprisingly, Alexandre de Lur-Saluces felt comfortable being interviewed for *La Revue du Vin de France* by Ginestet about his battle.

Alexandre presented his fight as the defense of eternal values against ephemeral capitalism. "The minority owners have indulged in a regrettable financial speculation," he charged. "Yquem is an exceptional product which belongs more to a dream than to finance."

In the summer of 1997, Alexandre threw a lavish party to thank his supporters. Many of France's leading intellectual lights, writers such as Bernard Clavel and Jean-Paul Kauffmann and philosophers Michel Onfray and Michel Serres, traveled from Paris to illuminate the château. The men wore black tie. The women strolled in silk evening dresses. In the courtyard, a chamber orchestra played baroque music, the count's favorite. Magnums of Krug Champagne—ironically, an LVMH brand—were uncorked as aperitifs. Foie gras and caviar were served, all paid for from Yquem's coffers. And for dessert, liveried waiters poured bottle after bottle of the golden nectar itself. For those who desired them, Havana cigars were offered. A whiff of Louis XIV at Versailles lingered in the air. "It was a celebration for kings," recalled one guest. Alexandre vowed to win his family battle.

The lawyers filed a total of twenty lawsuits on Lur-Saluces's behalf. They argued that under the terms of the document signed in 1968, Eugène shouldn't be able to sell any Yquem shares before obtaining Alexandre's permission. Arnault argued that the 1968 document carried no legal weight. "All the corporate documents drawn up and signed by Alexandre de Lur-Saluces show Eugène de Lur-Saluces as the owner of 48 percent of Yquem," he said. The judges would have to decide.

That could take months, if not years. During that time, Alexandre demanded that Yquem's capital be frozen. In March 1997, a commercial court in Bordeaux agreed. It allowed one-third of LVMH's purchase price to be paid out. The other two-thirds of the contested shares, Eugène's, the Hainguerlots, and even those of Alexandre's own children Isabeau and Philippe, remained in a blocked account, paying 2 percent interest per year. The sellers lost their votes on Yquem's board. Worse, they couldn't touch most of the money they expected to pocket from the sale to LVMH.

At Yquem's general assembly in June 1997, Alexandre emptied the estate's coffers and distributed $6 million in dividends. The payoff came after years when almost all the profits had been sunk into investments and shareholders had not received a cent. Now the count and his son Bertrand each received some $800,000 in cash. The Hainguerlots and other shareholders protested. Their dividends, as well as LVMH's, were placed in the frozen bank account. Alexandre had won round one.

BERNARD ARNAULT WAS FURIOUS. Although he owned a giant chunk of Yquem, because of the legal wrangling he could not set foot on the property. For a corporation with billions of dollars in sales, the Yquem investment was minor in financial terms, and yet it generated as much bad publicity as a billion-dollar deal gone wrong.

Throughout 1998 the lawsuits crawled through the French legal machinery. LVMH still was only a minority owner. Shares sold to it by Eugène, the Hainguerlots, and other minority owners remained blocked. Almost every day, Alexandre sent registered letters to Bertrand Hainguerlot demanding more information for the upcoming court trial. "I was bombarded," Hainguerlot said.

The Hainguerlots worried about a war of attrition. If the count could delay the day of reckoning, they feared LVMH and Arnault would give up and go away. Then Alexandre could buy out his family at a discount. Alexandre soon attempted a new maneuver to engineer a delay. Under French law, if a criminal charge was lodged, it would have to be resolved before any of the civil cases were even heard. Such a court procedure could drag out for years more.

Until now, lawyers drafted briefs and judges delivered their decisions in court papers. None of the legal battles pitted the protagonists face-to-face. But in December 1996, Alexandre instructed his lawyers to file a suit against "X"—which in French law is the equivalent to the American legal term "parties unknown"—for "abusing the weakness" of his brother. Five months later, the police summoned the seventy- six-year-old Marquis Eugène to Bordeaux to appear before the French equivalent of a grand jury. "When I received the summons to go to Bordeaux, I was overcome by shock," Eugène said. Soon, however, his shock was replaced by a compulsion to let the true story be known. He issued a press release on June 3, 1997. "My brother pretends that I was the victim of an abuse of weakness and that my signature was extorted," it began, referring to the signature required to sell to LVMH. "That is totally false. My brother, who owns only a small part of Yquem, is trying, against my will, to usurp all of my shares."

Alexandre had figured that his shy, retiring older brother would give up. Instead, Eugène went to Bordeaux. There he spoke with local journalists, including Didier Ters, the respected wine journalist for *Sud Ouest*.

The scenario was no longer Alexandre the Brave Knight against Bad Bernard the Raider. The press presented Alexandre as aloof, detached, pretentious, and stubborn. Bernard Arnault gave interviews extending a hand of friendship, but Alexandre refused to shake it. LVMH now took the offensive: the luxury group revealed how Alexandre had tried to buy Eugène's shares for a pittance during the early 1990s. "Alexandre de Lur-Saluces said his older brother Eugène is mentally incapacitated because he is selling out to LVMH for only $200 million," Ters commented in his column. "Eugène must be sane, even a smart businessman, to have refused because his brother Alexandre wanted him to cash out for ten times less." Ters revealed how even Alexandre's own son and daughter favored LVMH.

By now, Alexandre was frightened. His court case was weak. While he continued to argue that Eugène had agreed to divide Yquem with him in 1968 by creating a new company split fifty-fifty between the two brothers, the holding company created in 1992 made no mention of such a division. Eugène was listed in the corporate records as the sole owner of 48 percent of the shares. Worst of all for Alexandre, the Hainguerlots' lawyers discovered the $200,000 of Yquem funds spent on Madame Billé-Rode. Alexandre had filed criminal charges against LVMH in order to pressure his brother Eugène. The Hainguerlots were willing to do the same against their cousin. "We were zeroing in on him," Bertrand Hainguerlot said.

Arnault sensed the vulnerability. At the beginning of 1999, he flew to Bordeaux and met Alexandre at Château de Fargues. The two men talked. Alexandre demanded that Arnault sell his shares. Arnault replied that he had invested only because Alexandre's relatives had approached him. He wasn't a raider. He was an investor who would save Yquem. As proof of his goodwill, he offered again to let Alexandre stay on as president. "We weren't the aggressors in this affair and we tried to explain that to Alexandre," said Pierre Gode, who was also present at the meeting. And though the count still wouldn't budge, the mere fact that he agreed to the meeting showed that his resolve was wavering.

Arnault kept up the pressure. He invited leading Bordeaux estate owners to Paris for elaborate lunches and asked advice on dealing with Alexandre. Jean-Michel Cazes attended one and came away impressed. "Arnault convinced us he didn't want to change how Yquem was made or to produce an Yquem perfume," said Cazes. In comparison to Cazes's own bosses, the insurance company AXA, or to the pension fund buyers of Château Lascombes, both of which were financial operators seeking a good investment, Arnault was a luxury operator looking for an image enhancement.

Cazes listened and told Arnault he would talk with Alexandre. "I understood that Alexandre could be arrogant, so I played to his arrogance," he said. "I told Alexandre that Arnault wouldn't be interested except that Yquem was such a symbol of excellence." If Alexandre wanted guarantees, Cazes told him he would get them. Cazes and other Bordelais became tougher on Alexandre. They told him that Arnault wouldn't go away. With all the bad publicity he was generating, Alexandre would end up damaging Yquem's reputation, the reputation he was supposedly defending. "The battle had to come to an end, for the good of Yquem," Cazes said.

Finally, Alexandre approached Arnault, ready to concede defeat—on certain conditions. He wanted a premium on his 7 percent and his son Bertrand's 2 percent of the Yquem shares. Family members say the bonus demanded was up to 40 percent higher than that received by other shareholders. Alexandre also wanted revenge. Under the original deal signed in 1996, Eugène and other family members were guaranteed a number of seats on Yquem's board and a say in the management. In their own minds, the marquis and the other family members were selling but keeping a minority 35 percent stake in order to ensure the Lur-Saluces legacy. But Alexandre said he would never sell if Eugène and the others retained these rights. He demanded that Eugène and the other shareholders be barred from the estate. Arnault agreed.

ON APRIL 19, 1999, Bernard Arnault and Pierre Gode boarded the LVMH corporate jet and flew to Bordeaux. It was raining. The two businessmen stepped right into a limousine and sped off to Yquem. Alexandre greeted the victors graciously. A catered lunch was served. For dessert, as a peace offering, the count chose one of the rarest bottles in his cellar, an 1899. All three men raised their glasses and toasted. "You could taste the entire century in your mouth," recalled Gode.

The count now went to work for his former enemy as a simple employee, though one with a grandiose title. "I fought to save this jewel, but my family betrayed me," he said afterward.

The Hainguerlots and Marquis Eugène were dissatisfied. Having been barred from the estate, they would no longer receive invitations to parties there or discounted cases of Yquem. Although this may seem a relatively petty annoyance considering all that went on, it grated. And there was nothing they could do about it. At least they received their money from LVMH and could be happy that the battle was over. "It wasn't the outcome we hoped for, but at least calm was restored," said Bertrand Hainguerlot. Eugène was less philosophical. Alexandre kept pursuing his suit to obtain half his older brother's inheritance and the legal wrangling was ongoing in 2003. "The dragon still wants to slay me," an angry Eugène complained.

LVMH assured Alexandre that he could stay on as Yquem's president as long as he liked. The count's excessive entertaining? "We are used to spending a lot on publicity and the press," Gode replied. His poor marketing? "We will correct the problem," Gode said. Yquem's economic health? "The return on investment isn't as high as with Louis Vuitton handbags," he admitted. LVMH doesn't care. Yquem is "like *haute couture* for the fashion industry," Gode insisted. "He cultivates a culture of excellence in the group and that's all we care about."

Not even the potential time bomb of 750,000 bottles of unsold wine stored in the estate's cellars worried Gode. If Yquem's scarcity needed to be retained by artificial means, so be it. LVMH wouldn't lower prices to sell off the stock. "We won't put 100,000 extra bottles out on the market all of a sudden because we don't need cash," Gode said. His plan instead was to reduce the inventory slowly, selling a few thousand bottles of old vintages a year. The strategy pleased Alexandre. After denouncing Arnault and LVMH as the devil incarnate, he praised them as Yquem's savior. "Bernard Arnault understands this is a jewel to be protected," Alexandre said in late 2001. "I was wrong to suspect him." He was much less tender about his own family: "My family was motivated by childish jealousy," he said.

Wine lovers were left with a glass of uncertainty. Traditionalists wondered whether they would be drinking the same Yquem in the future. Would the count, pushed by his new corporate owners, seek to sell them what they considered a substandard elixir? Modernists such as Jeffrey Davies wanted a fruitier nectar. In their view, Alexandre's wine was old-fashioned and too heavy.

The debate erupted over the 2000 harvest. When the count went ahead and released 20,000 bottles of the millennium vintage in the summer of 2001 despite the storms of October 2000 that had damaged much of the crop, LVMH insisted it had remained hands-off. "We left the entire decision to Alexandre because we know that he is the ultimate guarantor of Yquem's quality," said Gode.

Bordeaux's merchants weren't allowed to taste the elixir and were nervous about buying it. Yquem's brokers phoned Jean-Marie Chadronnier of Compagnie des Vins de Bordeaux et la Gironde two to three times a day, demanding he take his annual quota of Yquem. Chadronnier had made a fortune reselling the millennium year's top red wines at two to three times the release price. But his business in sweet white wines was struggling. "You need to be heroic to sell Sauternes," he complained. "While it's extraordinary, people don't know when to drink it and with what food. The image is outdated." Chadronnier hesitated. He sent out feelers to his customers. They were lukewarm. The brokers kept telephoning.

One afternoon, Yves Bénard, head of LVMH's drinks division, called Chadronnier and personally asked him to take his quota of Yquem. By this time, the merchant was tired of the harassment. "Get Alexandre's dogs off my back," he told Bénard.

But Chadronnier feared upsetting the powerful luxury group. After several more days of reflection, he went ahead and ordered his consignment of Yquem. Even if LVMH could twist some of the Bordeaux merchants' arms, rot was in the air. The giant multinational was finding change easier to enact elsewhere in Bordeaux.

—

CHAPTER 12

Harvest Hurdles

DOZENS OF WORKERS SWARMED ABOUT CHÂTEAU CHEVAL BLANC, Bernard Arnault's other Bordeaux trophy. No garish Left Bank architecture here: the Right Bank institution is a sober complex of one- and two-story buildings surrounded by vineyards. The residence is a simple, square manor house with a wrought-iron portico entrance. Workers were gutting it, and the worn stone floors were already ripped up. Alongside the house the workers were creating a grand reception area out of the former workers' kitchen and harvesters' dining room. "We're sparing no expense," said Michel Gracia, reflecting on the overhaul of the château Arnault had ordered.

More than a decade before, Gracia had rebuilt Cheval Blanc's cellar and office. Now he was responsible for repairing the stonework in the new renovation. Instead of putting in new-looking floors, he wanted to preserve the original ambience. At first he tried to find old stone. When that proved impossible, he came up with a solution: a secret mix of varnishes and stains that made new stones resemble centuries-old tiles. "Michel's the most expensive stonemason in all of Bordeaux, but we chose him because he's an artist," said Gilles Lamerent, the project's architect.

Gracia likes to take visitors for a walk through Saint-Emilion, pointing out his village's medieval splendor. Midway up the village's hill, when he reaches the Monolithic Church, Gracia explains that he renovated one of the original stone front doors. Another mason did the other.

"Which is my work?" he asks his guests.

It seems impossible to tell the difference. Both look impeccable, the stone burnished with love, complete with intricate scrollwork. On closer inspection, though, one door appears a bit cleaner, its color more uniform. The other is slightly crooked, with spots suggesting wear. Most potential customers guess that Gracia made the sleeker, shinier one.

*Harvesters on the Médoc peninsula rush
to bring in grapes in September 2001.*

"Wrong!" the mason says, delighted. "The goal is to make the renovation blend in with the original, to give the piece patina, not to smooth it over."

When Bernard Arnault bought Cheval Blanc in 1998, his purchase could have degenerated into a struggle similar to that over Château d'Yquem. Cheval Blanc had twenty-nine relatives sharing ownership and squabbling over what investments needed to be made. In this case, director and family leader Jacques Hébrard, bitter though he was, decided early on they had no choice but to sell.

Arnault moved fast to make his mark at Cheval Blanc, replacing director Hébrard with a seasoned professional named Pierre Lurton. While the thirty-nine-year-old Lurton was part of an old Bordeaux winemaking family, he was hungry and ambitious. His only inheritance was a small estate called Château Marjosse in the Entre-Deux-Mers. There, Lurton built a shiny steel and glass winery and turned it into a commercial success story, signing up Jeffrey Davies to distribute his wine. Davies, in turn, presented Marjosse to Parker and won a "Best Buy" recommendation. At Cheval Blanc, Lurton hired a geologist to plot the character of the land and make sure that the appropriate varietals were planted in the appropriate places. He reduced yields and began harvesting later. The quality of Cheval Blanc's wines improved. Parker, whose encounter with Hébrard and his dog in 1989 resulted in his upward revision, gave the 2000 Cheval Blanc one of the highest ratings of the year, 98+.

The château's marketing received a similar face-lift. Lurton fired Cheval Blanc's old brokers and withdrew allocations from more than half of its longtime merchants. "You have to bring in new blood and open up the market in order to get the best distribution," he said. The price of a bottle of Cheval Blanc was soaring, reaching $250 wholesale in 2000. That might still be less than Yquem, but unlike the Sauternes estate, Cheval Blanc had no trouble finding buyers.

From a distance, Lurton watched with horror the developments at Yquem. He couldn't understand how Alexandre de Lur-Saluces could have refused to modernize either the estate's winemaking or its marketing. He knew Sauternes was a hard sell, but he thought that some dynamism could be restored if Lur-Saluces became less haughty and worked together with the other winemakers. "Yquem must become a locomotive for the rest of the *appellation*," he said. "Right now, it's detached from the rest of the rail cars."

While Arnault, out of fear of provoking poor press, allowed Lur-Saluces to go his own way at Yquem, he paid more attention to Cheval Blanc. One sign was the ambitious $1.2 million renovation. "After they finish the reception building and the château, Arnault's also thinking of redoing the cellar," Gracia said. Arnault and Lurton wanted the current work finished by the following March so merchants and journalists could be hosted in style at the annual spring tasting. The rushed schedule worried Gracia. It was now September 25, and sometime in the next few days he wanted to stop work to harvest his grapes. Some of his construction workers were scheduled to double as his harvesters.

"You've got to keep them working at Cheval Blanc," said architect Lamerent.

"*Putain!*" exclaimed Gracia with his usual mixture of excitement and incredulity. "When I did the first renovation, we never had so much pressure."

FOR YVES VATELOT, his Right Bank baby, Château de Reignac, could pretty much take care of itself, but at Château Lascombes the harvest was not quite going according to plan.

On September 28, pickers were out in the vineyards by 8 A.M. across Bordeaux. They began moving down the rows of vines in pairs. Since the grapes were clustered below the leaves, and only two to three feet above the ground, they had to stoop and squat to cut.

Click, click went the music of their scissors, accompanied by the murmur of low conversation. The grapes fell into gentle hands and were placed in the baskets. A burst of occasional laughter broke the monotony of hard work.

Around Bordeaux, almost all of the Sauvignon Blanc and Sémillon white wine grapes had already been picked. The Merlot was now mature and growers on both the Right and Left Banks were rushing to beat the onset of gray rot. Only the late-ripening Cabernet Sauvignon required more time. At Lascombes, about four dozen harvesters, a mixture of young housewives, students, and retirees, all united by the prospect of earning a

230 · *William Echikson*

few extra francs—$7 an hour—were busy bringing in the more precocious Merlot. "The Cabernet's one hell of a constipated grape," said Vatelot. "It only really gets ripe around here three years in ten."

On most estates, even the most prestigious on the Médoc peninsula, men strap plastic tubs called *hottes* on their backs and follow behind the female cutters. They are termed *porteurs*—carriers. When the cutters fill their baskets—a quick process, two, three vines and it is done—carriers come up behind them and receive the load. Soon, their *hottes* full, the *porteurs* struggle to the end of the row of vines. There, they pour their load into large bins that are pulled by tractor to the cellar.

If it is hard to hire harvesters to cut grapes, it is almost impossible to find the *porteurs*. Young mothers and retirees are good for cutting grapes. But they struggle to carry them. "We can't get men," lamented Dominique Befve. "The work is just too backbreaking." This system is also hard on the grapes. Each *hotte* holds some sixty pounds of grapes, and when these are poured into the larger bins, many of the berries are crushed.

The general manager was determined to bring in clean, unblemished grapes. He decided to adopt the same system at Lascombes that Vatelot had successfully developed at Reignac. Vatelot fitted a trailer, resembling an M-shaped sculpture fashioned from bed frames that straddled the vines so that it could be towed down the rows by a tractor of similar design. Using this deceptively simple contraption, pickers could now place their crates directly onto this specially designed trailer, eliminating the need for the *porteur* and his *hotte*. But more importantly, this technique meant that the plastic crates, each containing twenty-five pounds or so of grapes, could be quickly and easily stacked on top of each other without bruising the fruit. It also meant that the grapes could be more quickly towed to the winery, where the fruit of each lug was then poured onto sorting tables.

For this year's harvest, Vatelot bought hundreds of new plastic crates and several new tractors with their "crate-trailers." But to his dismay, the new tractors were too large to drive through the narrow rows of vineyards. Harvesting ground to a halt for a few days beginning on September 20. Extra pickers and *porteurs* needed to be hired and the crates carried much further to the tractors stationed at the edge of the rows. Eventually the tractors were adjusted and fit.

The newly refurbished cellar, though fully powered, was not quite completed. Only a temporary floor had been laid down, and the roof wasn't finished. When it rained, water poured down on top of the workers handling fruit, and since the drains weren't all installed, puddles formed on the cellar floor. "We'll have to wait until after the harvest is over before tackling those problems," Vatelot admitted. Fortunately, the electrician had satisfied his insistence on installing extra circuits so the cooling system was up and running.

When the harvested fruit arrived, the new cargo elevator took it in the crates to the third floor, where a dozen workers stood around the two sets of parallel sorting tables. A first sorting table, little more than a slow-moving conveyor belt, was positioned ahead of the destemmer. Carefully observing each passing cluster, the cellar workers discarded any unripe, damaged, or moldy berries, as well as stray green leaves and small bits of stems. After going through the destemmer, the individual berries rolled onto a second, vibrating sorting table, where it was easier to spot and remove any suspicious fruit and vegetal detritus. Another conveyor belt then carried the individually hand-sorted berries above the fermentation tanks. In Burgundy, where the delicate Pinot Noir grape dominates, some winemakers still retain a portion of the stems in the fermentation vats, believing that these will give the wine added structure. In Bordeaux, the Merlot and Cabernet Sauvignon are heartier and thicker-skinned and winemakers remove all the stems to eliminate the potential green or bitter flavors. Removing vegetal detritus and unripe or unhealthy berries promised to be more important than ever in the 2001 vintage. The rains in May and June had caused buds to shatter. Grapes from the same vine ripened unevenly or not at all. These needed to be discarded if the wine was to be a success.

Throwing out grapes raised tensions at many estates, particularly between generations. At the Raynauds' Château La Croix de Gay, Alain's mother cried every evening after the harvesters left.

"Look how many grapes they left on the ground," Geneviève moaned.

"But, Mother, you can't keep thinking like that," Raynaud reminded her. "If we used that fruit, it would ruin the wine."

"It's a little like the TV show *Dallas* here," added his teary-eyed sister Chantal. "I fear my mother's temper tantrums more than a devastating rainstorm."

At Lascombes, Befve struggled to convince many of the harvesters to leave unripe bunches on the vine. "They want to bring everything in," he reported. At the same time, his bosses Vatelot and Raynaud worried that Befve might be going too far. Their green harvesting was planned to reduce yields by about 40 percent. Now nature was being ungenerous and they probably would end up well below their already low target.

How best to put the ripe grapes into the fermentation tank is another subject of dispute. In most cellars, harvested grapes are destemmed, crushed, and violently pumped up into fermentation tanks. At Lascombes, with the new cargo elevator and sorting tables in place and grapes lowered by gravity, no pumping was needed. "We're treating the fruit like a precious baby," marveled Vatelot. Many longtime workers couldn't understand why grapes, so bountiful, needed to be pampered like a newborn. They resisted the extreme methods. General manager Befve found it necessary to stand guard at the head of the conveyor belt. He often stopped it to show sorters how to recognize and remove bruised fruit and any green stems. "You always have to be looking over their shoulder," he complained.

Similar conflicts erupted over how to conduct pumpover, or *remontage,* the process of pumping the juice up and over the thick cap of skins in order to extract tannins. Until recently, this punching down was done by hand. Machines do most of the work these days, pumping juice over the hard skins until they are submerged and break. Lascombes's longtime cellar master just wanted to press the button of a pump that did the work automatically. This was not good enough for Befve. He wanted someone to make sure that the pumps were running correctly, that they were breaking the cap gently. Many times, Befve himself turned on the pumps and controlled them manually. But the cellar master refused, saying the automatic system had worked in the past and was good enough for the present. "It's always a fight to get the workers around here to change," Befve complained.

The general manager pondered whether to fire the recalcitrant cellar master. In the end, he decided against the radical measure, fearing the move might spark a full-scale revolt among other workers. "It's a rotten atmosphere around here: everyone is a cousin and they will stick together against you," said Befve.

Indeed, strikes were becoming more and more common in the Médoc. A few days earlier, harvesters had threatened to walk out at Lynch-Bages. They arrived at 8 A.M. as required. Around noon, however, it started raining.

"Go home, we're not going to pick anymore today," said the estate's general manager.

"We're not coming back tomorrow unless you pay us for the afternoon," replied one of the workers. Jean-Michel Cazes was soon alerted to the simmering crisis. When he arrived, he found the workers sitting outside the front door. Some were getting angry. As the owner, he relented and paid the workers. "In retrospect, I could sympathize with their request," he admitted.

At Lascombes, Befve avoided such a crisis. But his patience was tried. All his workers insisted on leaving the cellar at 5:30 P.M. Their eight hours were over and that's all they would work, even if it was still light out and every minute of good weather was precious to bringing in ripe grapes before they rotted. Almost every harvest day, Befve said, he ended up staying till midnight, sorting the berries by himself and making sure all of them were put carefully into the fermentation tanks.

Time, he feared, was running short. When it rained at Lynch-Bages in Pauillac a few days before, it remained dry eight miles south in Margaux. "We've been lucky: some of our neighbors have suffered four times more precipitation than we have," Befve said. The extra precipitation caused the grapes to swell and spread rot—gray, not noble—forcing growers to speed things up. Workers at Bordeaux's main weather station chose September 28, at the crucial phase of the harvest, to go out on strike. More rain could fall at any time. Befve figured he had only a couple more days before gray rot set in at Lascombes.

IN CONTRAST TO THE morose Médoc, Sauternes was cheering. Pickers were out in Yquem's vineyards on September 20, one of the chateau's earliest harvest openings on record. During the entire twentieth century, harvesting had begun before the third week of September only four times. Each morning during harvesttime, Yquem's production manager, Francis Mayeur, arrived at 7 A.M., checked the weather, and made a quick tour to see how much fruit was ready to be harvested. Mayeur is Alexandre's right-hand man. He is trim, dark-haired, efficient, and quiet enough to work in Alexandre's large shadow. After Pierre Meslier's departure back in 1990, Mayeur, then in his early thirties, was appointed in his place.

Over the previous decade, even before LVMH assumed ownership, a number of staff changes took place. Yves Laporte, the vineyard manager, served in his post for more than four decades. When he retired, Antoine Depierre replaced him. Guy Latrille, a stocky man with an owl-like face, worked as cellar master for about forty years before turning over his post in the late 1990s to the striking Sandrine Garbay, who in 2001 was only thirty-five years old. "There was already a woman who directed Yquem, my ancestor Françoise-Joséphine," Lur-Saluces said. Even before Garbay assumed her position, he noted, half of Yquem's staff members were women.

Through the end of September and into early October 2001, the full 150-person contingent was called to Yquem almost every day. Rain fell from September 20 to 25, accelerating the development of noble rot. Even when it drizzled, the full team came. So far, the rain hadn't bloated the fruit.

Yquem's Sauvignon Blanc vines, located at the top of the hill near the château, were the first to mature. Next comes the capricious Sémillon. It is the dominant grape in Sauternes—almost 80 percent of Yquem's vines are planted with this varietal. Sémillon ripens and rots in less regular fashion than the Sauvignon Blanc. And yet by the beginning of October, the harvesters had moved down Yquem's hill toward the Ciron River to pick the Sémillon.

The open question with every harvest is how fast to proceed. Generations divide over the issue. Yquem's choice is clear: continue at the treasured, measured pace. Accelerating the harvest risks bringing in imperfect grapes. It means hiring more workers. It upsets the traditional rhythm.

At other estates, the answer isn't so clear. At Doisy-Daëne in 2001, patriarch Pierre Dubourdieu voted to go slowly because he feared not being able to process a quantity of grapes that looked to be greater than anticipated initially. His grandson Fabrice, Denis's son, disagreed. A student in enology at the University of Bordeaux, he was helping out for the harvest. He wanted to call in more workers and pick up the pace. "Nature is giving us a real break and we must use it to the maximum," he argued.

In Doisy-Daëne's cellars, new, still-fermenting wine soon was ready for a preliminary tasting. Workers filled small plastic casks with some of the fermenting juice and cut a hole in the top to let out the gas. Otherwise, the gas generated by the fermenting grapes would trigger a small explosion. Three- to four-day-old juice, which looked cloudy and troubled, tasted like tangy grapefruit nectar. Locals drink it to accompany grilled chestnuts.

"Don't drink too much, though," warned Pierre Dubourdieu.

It wasn't that the alcohol went to the head or created a nasty hangover.

"It's an incredible laxative," Dubourdieu said.

SHORT-LIVED BUT STILL brutal thundershowers struck around Bordeaux on October 3. That evening, the weather turned cold. The next day, it heated up. For Sauternes growers, this weather represented good news. Noble rot continued to spread.

For the last holdouts among makers of red wines, though, the fickle weather was a red flag: harvest quickly or risk a ruined crop. Many would have liked to wait a few more days for the Cabernet Sauvignon to ripen, but they couldn't risk it. "The situation is explosive, we're playing with fire," said Remy Fouin, owner of Château Belle-Vue, a small Left Bank estate a few miles south of Château Lascombes. Thundershowers hit both Belle-Vue and Lascombes. Vatelot ordered that some Cabernet Sauvignon be discarded. The quantity of fruit picked would be even smaller than expected—a full 50 percent less than the year before.

In Sauveterre, Rémi Garuz pushed and pushed his growers to hold off bringing in the still underripe, bitter Cabernet. In the end, he relented and the harvest was finished by October 17. The entire process took only four weeks, compared to five the year before. "It's a decent harvest, but not exceptional like 2000," he judged.

In Saint-Emilion, Michel Gracia waited until the last possible moment. His vineyards are located not on clay but on stony soil at the cooler northern limits of Saint-Emilion. Fruit grown there requires more time to mature than in the *appellation*'s southern areas dominated by clay. And Gracia believes in pushing for maximum maturity. He is fortunate to enjoy flexibility with his harvest crew—they are his own construction workers, after all, and they stay on the same payroll whether out in the vineyards picking grapes or at a building site. His acreage is small, too, which means he enjoys the flexibility of being able to decide in the morning whether to harvest or not, or to call off the picking and return to his current construction site. Even with such stops and starts, Gracia gets all his fruit off the vines and into the cellar within two days, though the two days may be spread over several weeks of picking. Compared to the supertanker Lascombes and other Médoc estates, his operation runs like a nimble yacht.

On October 11, Gracia finally swung into action. He abandoned the Cheval Blanc construction site for the day and sent his team of workers to his vineyards. Across the street from his garage winery, outdoors under a makeshift roof, he set up the receiving station. More than a dozen workers stood ready at the sorting tables. Gracia's younger daughter, Marina, was among them. His older daughter, Caroline, was spending the harvest in California, learning about New World winemaking techniques.

Gracia's number two was Marina's former boyfriend, Ludovic Pochard.

The fresh-faced, ebullient twenty-six-year-old had spent the previous year in Australia, working for Rosemount Estate. The experience shocked him. Winemaking in Australia goes against every grain of Bordeaux's new thinking. Yields are high. Harvesting is by machine, with lots of stems and leaves left in the juice. Then grapes are shipped hundreds of miles in refrigerated trucks, where enologists intervene to correct the wine with viper juice and oak chips.

But Pochard acknowledged the system's advantages. The weather is consistently hot, with almost no rain during the harvest season. Irrigation means vines receive plenty of moisture to ripen. Because grapes can be shipped from all around the country, a bad harvest in one area can be discarded. Grapes are picked at high sugar levels, up to 14 percent. If the fruit lacks acid, it can be added in the cellar. The result, Pochard conceded, is a consistent quaffable product.

What Australia lacks is the handcrafted purity of Bordeaux's best. At Gracia's garage when the grapes come in, bunches are placed on the sorting table. Even at top Bordeaux estates, the action moves quickly and workers rush to take off the stray leaves and stems, but leave the bunch whole. Not here. The workers pick up each individual cluster and take off each grape, one by one. Then they put them in sifters. Gracia got the idea from his construction work, where he shakes out impurities in limestone. Here he does the same with fruit, using a fine sifter to gently remove bits of stems and leaves too hard to be picked out by hand.

The stonemason was in a good mood. Eighteen merchants had approached him about distributing his latest vintage. They sensed that Gracia had an inside track to a good Parker rating. They had already witnessed how Thunevin's Château de Valandraud had exploded upon the world market, and they didn't want to miss the next opportunity to rake in a garage Big Buck. Since fewer than 7,000 bottles of Gracia were going to be produced this year, Jeffrey Davies was becoming concerned that he wouldn't get his full allocation.

With three years of successful vintages behind him and his daughters wishing to carry on when he no longer can, Gracia's passion was beginning to look like a serious occupation. On building contracts, he is one of several bidders—business is cyclical as well as tough. During the recession of the early 1990s, his firm struggled. He fired workers and cut margins. The last few years of the century were much better as the French economy swelled in the global upturn. But building is nothing like the Internet or telecom—or the Bordeaux wine bubble. Here, Gracia doesn't bid. Bidders come to him. Plus, the margins on wine are two to three times higher than in construction. If he could increase production the following year, it would mean more profit since the additional fixed costs were minimal. Best of all, wine remained fun. The workers' motivation wasn't money as much as having a good time. Lunch was a boisterous, jolly affair. Hams, salamis, and pâtés were spread out on one table. Cheeses were in plentiful supply, too, everything from a pungent Roquefort to a creamy Camembert and a hard Comté. Everyone laughed. This was construction work without the heavy lifting.

The harvest was coming to a close throughout Bordeaux. On October 21, it poured once again. Yquem's workers were put on hold. But Alexandre de Lur-Saluces wasn't worried. The vast majority of Yquem's grapes were already in the cellar. A short pause would let the workers take a needed break and allow the noble rot to continue developing on the remaining fruit. Work picked up again on October 23. The harvesters made their third, fourth, and fifth passes through the vineyards. On October 25, Yquem's 2001 harvest ended. It had taken only twenty-one days spread over six weeks. The number of passes through the vineyard was average—in 1964 pickers had gone eleven separate times through the same parcels in an effort to find the perfect mold-infected fruit. Rarely had a harvest finished so early. In a typical year, it stretched out at least through mid-November.

For Bordeaux's red wine, the 2001 vintage promised a relatively small amount of terrific wine for the hardest-working and most discriminating producers. For Yquem and the rest of Sauternes, the 2001 vintage looked set to be much more generous.

—

CHAPTER 13

Cellar Time

ONCE THE HARVEST WAS FINISHED, PREPARATIONS BEGAN FOR All Souls' Day, the Roman Catholic day commemorating the dead celebrated on November 2. Florists promoted pots of chrysanthemums to be placed at family graves. *Sud Ouest* reported that the shops sold an average of 30 million flowers each year.

The newspaper also described a colorful new phenomenon imported from the United States—Halloween. Carrefour and other hypermarkets stocked bright masks and electrically lit pumpkins. Two nights before visiting her grandparents' graves, Alain Raynaud's eight-year-old daughter, Marie, dressed up as a witch and went trick-or-treating. Some French decried the commercial desecration of their religious tradition. "This is the third or fourth year that we suffer from Halloween and I still can't get used to it," complained one M. C. Ferrey in a letter to the editor of *Sud Ouest*. "It's impossible to put one's foot inside a hypermarket without seeing one of those pathetic scenes of a ravishing little child convincing his mother to offer him the mask with the scrofulous scars. Pathetic!" Ferry lamented that it was impossible to protest against what he called "the Halloween horror" without being called "an ill-tempered peevish Catholic" or "a first degree anti-American."

The weather in Bordeaux usually turns gray and dreary for the holiday, but in 2001 a beautiful sunshine burst forth. In the fields, the vines turned golden. Children were out of school and many families took the holiday, even the week, off, to go to the beach.

During the vacation week, Michel Rolland was working. Action at wine estates moved from the vineyards to the cellars: it was a key time to check if the primary, or alcoholic, fermentation was finished and the wine was ready to be run off into tanks or new oak barrels for the secondary, or malolactic, fermentation. Since not all of his customers can afford 100 percent new barrels every year, Rolland suggests which lots of wine will go into new barrels and which into older ones. New oak imparts a strong toasted flavor and sweetness to the wine; wine aged in old oak has a less pronounced, more neutral taste.

At 7 A.M. one day that week, the Flying Winemaker was already in the front passenger seat of his black Mercedes sedan. While he was out consulting, his wife, Dany, stayed behind to run the enology laboratory and supply store, now located in Pomerol. The lab looks like a hospital pathology department, complete with microscopes and Pyrex measuring devices. Technicians dress in clinical white jackets. The store sells wine accoutrements—decanters, corkscrews, glasses—plus a wide selection of winemaking devices such as pumps, barrels, and tanks.

Rolland's Mercedes headed west on the highway from Libourne to Bordeaux. A chauffeur drove. "Otherwise, the police would be after me all the time—with reason," Rolland admitted, explaining, "I taste a lot." Rolland was wearing his work uniform—a dapper double-breasted blue suit—looking more like the CEO of a multinational firm than a man tied to the land. A full day in the Médoc was scheduled, with visits to ten different châteaux including Lascombes, where he was looking forward to seeing his old friends Raynaud, Vatelot, and Befve.

"We need to start early or we could spend hours in traffic jams," Rolland said. The Mercedes sped toward Bordeaux and over the Aquitaine Bridge to the Left Bank. Traffic was light. Rolland had beaten the rush hour. About forty minutes after leaving his home near Libourne, he arrived in Margaux. His first visit was scheduled for 8 A.M., so he stopped at a village café for a jolt of espresso. "I need some coffee to wake up my taste buds," he said.

He drank standing up at the bar and picked up the day's *Sud Ouest*, which was lying on the counter. Didier Ters reported on the vintage in

CHÂTEAU LASCOMBES

*Château Lascombes had a grand appearance
but its winery required renovation.*

sweet wines in his weekly wine column. "This will be a great year in Sauternes," Ters predicted. Even in a bad year, Rolland said, he can salvage enough fruit to create an acceptable red wine. At Yquem or another Sauternes château, the vintage would be lost. The news didn't stimulate Rolland's thirst because the enologist doesn't consult in Sauternes. "You are really a slave to nature with sweet white wines, and I don't like being a slave," he explained. "With red wines I can massage things—man plays a large role."

Rolland prefers California, Chile, South Africa, and of course his home, the Bordeaux Right Bank, to the Médoc. "This is the place where my message was the hardest to get across," he lamented. "It's so traditional: if you tell the Médocains that they let their vines be too prolific, they will run you out of town. They will say nature was generous and then blame nature when their wines are diluted." But the enologist loves a challenge and changing the Médoc mentality certainly represents one.

CHÂTEAU MOUTON ROTHSCHILD

In November, action in Bordeaux moves underground to cellars such as this one at Mouton-Rothschild.

At 8 A.M., the chauffeur parked Rolland's Mercedes in front of Margaux's Château Kirwan, a third growth that had fallen on hard times but was climbing its way back. The merchant house Schröder & Schÿler, of German origin and one of the proudest names on the Quai des Chartrons, bought Kirwan in 1926. Through the 1950s, the merchants had little money to invest. The estate became run down. In the early 1990s, Parker was scathing about Kirwan, calling it "another Margaux estate that would have a hard time holding its position in Bordeaux's 1855 classification." He described the 1991 Kirwan as "light, dull and bland" and gave it a pitiful 77 score.

During the 1990s, a new generation of Schÿlers began to renovate Kirwan and one of their first moves was to hire Rolland. Kirwan is a typical patient for Rolland, who prefers to take on underperformers and shies away from first-growth stars. "Myths refuse to change, because they are so steeped in history," Rolland explained. Without man's active intervention, Kirwan would remain an austere wine. "I try to add richness, roundness," Rolland said. When critics argue that this objective masks each estate's individuality, the enologist becomes incensed. "People who say that we don't respect *terroir* are being mean, defending old wines, bad wines, weak wines, weedy wines," he responded. Even in the United States, Rolland believes, French ideas of *terroir* are making a comeback. Whereas the goal was once to make uniform wines, now Napa Valley winemakers are talking about how the grapes grown on the hills turn out different from the ones on the plains, how the western side of the valley benefits from more sun in the morning than do the eastern slopes.

Rolland's touch soon revolutionized Kirwan. In 1997, a poor vintage, Parker rated Kirwan 87+ and described it as exhibiting an "impressively saturated dark purple color, as well as an elegant, sweet, moderately intense blackberry fruit and spice-scented bouquet, medium body, moderate tannin, and very good length."

When he arrived at Kirwan, Rolland avoided the château's grand reception rooms and headed straight to the cellar. Twelve bottles of wine were lined up on a long wooden table in the center of the room. They were divided into different grape types, Merlot, Cabernet Sauvignon, and Petit Verdot. Family representative Nathalie Schÿler and technical director Philippe Mottes greeted the guru.

"Let's start with the Merlot," Rolland suggested.

Madame Schÿler began pouring samples into large-bowled Riedel wineglasses, the beautiful Austrian crystal that is an industry standard. All of the juice had been fermented in stainless steel tanks. Some of the new wine would go into new barrels for its malolactic fermentation, the rest into tanks or older barrels. "We didn't have as much sun this year as last, so the grapes aren't as rich or weighty as in 2000," she said. "In these thin years, we need to use more new oak to give the wine a little extra oomph."

Despite the early hour, Rolland put the first half-full glass of Merlot to his nose, then to his mouth, spitting the wine out after he tasted it. He made no comment until he'd finished seven samples. "That tastes nice," he said reassuringly. More than the words, his smile conveyed a sense of encouragement. His professional manner combines diplomacy and psychology. During the entire day of tasting, he never criticized. He always praised and suggested.

Although the enologist jotted a few notes on a small pad, his approach was not academic or pedantic. He carried no computer in which to record data. "There is little you can measure here by scientific analysis," he explained. "You have to judge by tasting." Almost as soon as he finished spitting out the Merlot samples, he rendered his verdict. "Number one, fermentation finished. It could use a new wood barrel in order to make it rounder." Number two still was austere. Number three was good enough only to go into an older barrel. "It won't suffer much there," Rolland assured. Numbers six and seven required more time. Rolland proceeded with the same exercise for Kirwan's Petit Verdot and Cabernet Sauvignon, tasting a total of nineteen different lots. While judging, he charmed Madame Schÿler with a discussion of his recent hunting trip in the Sologne, in the Loire Valley, where the kings and princes of France had hosted their shooting parties.

By 8:45, only three-quarters of an hour after arriving, Rolland was ready to move on. He made an appointment to return the following week to decide where to age the still unfinished Petit Verdot and Cabernet Sauvignon. He headed toward Château Prieuré-Lichine, the property Yves Vatelot briefly considered investing in when he was looking for a Médoc estate. It had become prominent as the home of Alexis Lichine, the world-famous wine writer and wine promoter. Lichine was Russian by birth, American by adoption, and French by preference. His parents fled to Paris at the onset of the Russian Revolution, taking with them the then four-year-old child. He was a born salesman, and as a teenager began working for the *International Herald Tribune*. After Prohibition was abolished, he moved to New York and worked with the U.S. wine merchant and writer Frank Schoonmaker. During the war, he used his fluent French to arrange the wine list for General Eisenhower. After the war, he set up his own wine import business and decided that in Bordeaux a little American money could go a long way.

In 1951 Lichine bought Prieuré, at the time called Château Prieuré-Cantenac. It was a fourth growth in 1855, but absentee ownership and inept management had turned it into a run-down vineyard. True to its name, the property came with an uninhabitable house, built in the sixteenth century as a Benedictine priory. There were thirty-two acres in all, a patchwork scattered all over the Margaux *appellation*. Lichine bought more land, ending up with 170 acres, and renamed the estate in his own honor. He quadrupled the size of the cellars, built a handsome tasting room, and, almost unique in Bordeaux, welcomed tourists. Billboards along the road out of Bordeaux announced that Prieuré-Lichine was open for tours and the visitors' room offered T-shirts, corkscrews, and other souvenirs. The commercialism shocked Médoc's traditionalist elite. Lichine wrote best-selling books about wine, fulminating against the injustices of the 1855 classification. And he continued his profitable merchant business. "Lichine certainly was an innovator in marketing," said Rolland. "Problem was, he certainly was not an innovator in making wine."

Parker rated Lichine's 1982 vintage a catastrophic 74, saying, "It exhibited considerable dilution and seemed disjointed." In 1989 Lichine died and his flamboyant son, Sacha Lichine, then a wine merchant living in Boston, took over the estate and hired Rolland. But the enologist admitted his efforts had been hit-or-miss. In 1999 he put the estate up for sale. When Vatelot and his backers chose Lascombes instead, French investors stepped in and bought Prieuré-Lichine. Rolland now hoped he would have more funding and freedom to produce a top-flight wine.

At 9:01, Rolland's Mercedes rolled into Prieuré-Lichine's graveled courtyard. Once again, Rolland eschewed the main reception area, heading straight into the cellar and the tasting room. There, twenty-nine glasses were lined up. Rolland went to work, sniffing, tasting, and spitting.

About halfway through the tasting, the cellar door opened and a man fifteen years Rolland's junior entered, almost running.

"Sorry to be late," he excused himself. "Lots of traffic."

He had short clipped hair and wore black jeans and a black T-shirt, looking more like a SoHo artist than a professional in the wine industry.

"I left at 7 A.M.," Rolland said. "Only way to get across the bridge. Already did one tasting."

In a frantic effort to improve, Prieuré-Lichine's new owner had hired two consultants and the incumbent Rolland wasn't cutting his rival much slack.

"I get to bed late, that's my problem," the younger man admitted.

His name is Stéphane Deronencourt and he is Saint-Emilion's up-and-coming enologist, a challenger to Rolland's supremacy. Where Rolland is smooth and suave, the thirty-seven-year-old Deronencourt is rough and rustic. He was born in the northern French city of Lille and didn't grow up in the wine business. In 1982 he hitchhiked to Bordeaux following a girlfriend. Needing money, he harvested grapes and before long signed on as a simple worker at Count Stephan von Neipperg's Château Canon-La-Gaffelière. His ability in the cellar caught the count's eye and he rose to become chief technician. In that position, he popularized techniques such as micro-oxygenation—by which small amounts of oxygen are purposely injected into the barrels. The process helps get rid of vegetal tones and polish other potential rough tannic edges.

For Rolland, a consulting job means a maximum of ten visits a year. He comes before the harvest once a week to choose the best day to pick the grapes, follows up after the grapes are in the cellar to monitor the alcoholic fermentation, and continues visiting once a week through the end of the malolactic fermentation. Deronencourt spends much more time over the entire year. In particular, he surveys his clients' vineyards. "I can only vinify grapes that I know," he said. For Deronencourt, the Left Bank almost represents a trip abroad. "This type of contract at Prieuré-Lichine is new for me; I don't have a Mercedes and a chauffeur," he said. While Rolland addresses most of his clients in a formal French *vous*, Deronencourt insists on using the informal *tu*.

After their initial verbal sparring, the two enologists were polite to each other. Deronencourt respects Rolland for raising the profile of the profession. Rolland, in turn, recognizes Deronencourt's talent. Both agreed that the 2001 vintage in Bordeaux would produce less dense wines than in 2000. By 10:45, Rolland finished tasting all twenty-nine samples and was ready to leave. Deronencourt still had about fifteen to go. The two enologists discussed their findings. "Number nine needs to wait a while before going into barrel," Rolland suggested. "You're right: it tastes poor," Deronencourt agreed.

That morning, Rolland visited two more Margaux estates, Château Siran and Château Clarke. Both are typical Rolland patients, underperformers in need of rejuvenation. At each stop, Rolland tasted another twenty or so wines, encouraging his clients as he worked. Descendants of Baron Edmond de Rothschild, Baron Philippe's cousin, are the absentee owners of Clarke and they have poured money into the operation. "Bravo," Rolland told Clarke's managers. "This is the best I've ever tasted at Clarke and it shows what you can do when you reduce the yields by 20 percent."

After a business lunch with investors trying to interest him in their New World project, Rolland visited two more estates, one in Saint-Julien and the other in Pauillac, tasting an average of thirty samples at each. He finally arrived back in Margaux at Château Lascombes at 4:15. An afternoon sun-shower had sprinkled the front lawn. Alain Raynaud's Land Cruiser was parked in front. Raynaud, Vatelot, and Dominique Befve were inside waiting for Rolland.

The initial news from the laboratory was worrisome. Analyses showed a low level of tannins, suggesting that the resulting wines would be fruity but lacking in body and structure.

"The tannins register only 110," Raynaud revealed. A good level was at least 130.

"Let's see, you really can only tell by tasting," cautioned Rolland.

Lascombes is a large estate and the new proprietors had made an effort to study the individual parcels with greater than average care. A massive tasting was arranged in order to sample the wine from each parcel; four rows of forty-six glasses were set up in the tasting room. Silence enveloped the room. After about ten samples, Rolland paused.

"Clean and powerful," he judged.

"I'm agreeably surprised," said Raynaud.

The tasters moved on from the Merlot to the samples of Cabernet Sauvignon and Petit Verdot. Befve warned them that they weren't yet "dry"—their alcoholic fermentation wasn't yet finished.

"Number twenty-five is a little firm in the mouth, number twenty-six a bit better," judged Rolland. "Overall good fruit, good middle of the mouth." He suggested improving the extraction process by increasing the frequency of the *pigeage* to three times a day.

"Can you taste the Margaux signature?" asked Vatelot. His main worry was being accused of masking the *terroir* in an effort to Parkerize the wine.

"Yes, there's a difference between the different samples, between the ones on the gravelly soils and the ones on the clay," said Rolland.

The four men began to consult around the fireplace. Although Rolland wanted to begin moving the wines from the steel tanks to oak barrels, the new cellar wouldn't be completed for at least another week. They figured out a solution to store about half in barrels in a temporary holding area.

"What about the low tannin levels?" asked Raynaud. "Could it mean lack of structure? We know the fruit is there. But if there's insufficient structure the wine won't age well."

"A few samples are a bit rustic, but it's nothing dramatic," Rolland responded. "It's the tasting that counts, not the laboratory."

"What's your overall judgment?" Vatelot asked.

"Before, whenever I drove through Margaux, I knew where to find the worst wines—at Lascombes," Rolland began. "This is 100 percent better."

Everyone smiled. Rolland didn't have time for much more small talk. It was already 5:30, and he had spent longer at Lascombes than elsewhere, both out of friendship with Raynaud and Vatelot and because the estate had so many samples for him to taste. He still had two more visits to make in Margaux before heading back to the Right Bank. By the end of the day, he had tasted and judged almost 350 unfinished wines. His mouth was purple. Even for this professional, the senses were numbed.

In his Mercedes returning to the Right Bank, Rolland said he was encouraged about Lascombes's progress but considered it too early to determine a final verdict. "We can only tell when we do the final blending just before the spring tasting," he cautioned. Then he fell asleep.

BY MID-NOVEMBER, the weather began to turn rainy and cold—and in the vineyards the reddish golden leaves began dropping with the first frost. Tourists to Saint-Emilion were undeterred by the weather. While the village used to be overwhelmed only in summertime, the season now extends late into the fall, and this year the Tourist Office predicted the number of visitors would reach 1.2 million.

Even if tourists still flooded to Saint-Emilion, the professional wine world's attention now moved away from Bordeaux, to Burgundy. On the third Sunday in November, wine buyers congregate in Beaune, center of the Burgundy wine trade, for the annual Hospices de Beaune auction. The Hospices is one of France's great buildings, a mixture of Flemish-style fantasy and traditional French lines. Founded in 1443 by Nicolas Rolin, chancellor of Burgundy, as a hospital for the elderly and infirm, today it is a historical museum and Beaune's major tourist attraction. Almost from the institution's inception, it became customary for Burgundians to donate parcels of vineyard land to help finance its work. Since 1851 the wines from those vineyards have been sold at the annual November auction, providing operating funds. The auction always offers a sense of how the global market for top-of-the-line wines is turning. Hospices's prices increased steadily from 1993 to 2000, multiplying by a total of three. In 2001 they plummeted by an average of 24 percent. Although price fluctuations are exaggerated at the annual charity auction, the president of the Burgundy winemakers association, Hubert Camus, was worried. "Anything above 20 percent makes us ask questions," he said.

Back in Saint-Emilion, winemakers were already putting out a preliminary verdict on 2001: prices would fall. The question was how much—and how much wine would be available to sell. Michel Gracia gave his crew the week off for All Saints' Day. There was little to do in his garage cellar except check the evolving wine once a day. He could do this by himself. The stonemason was feeling good. His 1997 vintage had come out first in a tasting of top Saint-Emilions in Japan—ahead of his client Cheval Blanc. "Can you believe it, ahead of Cheval Blanc?" he asked with wonderment.

At lunch soon after the auction in Beaune, Gracia headed to L'Envers du Décor, at the top of Saint-Emilion's hill. Although owner François de Ligneris is one of Robert Parker's loudest critics, his establishment serves as a meeting place for new wavers as well as the old guard. The décor is simple: brown wooden tables, wall decorations of wine cases, labels, and posters, and a zinc bistro bar. The hearty menu features omelettes, chitterling sausages, duck *confits,* and other down-home delights. What makes the restaurant a particular favorite is a vast wine list with offerings ranging from the oldest, most traditional Bordeaux to the newest, most concentrated garage wines.

When Gracia arrived, he saw *Sud Ouest*'s Didier Ters holding court at a large table in the front room with a broker from Daniel-Georges Lawton's firm and a group of Saint-Emilion stars, including Jean-Luc Thunevin and Château Ausone's Alain Vauthier. Gracia ate in the back room with Count Stephan von Neipperg, whom he had known for more than two decades, ever since he did some renovation work on his estate. The owner of Château Canon-La-Gaffelière is a tall, ramrod-straight man with a small clipped mustache who looks as if he just stepped out of the pages of *Town & Country* magazine. His family, once one of the largest and most distinguished landowners in the former Austro-Hungarian Empire, came through the fall of the Hapsburgs and two world wars with much of its wealth intact. They bought their Saint-Emilion estate as a hobby in 1971.

But after Stephan studied in Paris at the university, he decided he wanted to live in France full-time. He proved to be an innovator, picking up lessons from the *garagistes* and integrating them into the making of his *grand cru classé.* He became a founding member of Florence Cathiard's Les Cinq group. He knows how to spot talent. Even though Neipperg looks and acts like the consummate count, he does not let pedigree cloud his vision. It was he who groomed Stéphane Deronencourt from mere technician to star enologist. Deronencourt still keeps his office at Neipperg's Canon-La-Gaffe-lière and considers the count his primary patron. Gracia appreciates the count's openness, even if he sometimes becomes the butt of jokes. "Michel's too expensive," explained the count, with only half a smile.

The mood at the table was morose. Gracia didn't want to let on to the count about his victory in Japan. Such self-promotion wouldn't be looked well upon by the village's aristocrats. "It makes them furious when they see that I am on top and they are on the bottom," he said. And despite the victory, he was worried about the price decreases in Burgundy at the Hospices auction.

"Bad news," he told Neipperg.

"We will face similar pressures this spring," the count concurred.

The stonemason and count shared another common worry, the same one that contributed to Yquem's ultimate sale—high inheritance taxes. Both men agreed that the taxes in France were excessive—a full 40 percent for all estates worth more than $1.75 million. Corporations such as LVMH don't pay the same tax rate, nor do foreigners who purchase wine estates through foreign companies. Neipperg said he was looking at investing in vineyards in Bulgaria rather than expanding in France.

Neipperg is far from alone. The Rothschilds' operations with Mondavi in California, LVMH's high-end Cloudy Bay in New Zealand and Cap Mentele in Australia, and Michel Rolland's new venture in Argentina are just a few examples of attempts to diversify and spread risk. Such ventures also export superior French know-how. But there is also another reason to go abroad.

"France puts so many constraints on you," complained Neipperg. "I want to go somewhere where I can do what I want, where I want."

"It's not fair," agreed Gracia. His construction business would be hard to hand down to his daughters and he knew that, sooner or later, he would have to sell it. He was also worried about the future of his small winery. How would his daughters pay the inheritance tax? How would they divide up the estate, small as it is? Fortunately, he felt he was at least a decade away from having to make these decisions.

In the meantime, he was planning for a happier occasion in the short term—a trip to California over Christmas. It was to be his first voyage ever to the United States. With his daughter Caroline working at a Sonoma Valley winery for six months and loving it, he wanted to see the New World for himself.

ON THE WEEKENDS in November, the countryside in the Entre-Deux-Mers sounds like a battle zone. Most of the male residents take their guns and dogs to go hunting. Under the ancien régime, the king and his nobles could forbid anyone else from hunting. The aristocracy could trespass on anyone's land and kill any animal they came across. If an unauthorized peasant hunter was caught, he faced hanging. When the revolutionaries overthrew the old order, one of their first priorities was to grant all citizens the right to *la chasse*.

The peasant growers at Sauveterre's co-op hunt in the forests around the town. Wealthier Saint-Emilionnais go further afield. Alain Raynaud often heads off to Spain to hunt birds. "I'm a hunting widow every weekend until January," lamented Raynaud's wife, Françoise Raynaud. She leads the tastings for visitors to Quinault during her husband's absence.

In Sauveterre, the co-op was already beginning to sell its white wine. The fresh Sauvignon Blanc would be bottled in February and ready to drink by March or April. Fermentation was done and merchants came to taste. Rémi Garuz had 3.5 million gallons of Sauvignon Blanc. Giles O'Connolly visited often to choose the blend to make the new wine tailored for export. "We're not looking for something complex, just pleasant and flattering on the palate," he said.

One cold November day, O'Connolly tasted at the co-op. The first sample smelled of green pepper. Too much underripe Sauvignon Blanc. Number five represented an improvement. "You begin to taste some fruit in here," O'Connolly said. In all, he rated seven out of the twenty-four samples as acceptable. The bad lots would be unloaded in French super-markets for less than $5 a bottle. "I admit it's not very good for Bordeaux's overall image to unload wine at that price and I know that the bottom end of the wine market is shrinking, but it's still better than nothing," technician Christian Caviole said. O'Connolly remained optimistic that he would find enough superior juice to launch the new brand.

Another morning that month, a representative from the Jacques and François Lurton merchant house tasted the Sauvignon at the Sauveterre co-op. The Lurtons are cousins of Cheval Blanc's director, Pierre Lurton. Their buyer is Oswaldo Hernandez, who came to Bordeaux from Chile to study enology, met a French woman, fathered two children, and decided to stay. He is dark-skinned and thickset and speaks French with a rounded Spanish accent. The Lurtons love having him on their team because, in addition to producing and buying wine in France, they work in South America. When he arrived in Sauveterre, Hernandez had already tasted at other co-ops. He believed this was a good year for Sauvignon Blanc in Bordeaux. "It wasn't too hot, so you get some real flavor," Hernandez said.

In Caviole's office, twenty samples were prepared. In comparison to the pomp and circumstance surrounding the spring tasting, the co-op tasting experience was basic. The office looked like a hospital attending room, pure white tile and Formica tables. Hernandez sipped and spat out the samples one by one. He chose two, buying about 125 gallons, only Sauvignon Blanc. "Sauveterre is one of the better co-ops in the entire Bordeaux region," he said. "Their Sauvignons are more interesting, longer in the mouth, than most others."

Caviole smiled, half out of pleasure at the compliments, half with wonder at how the merchants had such different tastes. The Rothschild buyers had come by the week before to make their choice for Mouton Cadet's Bordeaux white. "They picked only Sémillon, which they said had a rounder, plumper taste," he said. In Bordeaux, this represents another problem for consumers—its dry whites can be either crisp and clean or rich and robust depending on the individual merchant. The stylistic disparity is yet another reason why the sale of Bordeaux mass-market whites is falling fast.

Just as Lurton's Hernandez was on his way out the door, another broker arrived. He was there to taste the co-op's wines and determine which ones might interest his merchant clients. But his main preoccupation wasn't Sauveterre's Sauvignon Blanc. It was Yquem. Earlier that morning, Alexandre de Lur-Saluces had released his 1996 vintage. It was 14 percent alcohol but contained 7 percent unfermented sugar, more than the usual 6 percent. "It's more like syrup than wine," he complained. The wholesale price to the trade was $140. Not counting the extravagant $400 a bottle for the rare 2000 vintage, this represented a price rise: the 1995 had been sold at only $120 the year before, which was a superior vintage.

The timing couldn't have been worse. Yquem's 1995 and 2000 vintages were still moving—slowly—through the distribution system. The 1996s would be available in bottles too late to be in stores by the Christmas holidays. "The count's gone crazy," judged the broker. "At the least he should have sold them two months ago so they would be in the stores for the end-of-the-year festivities."

News of the count's commercial slipup spread fast. Merchants soon reported that he was discounting and offering bottles of the 1996 at $130 instead of the original $140.

The contrast was striking with Cheval Blanc. A few days after the 1996 Yquem was released, Cheval Blanc's Pierre Lurton decided to sell a few more 2000 futures. While brokers were advising Lur-Saluces to keep Yquem's wine in the cellars, they urged Lurton to part with some more of his stock. Lurton agreed, but he wanted $400 a bottle—the highest price ever for a red Bordeaux as a future. Despite September 11, despite Yquem's flop, the merchants gobbled up the offering of 6,000 bottles. Within a day, Arnault's Cheval Blanc coffers were bulging with an additional $2.4 million. "It shows what happens when you change your brokers, mix up your merchants, and modernize your winemaking," said a satisfied Lurton. "You can't use the same brokers from forty years ago and the same merchants as they do at Yquem."

Lurton began to fear Arnault might soon ask him to replace Lur-Saluces at the helm of Yquem. The challenge of modernizing Sauternes's

icon appealed to him. But the politics of replacing the aging count frightened him. He preferred to stay and make his own mark at Cheval Blanc.

AS 2001 CAME TO A CLOSE, the weather turned wintry. Vines, bushy
only a few weeks before, were "undressed": workers braved the cold
weather to prune them in preparation for their spring budding. They
used heavy clippers to cut away the long branches and their shoots that
gave fruit the previous fall. When all the excess wood was removed—
later to be used for barbecuing steaks—only naked stumps remained.

It was the season for indoor dinner parties and warming fires. Alain
Raynaud decided to host one of Alexandre de Lur-Saluces's lawyers, at
Quinault. Raynaud liked him, admiring him as one of Bordeaux's best
barristers, and the two men had socialized before. When the lawyer
arrived, Raynaud offered him a tour of his estate's impressive cellars.
They were spotless and lit like a theatrical stage. The 2001 wines were
maturing, finishing their malolactic fermentation. Raynaud explained
how he had adopted a new system to allow the barrels to be rotated with
ease. This process is called racking and means turning the barrels slowly
so that potentially harmful sediment cannot form. Wine is also transferred from one barrel to another on the theory that the air it is briefly
exposed to helps it grow up from a baby to a healthy child.

Champagne was uncorked and served as an aperitif. It was 9:30 P.M.
by the time the group sat down in the formal dining room, its table
resplendent with silver and porcelain. The first course was fish. In the
Raynaud household, that meant a traditional Bordelais stew featuring
the *lamproie,* or lamprey. Lamprey is caught in the Gironde River.
Françoise Raynaud bleeds the freshwater eel, reserving the blood to flavor the sauce. She cuts two-inch slices and puts them into a buttered pan
lined with sliced onions and carrots, adding leeks, ham, and red wine to
simmer together. "You can't get this in a restaurant, because they put
cheap chocolate in the sauce to give it the right color," she said. Her
wine-infused *lamproie* was accompanied by a 1989 Mouton Rothschild.

Parker wrote that it was "a superior wine" but in no sense "a compelling wine," and the diners agreed.

The main course was partridge that Raynaud had shot in Spain, served with the juicy mushrooms called *cèpes,* pan-fried with a hint of vinegar and plenty of shallots. This was a typical Bordeaux feast, where the food was chosen to suit red wines. Raynaud opened a Pomerol called La Conseillante. "I don't like to serve my own wine at a dinner party because people can't be honest about what they think," said Raynaud. La Conseillante is considered an inconsistent Pomerol, but its vines are located next to those of Pétrus and occasionally the wine soars. This was the case with the 1989 vintage that Raynaud served, which Parker scored a 97, calling it "perfumed, exotic, sweet, expansive, yummy wine that is hard to resist." The wine was smooth and silky and evoked oohs and ahs at the dinner table.

The conversation was even spicier. The lawyer was concerned about Alexandre de Lur-Saluces. Despite the victory in getting a premium for his shares of Yquem and his success in staying on as president, the count remained bitter, he said. "Alexandre feels he did everything to save Yquem. Eugène never set foot in the château for thirty years, and without Alexandre it would have been ruined." In his opinion, that was why Alexandre would continue to fight to gain half of Eugène's estate "even if the court cases drag on for years." Raynaud disagreed. He feared that the continued feuding was destroying one of Bordeaux's icons. "If Alexandre continues to run Yquem, it soon will be a shadow of itself," he said. "LVMH must replace him."

A few days later, Raynaud went again to Lascombes, this time to meet Château Margaux's Paul Pontallier. For the director of such an august institution, one expects a stuffy, uptight person. Pontallier is just the opposite, outgoing and affable. With his full head of curly brown hair and trim physique, he looks much younger than his forty-five years, and he has a quick and genuine smile. He is the most intellectual of the first-growth managers and was curious to see what experiments Lascombes's new owners were up to.

Raynaud had invited Pontallier to Lascombes in return for a promise of a tasting visit back at Château Margaux. "It's my way of seeing if we can make peace between us from the Right Bank and the traditionalists on the Left Bank," Raynaud explained. Michel Rolland and Dominique Befve also attended. Yves Vatelot was away on a business trip. The four men began tasting the Petit Verdot and Cabernet Sauvignon. Because of the delay caused by the dry ice and cold maceration, much of the juice from these grapes still had not finished its alcoholic fermentation in mid-November. "That's late," Pontallier said with surprise. "Most of our production is already into its malolactic fermentation."

The men began to attack the two dozen glasses of wine set up before them. As they tasted, their faces displayed a range of emotions: disappointment, caution, pleasure, and even a few expressions of joy. Numbers five and six were praised. Number twenty-seven had a fault and was discarded. "We're lucky," Rolland concluded. "These samples of Cabernet and Petit Verdot will fill out that empty middle left by the Merlot. They'll give a bit of the needed structure to produce a nice finale."

"The wines from Lascombes used to be thin and insipid and this is much more full-bodied, much more powerful," Pontallier observed, as others had done. But he feared the new owners were moving too fast and were going to break more than they fixed. "My worry is that your technique will hide aromas, rise fast in the mouth and then fall away," he said.

"Oh, no," Rolland disagreed. "You'll see, when we put together the Merlot and the Cabernet and the Petit Verdot, the wine will pick up and have real body and a real equilibrium."

After the tasting, Rolland left for another appointment. Raynaud and Befve headed to Château Margaux. Only a small sign points the way to the renowned château. At the entrance, a forbidding warning—"Private: No Admittance"—is posted. The elegant, white-columned edifice stands proudly at the end of a grand, tree-lined avenue. Inside the cellar, the visitors were welcomed into reception rooms decorated in Napoléon III Empire style. A worker brought bottles containing the 1998, 1999, and 2000 vintages. "It's really too early to taste our 2001," Pontallier said. "You have to wait until January."

"He's frightened to show them to us so young because he doesn't want to be shown up," a disappointed Raynaud whispered to Befve. Pontallier explained his philosophy. At Margaux, yields can remain higher, 50 to 55 hectoliters per hectare, because "God gave us great land." No dry ice and cold maceration is permitted because "it would mask aromas." "On such a magical *terroir*, you don't need any artificial fireworks," he argued.

Pontallier opened the bottles of wine and poured. The three men sipped. The wine was delicious, a mixture of aromas, fruits such as blackberries and cassis combined with earthy truffle and mushroom tastes and the texture of velvet and silk. It lingered on the mouth for a seeming eternity, epitomizing finesse and elegance.

"A magical wine," Raynaud admitted.

"*Terroir* counts," agreed Befve.

After Raynaud and Befve returned to Lascombes, they began discussing their visit. Both admitted that the Margaux was wonderful. Both understood why Pontallier was hesitant to change and upset a winning formula. If the wine was excellent, and it was, the changes might only result in higher costs and less wine to sell. Or it could result in something even more sublime. "What if Paul innovated on such a great *terroir*?" wondered Raynaud. "I still believe the wine would get better." Only half joking, he added, "We'll just have to take over Margaux and try out our ideas there."

Like all revolutions, Bordeaux's was running its course. The old order symbolized by the likes of Alexandre de Lur-Saluces and Paul Pontallier, as different as the two may be, remained under pressure. But success for the radical newcomers was not assured. Storms were buffeting global markets, and even Bordeaux's best winemakers risked getting caught in the downturn.

—

CHAPTER 14

Report Card

IN THE MIDDLE OF MARCH 2002, MICHEL ROLLAND VISITED Château Lascombes to prepare samples for the upcoming spring tasting. Some enologists believe the wines should be blended right after the primary fermentation. But Rolland blends late. He monitors the evolution of wine from different parcels, discards inferior barrels, and chooses the best possible combinations. "When it comes to mixing wines, Michel's the pope," said Alain Raynaud.

The enologist, dressed in his usual business suit, was tanned after spending most of the winter in Argentina and California. At Lascombes, Dominique Befve was waiting for him, wearing his customary Shetland sweater and corduroys. Alain Raynaud and Yves Vatelot arrived in casual dress. The four men congregated in a large reception room. It looked like a nightclub, with glossy black doors and black tiles on the wall, and an octagonal domed skylight. A total of forty-six bottles of wine were placed on the table. Rolland took off his jacket and went right to work. Once he had sipped a dozen or so samples, he picked up a chemistry test tube and a calculator, a cheap handheld model. He began pouring in small amounts from different lots and calculating percentages.

Earlier in the year, Rolland had found the Merlot rich and full-blooded. Now he judged the later harvested and fermented Cabernet Sauvignon and Petit Verdot, and his verdict was upbeat. "The basic Cabernet Sauvignon is super and the Petit Verdot is fabulous," he said. In his opinion, production levels could even be raised at the next harvest up to 5 percent without sacrificing quality.

WILLIAM ECHIKSON

*Enologist Michel Rolland is considered the pope of
Bordeaux wine blending.*

His next task was to blend the three different grape varieties to create a seamless whole. "Let's put in 3 percent of number three with 10 percent of number ten," Rolland ordered.

"Yes," said Befve.

"It looks so scientific," Rolland joked.

"Like alchemy," responded Befve.

"It may look like chemistry, but it's still done on feeling," Rolland insisted.

The enologist picked up another glass, tasted, and ordered, "Add 15 percent." Pretty soon the test tube was filled. Rolland, Raynaud, Vatelot, and Befve each took a glass, raised it to his nose, then the mouth. The faces were studies in concentration as they tasted. A few seconds went by as each collected his thoughts.

"A little diluted," Befve worried. "We need some more concentration."

"No, it's nice and soft," Rolland disagreed. "I'm happy because I added more Cabernet than I thought possible and the wine doesn't harden. It's much more appealing than the traditional austere Médoc."

He turned to the calculator and now began to determine whether he could make large amounts of the same sample as Lascombes's first wine. The figures began flying out of his mouth: 554 hectoliters of number thirteen, Merlot, plus 44 hectoliters of number seventy of Cabernet Sauvignon. He wanted a final combination of about 40 percent Merlot, 40 percent Cabernet, and 20 percent Petit Verdot. After calculating for several minutes, Rolland looked up and said, with a smile, "It all adds up."

Lascombes's new arrivals had met their first goal. Before they took over, the estate produced about 500,000 bottles of mediocre wine, about half of which was sold not as Lascombes itself, but as the inferior Chevalier de Lascombes. This year, their replanting and severe pruning of the vines, plus the reduction in the harvest because of the rain in early October, had slashed production to about 220,000 bottles. About 180,000 bottles would be full-fledged Château Lascombes. The small amounts of leftover would be sold as Chevalier—"but even that will be better quality than the old full-fledged Lascombes," boasted Vatelot.

Raynaud and Vatelot began to make financial forecasts. They hoped to sell the wine for $35 a bottle, almost a third more than the previous year. That looked ambitious, given the state of the global economy. Raynaud and Vatelot couldn't control the marketplace. But at least they had made 180,000 bottles of top-quality wine and could present it to the world's most important taster. Raynaud looked happy as he said, "We're ready for Bob."

MANY BORDEAUX WINEMAKERS were confident they had produced good wines, not up to the quality of 2000's magical vintage, though still quite good. Brash Gérard Perse underlined this confidence by announcing on March 18 that he was paying $44 million to buy the twenty-seven-acre Pomerol estate called Petit-Village. Although Petit-Village had made unexciting wines in recent years, it is located right near Pétrus and the possibility for greatness seemed clear. The price of $1.6 million per acre set a new record for Bordeaux. Production was only about 60,000 bottles a year.

Yves Vatelot and Alain Raynaud didn't know whether to celebrate or to cry. On the one hand, the price suggested that the investment in Lascombes as a real estate venture would pay off. On the other hand, Raynaud worried that his family's nearby La Croix de Gay, of which he owned 25 percent, would have to be sold in order to pay inheritance taxes after his mother died. "Gérard may be exaggerating," Raynaud said. "If this continues, no family estates will be left in Bordeaux."

As usual, Parker skipped the formal Union des Grands Crus tastings, scheduled for March 25 to 29. He came to France a week earlier and made his own personalized tour. On Sunday, March 17, he tasted at Jeffrey Davies's office. Parker arrived at 2:30 P.M., dressed all in black. Davies asked if he was in mourning and Parker answered yes. His father had recently died of cancer and his mother had just been diagnosed with the disease. Parker plunged into his work, bringing his usual devotion to the task. He stayed at Davies's office for five hours and tasted a total of 130 wines, among them Gracia and Lascombes.

The following Tuesday, Parker visited Alain Raynaud socially at Château Quinault. The two friends spent much of the time discussing their respective diets. Raynaud found Parker much more upbeat than Davies had. Parker had lost weight and was looking much trimmer than he had a few months before. "Bob seemed in good health," Raynaud reported. A chunky man, Raynaud vowed to keep up with his friend in the struggle to lose weight and to spend more time pedaling away on his stationary bicycle.

Most important, Raynaud was confident the guru's verdict about Lascombes would be positive, at least a 94. Although Parker refused to let him have an early look at his scoring, he did tell him that the "2001 were great and that it was the best Château Lascombes ever."

On March 22, Parker left Bordeaux. He traveled to Paris to spend the weekend with his colleague Pierre Antoine Rovani. There, Parker broke his diet for at least one evening to visit the luxury bistro L'Ami Louis. When French president Jacques Chirac hosted Bill Clinton, the two presidents dined there. A place for gourmands, not for the fainthearted, it hasn't changed much since opening in 1920. The décor looks straight out of a railway carriage, with a tiny kitchen at the far end filled with three fat chefs cooking huge pieces of beef, veal, and lamb over a wood fire. There is no printed menu, just a handwritten scrawl on a blackboard. Generous portions arrive at the table on plain, heavy porcelain or cast iron. "Even if he's on a diet, Bob said he just couldn't go to Paris without eating at L'Ami Louis," Raynaud reported.

Formally, the Union discourages tastings before their official week. But the Union could not prevent Parker or numerous other journalists from coming to Bordeaux before the tasting week commenced on March 25. One was the *Wine Spectator*'s James Suckling. In an effort to beat the competition, he set up a command post at Saint-Emilion's luxurious Hostellerie de Plaisance and asked winemakers to bring him samples. On Friday, March 22, he posted his first ratings on the *Spectator*'s web site. "Members of the trade will find many very good to outstanding quality reds, as well as super-quality dry and sweet white wines," he promised.

This praise was accompanied by a warning. "The vintage doesn't match the quality of 2000, when everyone from the big names to tiny unknown châteaux made wines of spectacular quality," Suckling wrote. "Nor does it compare marketwise with 2000, when the global economy was still running at a fever pitch." His verdict was more commercial than gustatory. "It makes little sense for consumers to tie up their money in 2001 futures. They can buy the wines when they are in bottle."

Vatelot and Raynaud were furious. Though they agreed with Suckling's overall judgment, the specific numbers angered them. Suckling gave his top 95–100 scores to the traditionalists, first growths such as Lafite Rothschild and Mouton Rothschild. New wavers scored much lower. Raynaud's Quinault L'Enclos received a disappointing 89–91.

Raynaud believed his wine was much better than an underperforming Mouton Rothschild. In his opinion, Suckling was not confident in his own tastes and was picking on him for his friendship with Parker. "Suckling is grading to separate himself from Bob," he said. In the end, it was Parker's, not Suckling's, words that counted, and Raynaud remained confident that their favorite critic would give Quinault and Lascombes at least 92s.

THE FORMAL TASTING marathon began in Sauternes. Given the small commercial following for sweet white wines, most journalists considered this first stop a prelude to the more important action later in the week with red wines. Growers in Sauternes debated how best to participate. A majority voted to set up a tasting center for the entire week in Pomerol. "It's hard to get people to come all the way to Sauternes," explained Nicolas Heeter-Tari of Château Nairac, a well-respected second growth. "We need to be closer to the real action."

Despite the decision to move most of their tastings to Pomerol, the Sauternes *grand cru* châteaux agreed to host a single Union press event. At 2 P.M. on the afternoon of March 25, tasting week's opening day, journalists, merchants, and importers congregated at Château Giraud, a first growth located next door to Yquem. A long, bumpy drive led to the front of a symmetrical, elegant nineteenth-century house.

As usual, tasters divided up into blind and nonblind groups. All twenty-four great growths representing Sauternes were available, with, of course, the notable exception of Yquem, which never permitted tasting before bottling. The journalists went to work. All the wines exhibited a deep golden color, a floral bouquet in the nose, and a delicious, smooth, and long taste in the mouth. Each sample seemed better than the last. After only a few sips, it was clear that this was an exceptional vintage, rich and powerful, perhaps the best in decades. When some excited journalists broke into animated conversation, a severe woman from a French wine magazine soon restored order with a hiss and reprimand, "Don't talk, we'll be late."

Their next stop was Yquem. While Alexandre de Lur-Saluces refused to allow Yquem's own wines to be tasted the spring after harvest, he did host a cocktail party for the tasters. In the late afternoon sun, the vines lay barren and dormant, waiting for the warm weather to wake them up. Cars made their way up the magnificent avenue leading to Yquem's château. Most of the guests were dressed in their Sunday best.

The reception was set up in the main part of the building, on the ground floor, in a room typical of the rest of the château: antique furniture, doors framed with brass, walls hung with eighteenth- and nineteenth-century portraits and Flemish tapestries. Neither Bernard Arnault nor Pierre Gode nor any other high-ranking LVMH executive attended. Alexandre greeted his guests, who numbered about 120, with a welcoming speech. He began by explaining why he did not participate in the spring tasting. No apologies were offered. "In my opinion, an Yquem needs ten years after harvest before it becomes an adult," he said. Guests were treated to a taste of 1996, the vintage he released, with great commercial difficulty, just before the end of the previous year. Alexandre warned that it was "still young, like a teenager."

In the back of the reception room, the head of Sotheby's wine department, Serena Sutcliffe, became impatient. "Where's the foie gras?" she asked her neighbor. Sutcliffe had flown to Bordeaux straight from Miami and a gentle tan set off her striking white hair. She was tall and thin, dressed in designer clothes, perhaps even Dior, and carried herself with aristocratic bearing. At her side, though considerably shorter than she, stood her husband, David Peppercorn, another English wine notable, a master of wine, writer, and consultant. "I heard Bernard Arnault forced him to cut back on the foie gras because he isn't selling enough Dior," Sutcliffe stage-whispered to him.

After a seeming eternity, Alexandre ended his speech and turned to Yquem's cellar master, Sandrine Garbay, to lead the tasting of the 1996 vintage. Several bottles were uncorked. The young cellar master put a glass to her nose, then to her mouth, and sipped. She didn't spit out. Her description represented a masterpiece of winespeak. "It's full of the nectar of apricot, fig, quince, honey—the classic Yquem notes," she began. Compared to most of the 2001 Sauternes sampled at the previous tasting, the Yquem was a blockbuster, heavy and rich in the mouth, delicious but also verging on the cloying. The Yquem punched. The younger Sauternes tapped and teased.

As Garbay continued her description, white-tuxedoed waiters began gliding through the room carrying glasses of Yquem and warmed bits of foie gras on small squares of toast. Serena Sutcliffe smiled. Bernard Arnault was not cutting costs too much. She ate several of the bite-size morsels and sipped a glass of Yquem. Her trip to Miami was successful, she reported. "The Americans are still buying." But her customers weren't purchasing the same wines as before. Their interest focused on older vintages rather than futures. "I think the price of older classic vintages will continue to rise while the new futures fall," she predicted.

Guests began to leave the cocktail party as an early evening sunset fell over the vineyard. Count Xavier de Pontac, a descendent of the seventeenth-century owners of Haut-Brion and owner of the second-growth Sauternes Château de Myrat, was celebrating. In 1976, his father had uprooted his vines because the price of Sauternes was so low. Although de Pontac replanted a decade later, he was still struggling. The count looked unkempt, his face worn, as if it had been trampled on. "Owning an estate in Sauternes represents such a burden," he said. But he had great hopes for this year's vintage. He predicted that prices of elite red Bordeaux would fall by 25 percent, while the first-growth Sauternes would rise by 25 percent. "After ten years where the prices of Sauternes haven't budged, we need the boost," he said, sitting down in the driver's seat of his car, a battered Volkswagen Polo subcompact.

The clock on Yquem's tower read 6:30 P.M. After years of neglect, it was finally restored and running.

Early the next morning, James Suckling posted a new review on the *Wine Spectator* web site titled "Sweet Dreams." The subheading read, "For Sauternes, 2001 is the best vintage in decades." Top ratings, 95–100, were reserved for ten of the twenty-four first and second growths. They included Nicolas Heeter-Tari's Château Nairac, which was described in winespeak as "intensely botrytised, with loads of allspice and mineral character, yet lively and exciting, full-bodied, racy and very long." Pontac's Myrat received 92–94 points and praise for "loads of botrytis spice character and dried pineapple fruit." The best single score went to the Dubourdieus' Doisy-Daëne's Extravagant, a perfect 100. "Unbelievably powerful, with loads of spice, clove, honey and flowers," Suckling wrote. "The palate goes on and on. I'm speechless. We may never taste a wine like this again."

AT BREAKFAST THE MORNING of the twenty-seventh, Alain Raynaud was in a foul mood. Suckling had just published a new, full listing of Bordeaux 2001 on his magazine's web site and scored Lascombes a pitiful 85–88. "The idiot," Raynaud thundered. When Raynaud was president of the Union des Grands Crus two years before, he tried to stop Suckling from publishing his ratings early by telling Union members not to send him samples before other journalists had tasted. At least, he consoled himself, while the *Spectator* score may count among consumers, it matters little among the all-important merchants and importers. "Parker is the king," he said.

Later in the day, journalists headed for the main Union tasting in Margaux. To Raynaud's dismay, a rival second-growth estate named Rauzan-Segla hosted the event. Raynaud and Vatelot both directed scorn against their colleagues in the Union des Grands Crus. They had petitioned for a special presentation at Lascombes during the spring tastings, but Rauzan-Segla was chosen instead. "We had something new to show at Lascombes and they preferred to go with the old guard," complained Raynaud.

Perhaps even more annoying to Raynaud, the Union rejected his membership application for Château Quinault. Pierre Lurton of Cheval Blanc and Michel Rolland sponsored him. But more than half the Union's members voted against admitting Quinault, so it was excluded. Raynaud said he felt like an Impressionist painter in the nineteenth century. When the academy prevented them from exhibiting their paintings, the Impressionists organized their own showings. Raynaud vowed to do the same.

Raynaud's successor as the head of the Union, Patrick Maroteaux of Château Branaire, disputed Raynaud's version. According to Maroteaux, Quinault would have won admission to the Union, but Raynaud insisted on being voted in unanimously, while a simple majority vote would have sufficed. "Alain is sometimes like a kamikaze, sacrificing himself on purpose," he said.

At the Rauzan-Segla tasting, guests differed in their reaction to Lascombes. Agreement was found on one point: the powerful product stood out among the other, much less concentrated Margaux offerings. Half in admiration and half in disgust, Fabien Teitgen, chief winemaker at the Cathiards' Château Smith-Haut-Lafitte, called it a "technological monster, a Gladiator wine." Steven Spurrier, the critic who organized the 1976 Paris tasting between French and Californian wines, was in Bordeaux for the English magazine *Decanter*. The new Lascombes horrified him. "Wines from Margaux should be fine, perfumed, and elegant," he told Raynaud. "But your wine is massive and meaty."

"Steven, if we stay with weak wines, Bordeaux will be dead in a decade," Raynaud replied. "We must change." Other brokers and journalists agreed and were enthralled. Michel Bettane of *La Revue du Vin de France* called Raynaud over and offered effusive praise. A broker named Damien Mortet described Lascombes as "rich, rich, rich." His colleague Stéphane Barreau reacted with religious language: "Lascombes has been resurrected." Barreau was convinced Parker would give the wine a "huge" rating.

Both detractors and supporters wondered whether commercial success would follow critical praise, however. Barreau watched how Gérard Perse improved quality and raised prices—only to go too fast and too far. "Even with big Bob, you have to remain lucid and take it up in little, not big, steps," he cautioned. For him, Lascombes's fate represented a good test of the limits of Parker's power.

In the evening, Vatelot and Raynaud hosted a private candlelit dinner for a dozen journalists and merchants at Lascombes. Before serving an aperitif of Champagne, the two took the guests on a tour of the cellar. The renovation was finally finished and the oak barrels containing the 2001 harvest were poised on metal racks bathed under soft, discreet light. The building looked immaculate and the two men spoke proudly of their accomplishments.

The feast, prepared by two-star Michelin local chef Thierry Marx, started with a foie gras soup, followed by scallops and figs and a main course of filet mignon. Vatelot served a Reignac with the foie gras, a Quinault L'Enclos with the beef. "These are wines that van Gogh could have painted," Vatelot said. Then he opened two bottles of the old Lascombes, one from 1995 and another from 1982. Both were ruby rather than purple, with a watery rather than jammy consistency. "These are academic wines," he said, picking up a glass, and concluded, "Delacroix could have painted them."

All the dinner guests lifted their glasses and toasted Lascombes's entry into the avant-garde.

IF THE MAIN UNION tastings were like Broadway, true connoisseurs flocked to the off-Broadway presentations where the *garagistes* and new wavers were presenting their superb, but non-*grand-cru,* offerings. In downtown Saint-Emilion, almost every public space was turned into a tasting site. Jean-François and Véronique Julien showed La Fleur Morange in an art gallery, along with other local and foreign growers, one from as far away as Israel. "No one invited us to display our wines, so we did it among ourselves," Jean-François said.

Yves and Stéphanie Vatelot presented Reignac, alongside Michel and Dany Rolland's Château Fontenil, at a pottery gallery. A few years before, Stéphanie had redesigned Reignac's label, removing all the Gothic excess common in Bordeaux. She printed it on thick beige paper with only the word "Reignac" and no mention of a château. Before the press tasting this year, she had wanted to do a similar makeover for Lascombes's "busy" label, but the American investors from Goldman Sachs and Colony Capital resisted. "They want to keep the traditional bottle with the coat of arms in order to avoid shocking anybody," she said.

The largest, best-attended, and hottest off-Broadway presentation took place at Jean-Luc Thunevin's home. Each day during the week, top winemakers from all over the world converged there. Spanish wines starred. Peter Sisseck brought cases of his Pingus. A more traditional name in Spanish winemaking, Vega Sicilia, also set up their headquarters at chez Thunevin. Founded in 1864 and located near Sisseck's property in the Ribera del Duero, the estate's premier wine, Vega Sicilia Unico, is made from grapes from the oldest vines and spends ten years or more in wooden casks and barrels. But now the Vega Sicilia team showed a new wave wine called Alion, a rich, concentrated mixture with coffee-roasted oak. English critic Jancis Robinson, otherwise critical of the *garagistes* and new wavers for "trying too hard" and producing "over-extracted and overdone" wines, praised Alion for "amazing but gentle concentration." Italians were there, too. At his Tuscan estate called Tenuta di Trinoro, Andrea Franchetti, a wealthy aristocrat and self-trained winemaker, produces new wave, low-yield wines, a Bordeaux-style mix of Cabernet Franc, Merlot, Cabernet Sauvignon, and Petit Verdot matured in 100 percent new French oak barrels. Parker gave the 2000 vintage a 92+ and Franchetti was aiming higher with the 2001.

At Thunevin's, the wines ranged from the superexpensive to the affordable. Peter Sisseck's Pingus ran $200 or more a bottle to consumers. But the Thunevin magic was spreading into less exalted realms, deep in the heart of the Entre-Deux-Mers, where Rémi Garuz's cooperative was struggling to fend off New World competition. There, Thunevin located a young poet turned winemaker named Guillaume Queyran, who used new wave wine-growing and winemaking techniques to produce a concentrated, fruity $10 bottle of wine called Villa Mongiron. Queyran brought samples of his wine to Saint-Emilion. Thunevin tasted and bought the entire production.

A few days later, a broker brought a sample of Villa Mongiron to Jeffrey Davies, who tasted and was also interested. Several of Davies's importers had asked him to scout out inexpensive wines. "The market wants value," he explained. When Davies discovered that Thunevin had bought out Queyran's entire production, he railed, half in true anger and half in recognition of his formidable rival's talent, "Jean-Luc is stealing again from me." He went out and found another estate in the Entre-Deux-Mers called Au Grand Paris, producing a fruity red table wine.

Michel Gracia also presented his wines at Thunevin's house. His trip to California had been a success. He enjoyed San Francisco. Caroline had returned home to help take over the family production. Now she helped her father prepare the samples and bring them to Thunevin's for tasting. Both she and Michel were wearing jeans and sweaters and big rubber boots, as if they were working in the garage cellar.

Over the winter, Parker had raised his rating on Gracia's 2000 vintage from 94 to 95. Work was continuing on the renovation of Cheval Blanc, and even though it wasn't finished in time for the spring tasting, director Pierre Lurton seemed to hold no grudges. Just a day before the tastings began, Lurton came over to Gracia and shook his hand. "I read about your wine at the Japan tasting," he said. Gracia's 2000 vintage, like his 1997 one, finished ahead of the august Cheval Blanc.

"Whatever happens with everyone else this year, I am confident we will be one of the few that is able to raise prices," Gracia said later. "We are producing the wine equivalent of Beluga caviar."

—

CHAPTER 15

Reality Check

THE ARTICLE WAS TITLED, PROVOCATIVELY, "THE SCANDAL THAT Shakes the House of Parker." Weekly magazine *Le Nouvel Observateur* published the exposé in mid-April, only days before Parker's ratings for the 2001 Bordeaux were scheduled to be released. Though some rumblings about the affair were already making their way through the Bordeaux wine community, the magazine broke the scandal to the wider world.

The article described a bizarre imbroglio involving Parker and his representative in Bordeaux, Hanna Agostini. Agostini organized Parker's wine tastings in Bordeaux and translated Parker's writings into French. In the acknowledgments to the successive editions of his *Wine Buyer's Guide*, Parker wrote, "Words cannot express my gratitude to Hanna Agostini." In 1999, without Parker's knowledge, she created a wine consulting company. Three years later, *Le Nouvel Observateur* cited six invoices for consulting services allegedly sent by Agostini on Parker's *Wine Advocate* stationery to local vineyards.

One of her clients was a Belgian named Roger Geens, who owned about 2,000 acres of Right Bank vineyards. On February 13, 2002, only a month before the spring tastings, Geens fired his manager, Isabel Teles Pinto, claiming she had stolen $300,000 from him. She took revenge by going to the police and charging that Geens falsified documents about the yields and origin of his wine. On February 14, the police raided fifteen of Geens's châteaux. Several days later, one of the cellar masters committed suicide.

The scandal now enveloped other Bordeaux luminaries, such as Eric Agostini, Hanna's husband and an attorney well known as an expert in copyrighting wine labels. For copyrighting forty different château names for Geens, the magazine said, he had received about $200,000. His wife had earned another $100,000 by advising Geens to hire as consultants Jean-Luc Thunevin and an Italian enologist named Ricardo Cotarella. Was the advice an innocent way of helping the investor to improve his wines? Or was it a way of getting Parker to give the wines good scores, since she knew that the American critic respected both Thunevin and Cotarella and would taste their recommendations?

Thunevin admitted that Agostini had introduced him to Geens, allowing his *Tue-le-vin* critics to snicker that he was getting paid for presenting wines to Parker. But Thunevin said he thought Agostini was only doing him and Geens a professional courtesy. "I could not imagine that she was paid for putting me in contact with the Geens group," he insisted.

Parker learned about the invoices three months before the story broke, when he visited Bordeaux in January. Later he told visitors to his web site that he was "shocked." He made an appointment at the Geens company with "a guy named Laporte, who manages an obscure Saint-Emilion estate called Cauze." Laporte showed him photocopies of invoices for consulting work. They were on *Wine Advocate* stationery. That night he met with the Agostinis. "This is where the scenario becomes Byzantine," Parker wrote. "She admitted doing consulting work for her clients in Bordeaux because 'they wanted to improve their wines.'" But Hanna Agostini insisted that all the invoices had been sent on her own consulting firm's stationery. The six with *Wine Advocate* letterheads were counterfeits, she insisted. One day when she and Cotarella were at one of Geens's estates near Saint-Emilion, she claimed she had left behind her attaché case that contained some *Wine Advocate* stationery. Driving the enologist back to the Bordeaux-Mérignac airport, Agostini realized that she'd forgotten her attaché case and mentioned this to Cotarella. Cotarella later vouched for Agostini's alibi.

Parker suspected the photocopies he saw were forgeries designed to discredit him. If his associate wanted to leverage his reputation for money, he noted, she could have made much more by insider trading on wine futures based on her advance knowledge of his scores. In principle, he had nothing against her efforts to help some winemakers improve the quality of their product. But to avoid any appearance of impropriety, Parker asked Agostini to stop doing paid wine consulting as long as she worked with him. He also warned her that if the six invoices on *Wine Advocate* letterhead were genuine, "our working relationship will be terminated."

Bordeaux buzzed with malicious gossip. Even his friends and supporters believed Parker should have cracked down harder on his associate. "Bob is just too loyal to his friends," said Alain Raynaud. "Bob is a pure man—he finds it hard to see evil," concluded Dany Rolland.

IN THIS CHARGED ATMOSPHERE, Parker finally released his ratings. The title in his annual April newsletter on Bordeaux read, with a wink at his favorite musician, Neil Young, "After the Gold Rush: 2001 Bordeaux, an Irregular Yet Good Vintage." Although he praised the wines' "classic style with fresh acidity, a cooler-climate taste and more noticeable tannin," the comparison with the millennium vintage was not flattering. "The style of the vintage is far lighter, less impressive, and less concentrated than 2000," he concluded. No mention was made of the excellent Sauternes vintage, a reflection of how Parker concentrates on Bordeaux's reds.

Although most estates received scores three to four points lower on average than in 2000, some exceptions emerged, primarily for *garagistes* such as Gracia. Parker gave his wine a 90–92, nearly as good as the 93 he garnered for his 2000, and praise for "another top-notch effort" that was "fleshy and seductive" with "ripe, sweet, lush black cherry fruit nicely wrapped in smoky, toasty new oak."

He also upped Lascombes's score to 90–93, calling it "the revelation of the Médoc." Parker explained how "hot-shot gurus" Vatelot, Raynaud, and Rolland "were given *carte blanche* to make all the necessary changes in the vineyard and cellars to produce the finest wine possible." The 2001 Lascombes "reveals the *appellation*'s savory elegance and lightness, but more fruit, purity, texture and intensity than any Lascombes I have ever tasted. Beautifully balanced with a dense ruby/purple/plum color, and a gorgeous nose of smoky black currants, minerals, flowers and blackberries. It is sweet, ripe, light on its feet, and textured with an extraordinary seamlessness. It is undoubtedly better than the 2000, no small achievement. Anticipated maturity: 2007–2018. Bravo!"

Despite such praise for overachievers, Parker's overall tone was damning. He lambasted greedy Bordeaux winemakers and predicted a tough selling season. "This is not a vintage that will draw interest from speculators and it is hard to imagine these wines will be significantly more expensive a year and a half from now when they are bottled and released."

Four questions must be answered "yes" for anybody to buy Bordeaux futures, Parker declared. First, "Are you buying wines from what will be considered an undeniably great vintage?" he asked. "The answer in 2001 is 'no.' Are you buying wines that will appreciate significantly in price? The answer in 2001 is 'no.' Are you buying wines because there are only limited quantities produced of exceptionally fine wines, and such wines are generally impossible to find once they are bottled? The answer depends on the property, but obviously the limited production of Pomerols, Saint-Emilions, *garagistes* and some Graves wines are often best purchased as futures." These wines in 2001 "do merit interest." Lastly, Parker asked, "Are you buying wines to guarantee the format you desire, half-bottles, magnums, double magnums or larger formats? Any wine, if purchased as a future, can be bottled to your command."

In the end, a simple law of economics doomed the 2001 vintage: too much supply and too little demand. Large amounts of fine Bordeaux were available, making it unlikely for futures to increase in value. Over-supply would make it easy to purchase the wines later, once in bottle. The powerful American critic's thumbs-down reflected this reality. "When Parker stabbed the vintage in the back, it sent the fear of God into everybody," said Davies.

At the end of May, estates finally began releasing their 2001 futures at dramatically lower prices. First growths Haut-Brion, Lafite-Rothschild, Latour, Margaux, and Mouton Rothschild came out at $80 a bottle for merchants compared to an average of $200 the year before. "After the crazy 2000, the time was ripe for a price cut," Margaux's Paul Pontallier admitted. The huge discounts did the trick. With only five formal first growths and a few Right Bank equals such as Pétrus, Cheval Blanc, and Ausone, these top labels would never have too much to worry about. "Even if they aren't the best, the first growths will always have a clientele of connoisseurs, people who have money, who are snobs, who think it is important to have the label like Cartier or Van Cleef," said Dany Rolland.

For the other Médoc classified growths, however, proposed price reductions, ranging from a few percentage points to more than 30 per-cent, were not enough to stimulate a thirst. Cazes dropped the price on his Château Lynch-Bages to $22 from almost $40 the year before. Even so, Lindsay Hamilton, a partner at Farr Vintners in London, one of the world's largest futures traders, said his company's own futures sales were down 80 percent from the previous year.

Sauternes represented a minor exception: the best estates sold out. "People know this is the year to buy them because the quality is good," Hamilton reported. Even here, though, success remained limited. Prices rose only marginally. At Doisy-Daëne, for example, Pierre Dubourdieu complained he received only $20 a bottle, "a small increase of 7 percent." Since Yquem's 2001 vintage would not be released for four years, it missed the opportunity to cash in on this small but modest boost.

In this difficult environment, Raynaud and Vatelot came out swinging at Lascombes. Armed with Parker's endorsement, the ambitious new wavers requested one of the highest price rises in the region, a 35 percent hike to $24 a bottle. Merchants' reactions were frosty. "The price was just outrageous," Lindsay Hamilton complained. Farr Vintners sold eight cases—compared to 224 cases the year before. Another major UK futures seller, Lay & Wheeler, did not carry 2001 Lascombes. "At that price we didn't want to take the risk," managing director Hugo Rose told *Decanter*.

Raynaud and Vatelot refused to back down and to lower their price. They criticized the British wine world as being slow to recognize improvement. The American market did display a little more interest and half of Lascombes's production was sold. Although Raynaud admitted this was not a brilliant result, he insisted the investors were not looking for a quick return. They decided to build up inventory and wait for the market to recover. "We are well financed," Raynaud said. "We can be patient."

Dominique Befve stayed on as Lascombes's director. He fired the recalcitrant cellar master who had refused to follow his instructions during the harvest. In his place he brought in a well-respected outsider. He also appointed a quality-control manager, a first for Lascombes. With those moves, he saw a decline in the social strife. "The workers have come around," he said. "They now understand what we are trying to do and appreciate it." He pledged to cut yields further and produce an even better wine in 2002 than in 2001.

Among the *garagistes*, Michel Gracia remained realistic, selling his wine at $40 a bottle, the same as the year before. In early May, broker Thierry Castells met Gracia for coffee at the Saint-Emilion café. "Michel, you could be a diva, raise your prices, and still sell your wine because you have such a good score and so little wine to offer," Castells told him. "But let's face it: the market is a bubble, just like the stock exchange." While the upstart Right Bankers working at Lascombes resisted similar entreaties, Gracia had listened. "He is a stonemason, who knows that you cut stones to last for years, and he is taking the same strategy for his wine," Castells said of him.

Even so, Davies and other merchants struggled to resell the *garagistes'* wine. As the campaign wound down in late June, he still had unsold stocks of Gracia. "Customers only are interested in price cuts in 2001," he complained. "They preferred 'name-brand' classified growths from the Médoc whose prices dropped by as much as 35 percent to the improved quality of such wines as Gracia and especially Lascombes. It doesn't make sense. If new owners or a new management team come in, invest a lot of money, and significantly improve the quality of the wine, they ought to be able to get a better price for it."

In the end, Davies managed at least to make a profit on Gracia thanks to a surprising new market—Japan. A prominent Japanese wine critic, influenced by Parker, put Gracia's wine on the cover of his influential glossy magazine alongside Ausone and Cheval Blanc. Gracia was ecstatic. Davies traveled to Japan and found an importer who took the balance of his allocation at the full futures price. At a dinner a few months later, Davies told Thunevin about his Japanese salvation. Thunevin agreed that Japan, with less exposure to the garage movement and little wine history of its own, was ripe for the picking when it came to the fresh, fruit-driven garage wines. "I've hired two Japanese speakers for my merchant business," he said.

WHILE MOST TOP estates struggled, Bordeaux co-ops made a surprising mini-comeback. They were less dependent on export markets than the most prestigious estates, and sales in France for their basic wines suffered less damage. At Sauveterre, prices of the co-op's Sauvignon Blanc actually rose almost 20 percent in 2002 because so many vines had been torn up over the past decade that a supply shortage was created.

Giles O'Connolly finally found an acceptable name for the Sauvignon Blanc he was going to launch in the States—Jacques-Yves Entre Deux Mers, with a single large scallop on the label evoking wine to be drunk with seafood. O'Connolly went to New York, where he found an importer, the prestigious Frederick Wildman company. "Cross your fingers," he said. The *Wine Spectator* gave it a respectable 85 points, calling it "clean, fresh and fruity," and the Aqua Grill in Manhattan began serving it by the glass.

O'Connolly also overcame Garuz's resistance to the heart logo for the red wine. Although the peasant president had thought the idea wimpy, marketing surveys showed that the best hope for the future of Bordeaux wine was to make its packaging more attractive to women. The labels were the same as originally proposed, a whimsical red-lined heart with a gold crown drawn over a black background. It was a simple yet elegant concept. Inside the heart hung a bunch of grapes. In modern, almost Australian fashion, the label indicated the grape type—Merlot, Cabernet Sauvignon, or a blend of the two. It also told consumers in straightforward English how the wine was made, whether it was aged in oak barrels or not. "We're going to make Bordeaux simple," O'Connolly vowed. "We're not appealing to the people who know Bordeaux and have drunk Yquem, but the 80 percent of the world that knows almost nothing about Bordeaux."

And yet selling Sauveterre's reds proved difficult. Among brokers, the 2001 Merlot and Cabernet Sauvignon from the entire Entre-Deux-Mers remained problematic. They pushed for large quantities to be disqualified from receiving the Bordeaux label. *Appellation contrôlée* committees were convened to taste the wine from the various co-ops. About 40 percent of the samples were rejected and would be dumped in bulk on the marketplace. "They are weak in color and thin," criticized broker Damien Mortet. Cellier de la Bastide's chief technician, Christian Caviole, admitted that their crop was "irregular." The Merlot was too "wet," he said. The Cabernet "hadn't quite ripened." The *appellation contrôlée* committee rejected some of the co-op's samples. They were going to have to lower prices, and still only the best lots looked saleable at the level near the price of the previous year. The rest would have to be discounted, up to 20 percent. "It's a struggle," the technician admitted.

Garuz traveled to Australia and the trip underlined the depth of the competition facing France. But it also gave him new determination. While he was envious of the Australians' weather, their freedom in how they make their wine, and their marketing heft, he no longer felt in danger of being overwhelmed. The reason was simple. "They lack our centuries of tradition," he insisted. "In these hard times, though, people will search for roots."

The Sauveterre co-op completed its ambitious building project.

Garuz took visitors on tours. With pride, he opened the doors to the new winery and watched them gasp in admiration. In this little town in the far reaches of the Bordeaux countryside, with its squat, weathered medieval structures, the shiny new 150-foot-high fermenting and storage tanks looked almost like science fiction props. Garuz liked to walk up the four flights of galvanized steel staircase to the top and look down with pride over the football-field-size structure.

The co-op president himself was planning to step down at the end of 2003. Garuz had held the office for thirteen years, and with the new cellar built, he felt his mission was accomplished. "This place has become a big administration and I don't want to deal with the paperwork anymore," he said. But he was still driving fast. In June 2002, police stopped him driving his BMW at 90 miles per hour. He was fined $150 and warned that he would lose his driver's license if he was caught speeding again.

Even though he was leaving his co-op position, Garuz was staying on as Producta's president and spending more time there than before to make sure the new Jacques-Yves wine succeeded. He was also appointed to the regional board of the Crédit Agricole bank. Crédit Agricole is a cooperative, owned by its farmer members. But it has France's largest retail branch network. While the Paris-based city slicker banks suffered from the stock market downturn, Crédit Agricole thrived thanks to its literally down-to-earth approach. In late 2002, the bank even bought the venerable Crédit Lyonnais and extended its reach into urban France.

Crédit Agricole participated in the loans to the buyers of Château Lascombes. When much of Lascombes's 2001 vintage went unsold, Vatelot and the other investors had to go back to the bank for bridge loans. Who was reviewing their financial plans? None other than Rémi Garuz. He planned to squeeze the investors. "All those big rich guys who just pour money into a project without thinking hard better start thinking harder," he said. Any extension of the loans would be granted on tough terms, he warned.

Garuz was convinced that the *garagistes'* peak of prominence had passed. He believed the market for high-end wines was going to dry up and that Parker's scores would no longer be enough to sell wines priced to consumers at $40 and up. Lascombes's strategy of halving the amount of wine produced and doubling the price to make up the difference was going to become more and more difficult. "The merchants just won't put up with it anymore," Garuz predicted.

HIS PREDICTION CAME TRUE in the next vintage. The summer of 2002 was cool and gray, not promising, and autumn was cool throughout much of France. On the other side of southern France, in the Rhône Valley, it rained for more than a week straight before a catastrophic twenty-four-hour deluge started on the evening of September 8. Parker, who was visiting the region, found himself tasting at Château Pégaü in Châteauneuf-du-Pape, "with several feet of water inundating their cellars." It took him two hours to make the normally ten-minute drive back to his hotel. The next day, he kept soldiering on to his appointments. Back in Châteauneuf-du-Pape, his car hit high water and flipped at a sharp angle. He walked to a friend's house "through such intense lightning that you could feel the electricity in your hair." Parker felt lucky. More than forty people in the immediate area were swept away and drowned. Much of the southern 2002 Rhône Valley harvest was ruined.

Although Bordeaux avoided the tempest, the poor weather resulted in uneven flowering and a cool summer followed by a sunny autumn resulted in many bitter, diluted reds. In some cases, as at Château Cos d'Estournel, the results looked better than in 2001. But caution was the watchword. At Châteaux Margaux, Paul Pontallier said he would have to produce more of his second wine than usual. "We had to be very careful with our selection," he said.

Economic and political worries were even more unnerving. Through 2002 the dollar fell more than 20 percent against the new European single currency, making high-priced French and other European wines that much more expensive in their prime American market. In effect, the currency shift wiped out many of the price cuts made the previous spring. French-American tensions over Iraq spilled over into an informal boycott by American consumers of fine French wine.

In Bordeaux, the impact was immediate. Gérard Perse backed out of the offer to purchase Château Petit-Village he'd made only six months before. He said the deal no longer made sense financially. There was a touch of bitterness in his retreat. "It's like a woman you love and then you fall out of love," he said. He sensed that the Bordeaux bubble was bursting and that, for the moment, further acquisition of wine-producing châteaux was not the best investment strategy.

Specialty merchants such as Davies and Thunevin responded to the changing environment by searching out inexpensive yet high-quality wines. Jean-Luc Thunevin signed a cooperation agreement with a local co-op and helped them through their entire growing season and harvest. He encouraged members to reduce yields by paying them the difference between what they made and what they would have received if they grew more grapes. He also called Rémi Garuz and discussed visiting the Sauveterre co-op to see the newfangled GrapeScan computer system.

Michel Rolland remained as busy as ever, globe-trotting, his energy and ability to taste two hundred wines a day undiminished. Even as Argentina plunged into near chaos, he remained optimistic. If anything, the country's financial meltdown helped, he argued. It lowered his costs and he planned to export most of his new wine anyhow. France and Bordeaux would soon face another formidable new competitor.

But the business of wine consulting was changing. At Prieuré-Lichine, Rolland resigned, leaving Stéphane Deronencourt as the lone enologist. "Stéphane has more time to give to each property, he is a real winemaker, not a consultant like Michel," said Dany Rolland.

Parker faced new challenges both personal and professional. When he visited Bordeaux at the beginning of 2003, he was again in mourning. Only months after his father's death, his mother died as well. He had been close to her—and she helped out with his correspondence. In that position, she only rarely showed him the many effusive letters of praise he received. She preferred to give him the critical letters to keep his ego in check. "This has been my *annus horribilus*," he told Davies, echoing the famous pronouncement of Queen Elizabeth a few years earlier. He felt his life's work was in danger from the Franco-American political contretemps. On his web site, one reader berated him as "an Iraqi-loving pussy" because of his support for French wine.

In spite of, or perhaps because of, his pain, Parker plunged into his work with renewed energy. One day in early January 2003, he arrived at Davies's house in Bordeaux at 10 A.M. and left only at 5:30 P.M., sampling two hundred of the 2001 wines. He departed only because he still had more tasting on the day's agenda. Before leaving, he said that the 2001s were "looking good" after more time in barrel and that he planned to rerate them upward in April 2003. "We're hoping, perhaps against hope, that his reassessment of the vintage will rekindle merchants' interest in the 2001s," Davies said. "There's still a lot of wine out there to be sold."

Just after Parker returned home to Maryland in mid-January, however, the Agostini scandal widened. On January 23, 2003, prosecutors filed criminal charges against his Bordeaux representative for forgery and "profiting from a breach of trust." Police said they believed that, rather than being duped, Hanna Agostini had conspired with Isabel Teles Pinto, Geens's former employee. Agostini's invoices on the *Wine Advocate* letterhead represented part of an embezzlement scam against Geens, they maintained. Police searched Agostini's home and arrested her. She was held in jail and questioned for forty-eight hours before being released on $38,000 bail. No trial date was scheduled, but if proven guilty, Agostini faced a maximum penalty of five years in prison and a fine of more than $1 million. When reached on the phone just before her arrest, Hanna Agostini threatened to sue journalists who wrote about the affair. Even after the formal charges, Eric Agostini continued to claim his wife's innocence, saying someone wanted to embarrass the powerful, controversial American critic.

Parker himself withheld judgment, saying, "It is my belief that one of the cornerstones of our judicial system, indeed of a democracy, is that every individual is innocent until proven guilty." In another of his web site postings, he insisted that Agostini was innocent but admitted that she had displayed "negligent judgment in doing consulting work" and that, "while not illegal, this work has placed me essentially in a very delicate situation."

His critics and rivals pounced. The *Wine Spectator*, which had almost never mentioned Parker's name before, published an entire article on the affair. Parker himself felt on the defensive. He hired a French lawyer and filed a civil suit in order to be able to examine the evidence against Agostini. Although insisting he "won't fire someone before being proven guilty," he suspected forgery by "enemies to embarrass me through her."

In September 2003, Parker met with the Bordeaux police, who showed him their dossier on Agostini. He posted a note on his web site saying he was shocked by the evidence of "embezzlement of large amounts of money." He asked Agostini for her resignation. She handed it in and he began searching for a new translator who would be based in the United States.

While digesting these legal challenges, Parker had skipped the 2003 spring tasting and not published any commentary on the 2002 vintage until after the entire futures season was closed. It pained him not to taste new wines for the first time in twenty-five years. It pained him, too, that after having been such a staunch defender of the wines of Bordeaux over the last quarter century, a number of well-heeled wine merchants there seemed to revel in the fact that he was not coming to taste the new vintage. A curious situation indeed. "With the world economy, the Iraq war, and the marketplace saturated with wine from 2000 and 2001, there's no real compelling reason to issue a report early on this year's harvest," Parker said from his Maryland home.

The impact was immediate. "Since Parker is without a doubt the most powerful journalist, his absence hurts," said Michael Aaron, CEO of the renowned New York wine store Sherry-Lehmann, who, like other U.S. merchants, slashed his orders of 2002. The only 2002 Bordeaux wines that sold well were the first growths and a handful of so-called super-seconds. Even the first growths dropped their prices once again to about $60 a bottle wholesale. "At this price, people still want the first growths," observed Lindsay Hamilton at Farr Vintners.

For Bordeaux's Parker-fueled new wavers, life became much more difficult. At Château Quinault L'Enclos, Raynaud lowered his price by another 35 percent to $30—but the market only absorbed a quarter of the estate's production. "In the past years, we sold out in a single day," reported Raynaud. "This year, the merchants are too scared to take a position, particularly without Parker." At Lascombes, Raynaud and Vatelot lowered prices 40 percent from the previous year to $20 and still tempted few buyers. *Garagistes* Thunevin and Gracia similarly struggled. "Without Bob to help prop them up, I fear many garages may end up closed," warned Jeffrey Davies.

Despite their setbacks, the revolutionaries continued on the offensive. A frustrated Raynaud escalated his feud with the Union des Grands Crus, launching the Cercle Rive Droite de Grands Vins de Bordeaux in the fall of 2002. The 150 members are innovators, many of them overlooked by the Union des Grands Crus. They include most of the garage winemakers, led by Thunevin and his Valandraud. All come from the Right Bank and many are from unappreciated *appellations* such as Fronsac and the Côtes de Castillon. They pledged to hold separate tastings and promotional events. In order to promote the association, photographs were taken in the middle of a verdant vineyard, with Raynaud in the front row and his members holding hands in back of him. "It's a circle of friends, driven by a common quest for perfection and constant innovation," said Raynaud in his public announcement of the new group. In private, he was more blunt. "This is revenge against the Left Bank and the Bordeaux snobs."

BORDEAUX'S REVOLUTION was coming to a close. Most monumental political, economic, and social changes overstep and devour their instigators, provoking an almost inevitable reaction. The coming years looked tough for Bordeaux. Many garage wineries would close up. Many ambitious new wavers might well go bankrupt. Even the well-established estates also looked set to struggle. Consumers would turn more and more to value, putting pressure on almost all top-notch wines. In the spring of 2003, Giles O'Connolly noted that the hottest wine in America was a $1.99 California concoction nicknamed "Two-Buck Chuck."

But the revolution's work would leave a positive legacy. When Parker finally published his 2002 ratings at the end of the year, he accompanied them with a three-page essay on why "Bordeaux is significantly better today than it was 25 or 50 years ago." He attacked the "ignorant belief that Bordeaux wines of today are more forward," and therefore shorter-lived. "Think it over," he asked his critics. "Does anyone want to return to the Bordeaux of 30 or 40 years ago when (1) less than one fourth of the most renowned estates made wines proportional to their official pedigree, (2) dirty, unclean aromas were justified as part of the terroir character, (3) disappointingly emaciated, austere, excessively tannic wines from classified-growths were labeled 'classic' by a subservient wine press that existed at the largesse of the wine industry, and (4) wines were made from underripe grapes that were too high in acidity and tannin to ever become fully harmonious?"

The answer, of course, was no. In his opinion, the *garagistes* and new wavers were responsible for most of the improvement. "When the history of Bordeaux is written, Jean-Luc Thunevin will be the hero," Parker said. The august first growths with their 1855 pedigrees can no longer rest on their laurels. Despite resisting garage methods, Margaux and the other Left Bankers had improved during the 1990s. At their price and prestige level, competitors had emerged over the centuries, including Ausone and Cheval Blanc. All are affected by the ferment overtaking Saint-Emilion.

Even at Yquem, change was coming slowly. At the end of 2002, LVMH installed a new marketing director with years of experience in the company's Champagne business. Bordeaux insiders speculated that Count Alexandre would not last much longer, pressed as he was by the company to improve performance. In February 2003, Russian leader Vladimir Putin visited Bordeaux. A half century before, his predecessor Nikita Khrushchev had done the same and met with Marquis Bertrand. Putin agreed to visit an LVMH estate and meet with Bernard Arnault. Instead of Yquem, though, the Russian leader went to Cheval Blanc. The star of Lur-Saluces had lost some of its luster. In 2004, Cheval Blanc's Pierre Lurton was hired to replace the count. Lurton introduced reforms, offering Yquem as a future. LVMH renovated the château, and work was accelerated so Bernard Arnault could hold the marriage of his daughter Delphine there in September 2005.

Around this time, on a crisp winter day, Yves Vatelot invited Jeffrey Davies to Château de Reignac for lunch. Like Thunevin, Vatelot wanted to end his feuding with Davies over his decision to market his Reignac through the *place de Bordeaux* and bring the American back on board as one of his key distributors. The two men visited Reignac's exotic tasting room, the entire ground floor of a small turreted building that once served as a home for pigeons. They tasted the 2001 and 2002 Reignacs. Davies believed them to be superior to the earlier vintages and said so.

They sat down to lunch. Stéphanie Vatelot had prepared the menu that morning before leaving for Paris. The meal started with fresh asparagus, drizzled with a light vinaigrette, accompanied by a perfumed white 2001 Reignac. The main course was a perfectly roasted chicken. Three decanters full of wine were brought to the table. They were numbered one, two, and three. All looked rich red in color, their robust appearance signaling youth.

"They're all from the same vintage," Vatelot announced. "And one is a Reignac."

Only he knew the identity of the other two wines, but not which had been poured into which decanter. His housekeeper had uncorked the bottles and decanted them. Three full glasses of wine were poured for each taster. The two men smelled and sipped number one. It exploded with strong cherrylike flavors, backed by a pleasant, slightly chewy, mushroomlike aftertaste.

"Superior," judged Davies.

"Terrific," agreed Vatelot.

They moved on to number two. Slightly lighter in color than its predecessor, it had a pleasant perfume but lacked power on the palate.

"After the first sample, this wine seems closed tight with rather tough tannins in the background. This is distinctly less 'sexy' than number one," criticized Davies.

Number three benefited from a particularly lovely appearance. It was deep ruby-purple in color, its brilliance highlighted by the early afternoon sunlight. Its heady bouquet revealed more dark cherries together with cassis and just a subtle hint of truffle.

"Stylistically it resembles number one, but with just a bit more depth and complexity," said a satisfied Davies, setting his glass back on the

288 · *William Echikson*

table. "I think number one is probably Reignac, number two is a disappointment in this flight of wines, and number three is very good, possibly a first growth from Médoc, perhaps from Pavillac."

"Number one and number three are ahead of the pack," Vatelot agreed. He stepped away from the table, walked into the kitchen, and brought back the three bottles.

The first was Château Reignac, 1999. The second was Lafite Rothschild. The third was Mouton Rothschild.

"You can only judge how you are doing when you taste against the best," Vatelot said. Every year, he bought a case of each of the first growths, and when special visitors came, he held similar blind tastings. His 1999 Reignac cost $20 a bottle in retail stores in the United States. In 2001 he had come out around $12 a bottle, which meant that his wine would ultimately sell in U.S. wine shops for about $24. Merchants, even Davies, had balked and Vatelot had slashed his asking price to $10. Initially, his decisive action infuriated other merchants who had bought at the higher price, but when Vatelot granted them a compensatory discount, much was forgiven.

The Lafite Rothschild and Mouton Rothschild sold for as much as ten times the price of Reignac. The difference was a function of their first-growth label versus Reignac's simple, unclassified, Bordeaux *supérieur* status.

"Reignac is such a better value," Davies said.

But Vatelot disagreed.

"The Mouton and Lafite aren't too expensive," he cautioned. "It's Reignac that's too cheap."

Davies laughed. "Yves, you may be a pain in the ass to work with, but you sure make one helluva wine," he said.

Although the economics of fine wine may no longer look so bright, the quality of elite Bordeaux has taken a giant leap forward. If innovators like Vatelot and Davies retain their determination to keep improving despite the inevitable, often cyclical commercial setbacks, wine lovers around the world will benefit. With these thoughts in mind, Davies proposed a toast. He and Vatelot raised their glasses of Reignac and drank to their success in breathing new life into Bordeaux's old order.

ACKNOWLEDGMENTS

—

Most of the research for this book was conducted while I lived in Bordeaux for six months during 2001. I followed that year's harvest and winemaking. I picked grapes and watched them being transformed into fine wine. I savored the results during the climactic week in spring of 2002 when the precious liquid was tasted and sold to wine merchants around the world.

It was a dream assignment. My family—my wife, Anu, and our children, Sam, Julia, and baby Ben—accompanied me for much of the stay. And while for me the joys of visiting a cold wine cellar are numerous, there's nothing more boring for a one- and three-year-old. Yet all the children put up with the visits and reporting with unfailing good humor.

Many of Bordeaux's most passionate players opened their homes and shared some of their best bottles with me. The Raynaud family graciously lent me a house; Geneviève, Alain, and Françoise Raynaud and Michel and Chantal Lebreton were also excellent teachers about past and present Bordeaux.

I owe special thanks to Jeffrey M. Davies. My fellow American introduced me to the Raynauds and opened up the world of Bordeaux's revolutionaries to me. Davies, Michel Rolland, and Denis Dubourdieu deciphered the mysteries of winemaking. Michel Gracia, Jean-Luc Thunevin, and Murielle Andraud, Alain Vauthier, Jean-François and Véronique Julien, and Christian and Anne-Marie Dauriac enabled me to better grasp how Saint-Emilion had been transformed from a provincial village into one of the world's most exciting wine capitals. Jean-Michel Cazes, Dominique Befve, Paul Pontallier, and Anthony Barton explained the passions of the historic Médoc. Daniel and Florence Cathiard of Château Smith-Haut-Lafitte were unfailingly generous and warmhearted. Pierre Dubourdieu, Bertrand and Louis Hainguerlot, Jean de Pouilly, and others who wish to remain nameless opened the door on the secretive world of Sauternes. Rémi Garuz showed me how the ordinary Bordeaux winemaker lives and works. Giles O'Connolly's marketing man's point of view on the Bordeaux scene was particularly helpful.

Special thanks also to historian Dewey Markham Jr., who took more time, energy, and care than I ever could have hoped when he kindly and carefully read a draft of the manuscript and saved me from numerous errors. Those that remain, it goes without saying, are entirely my own.

Michael Carlisle and Michelle Tessler of Carlisle & Company jumped on the idea for a realistic book on Bordeaux. Freelance editor Sarah Flynn came up with the structure that turned my reporting into a coherent narrative and then pushed me to provide the necessary precision to ensure that everybody, not just wine lovers, could understand Bordeaux's revolution. And in the end, this book is being published because a great editor, Starling Lawrence, believed in it.

INDEX

—

WILLIAM ECHIKSON is the Brussels bureau chief for
Dow Jones Newswires and a wine columnist for the
Wall Street Journal Europe. He has been a foreign correspondent
based in Europe since 1982, working as a staff correspondent
for the *Christian Science Monitor*, the *Wall Street Journal*,
and *BusinessWeek*. His articles have also appeared in
the *Wine Spectator*, *The New Yorker*, and other periodicals. From
1985 to 1990 he reported from Poland, Czechoslovakia, Hungary, and
the Balkans and wrote *Lighting the Night: Revolution in Eastern Europe*.
He is the author of *Burgundy Stars: A Year in the Life of a
Great French Restaurant*, about the late three-star chef
Bernard Loiseau. Echikson also collaborated with Pierre Franey
on the PBS series *Cooking in France* and *Cooking in Europe* and
with Jacques Pépin on his PBS special *Cooking Chez Moi*.
He lives in Brussels with his wife and three children.